Through the Eyes of Christ

How to Lead Muslims into the Kingdom of God

by

Harry Morin
and
Nikki Arana

Through the Eyes of Christ: *How to Lead Muslims into the Kingdom of God*

All Qur'anic references are from *The Holy Quran:Translation and Commentary* by A. Yusuf Ali, c.1977, Amana Corporation, USA. All biblical references are from the Holy Bible: New International Version, c.1984, International Bible Society.

Contact Information: info@avoiceforthepersecuted.com

Publishing History
First Edition, 2009
ISBN-10: 1442181087
ISBN-13: 9781442181083

Published in the United States of America

TABLE OF CONTENTS

Preface

We are at war.

The radical Islamic fundamentalists are on fire for their God and their faith and have committed themselves unto death to see their brand of Islam spread throughout the world. As these jihadists pursue their ambitious and terrifying goals, most American Christians feel powerless to respond. What should the body of Christ do? How can we respond in a way that will make a difference? Should we initiate an all-out war with them?

The answer is yes. And "**Through the Eyes of Christ**" lays out the battle plan.

But it doesn't forecast victory through any military or political solution, because the struggle is spiritual. And the American Christian church has been given a strategy that is God ordained. It begins with looking at our enemy through a prism of compassion. Seeing the Muslim people as lost and meeting that reality with the living Word of God, the love of Jesus Christ. We must equip every believer with the information he or she needs to reach out to moderate Muslims here in America, establish relationships with them, and through the power of the Holy Spirit, share the Gospel with them.

This can't be accomplished with a confrontational approach, slamming Islam, focusing primarily on its faults and failures, and promoting the Christian religion as superior to the Islamic religion. But it can be done with a *relational* approach, whereby the dedicated lay Christian primarily promotes "Christ in him" by establishing a mutual relationship that will allow the love of God to flow from his heart and touch that of the Muslim. "By their fruit will you recognize them." "But the fruit of the Spirit is love. . . ." Rather than conflict, the reader will be encouraged to look for commonality that will build bridges from general revelation of God to specific revelation of God in Christ Jesus.

Establishing these kinds of relationships will require empathy on the part of the Christian, a sincere desire to know the Muslims as human beings. It will require a servanthood mindset modeled after Christ, who descended to identify culturally with humanity. That is the heart of this book: encouraging and helping the Christian to share in the humanity of the Muslim so that the love of Christ and the gift of salvation in Christ become relevant and accessible to the Muslim people.

How many times have you heard that we are in a "new kind of war"? It's true. We must beat our swords into plowshares, take up the cause of Christ and reach out to Muslims here in our homeland. We do not have to sit helplessly and hope that somehow a military or political solution will materialize. Instead we can mobilize the body of Christ here in America. And it can begin with you.

1

Why I Should Care

Blessed are the peacemakers, for they shall be called sons of God.

Matthew 5:9

Terrorism, fanatical fundamentalism, suicide bombings, black-veiled women, holy wars, Arab sheikhs—these are the common words and images that come to the minds of most Westerners when they look at Muslims (pronounced "Moos-lims") in today's world. But did you ever wonder, "What does God see when He looks at Muslim people?" In many cases, God sees hungry hearts bound by the fear of evil spirits and haunted by the uncertainty of eternity. God sees a growing swell of young people in third-world poverty, frustrated by unemployment and deeply resentful of the luxuries of the extravagant West. He sees men groping for meaning and direction in a dark existence. He sees women aching for some measure of self-worth in the eyes of both community and heaven. God sees worried fathers struggling to maintain a respectable livelihood and fearful mothers struggling to arrange the next meal. God sees countless Muslims drifting in a sea of hopelessness and trapped by a fatalistic worldview that offers no escape from the miseries of life. He sees millions of innocent Muslims victimized by the whims of politics and the excessive demands of the radical few. God sees the lostness of souls that are either depraved by the onslaught of evil or deceived by a religious righteousness that eclipses the righteousness in Christ.

God yearns for the hearts of the Muslim people, but for centuries the Christian Church has ignored the spiritual plight of Muslims. It was far more expedient to write them off as cursed of God, impossible to reach, and unworthy of Christian sweat, tears, and sacrifice. Furthermore, acclaimed historians insisted there was no need to be concerned about Islam. They said it was a barbaric and rigid religion that was born in the desert and would die in the desert. They assured the Christian world that in time, Islam would simply fade away in the glory and splendor of Western civilization. But the night of ignorance has passed, and American Christians are awakening to the reality that Islam is now the fastest growing religion in many parts of the world, including the United States of America, and embraces a global community of 1.3 billion people. Islam is here to stay.

More and more, Americans as a whole are seeing what Muslims look like. In the sixties, it was the Nation of Islam, Malcolm X, and Cassius Clay turned Muhammad Ali. In the seventies, it was the Iranian Revolution and the hostage crisis. For the first time, bearded mullahs, headed by the Ayatollah Khomeini, entered American living rooms via nightly news telecasts. In the nineties, it was the beginning of an influx of Muslim refugees from war-torn places like Somalia and Bosnia, and from drought-ravaged countries like Ethiopia. Today, Americans see Muslims everywhere. They are in the shopping malls and corner stores. They are doctors and professors. They are athletes on the professional basketball courts and football fields. They are taxi drivers and bellhops in the big cities. They are students scattered all over university campuses. They are our coworkers and our neighbors.

Demographers estimate there could be as many as six million Muslims in the USA. About two million of them are African American converts. Many African American Muslims began their sojourn into Islam in the sixties through the Nation of Islam (a racist sect of Islam presently headed by Louis Farrakhan). Most of these people, however, have shifted to mainstream Islam, which avoids racial identity. Another 2.25 million American Muslims are immigrants who are mostly uneducated and speak limited English. Only about 500,000 of them are professionals or students with a good command of English. Another 1.75 million are the children and grandchildren of these immigrants who represent the bulging Muslim population of tomorrow in the USA.

Truly, Islam is a dynamic force that must be reckoned with. In a spirit of repentance for both ignoring and hating Muslim people, Christians must resolve to break down the walls of antipathy and invite the Holy Spirit to transform Christian attitudes and inspire Christian outreach. In the last twenty years, evangelical Christians have promoted prayer emphases for the "unreached" people groups of the world—animists, Buddhists, Hindus, and of course, Muslims. In miraculous fashion, God has honored those prayers. Christians around the world are now beginning to see Muslim people in the light of God's love. And in that light comes a compelling urgency to share the gospel message not only in the uttermost parts of the world, but also right here in America. We must reach out to the Muslims among us who have yet to receive an adequate witness of Christ, and then we must follow through by supporting, spiritually and materially, those Muslims whose hearts are changed by the working of the Holy Spirit.

As never before, Muslims themselves are relating testimonies of dreams and visions of Jesus, healings and supernatural miracles that have opened their hearts to the biblical message of God's love in Christ. As a result of technological advancements, economic turmoil, natural disasters, sociopolitical upheavals, and most recently, militant Islam, Muslim people all over the world have become inquisitive, restless, and dissatisfied. The opening years of this twenty-first century are witnessing an era of openness unlike any other in our past.

Opportunities for Christian outreach abound. Not only is God opening up new fields of opportunity, He is also raising up laborers to reap the harvest. But laborers need to be trained. With the help of the Holy Spirit, it is hoped that through this book, the reader will realize that with a passion for souls, there must come a passion for relevancy. For the gospel message to be viable, it must come from a heart of love, and it must relate to people in a language and manner they can understand.

It is important to know that not all Muslims are the same. They represent a wide diversity of national cultures, Islamic sects, superstitious beliefs, and social strata. Most Muslims around the world fit into one of the following general profiles.

Poverty-Stricken: Some Muslim people live in extreme poverty with barely enough food to survive from one day to the next. Some are refugees, forced to leave their homeland because of war. Some live in natural disaster-prone areas where floods, windstorms, or droughts inflict heavy damage and physical suffering. Many of these people are so poor and destitute that they will listen to almost anyone who can offer hope and a better way of life, regardless of cultural background. They are open to a compassionate and holistic approach to ministry that can offer both a "cup of water" and the "bread of life."

Animistic-Background: Some Muslim people come from a strong animistic background and embrace an Islam that has become heavily syncretized with witchcraft practice and folklore. This is what is commonly referred to as *Folk*

Islam. These Muslims are distant from mainstream Islam but nevertheless are resistant to any intrusion of a foreign religion that would threaten a disturbance of the cosmos or a war of the spirits. They generally are suspicious of any outsiders, believing that evil spirits can disguise themselves in human forms. These Muslims are mainly impacted by Christians through a demonstration of power in the name of Jesus, and are often reached through the approach of ministry referred to as power encounter.

Progressive: As more and more Muslims become exposed to the outside world and the living standards of developed countries, a number of them are joining the ranks of what are known as progressive Muslims or modernists. Though they may hold to religious values, they project a more liberal view toward the Western world and culture. They are especially attracted to Western education and technology and are eager to integrate these ingredients into their own Islamic society. As a result, Muslim modernists are more than willing to identify with Western-oriented people, but generally avoid religious discussion in order to preserve their friendships.

Discontented: There are some Muslims who are just simply fed up with Islam and refuse to involve themselves in any of its practices and teachings. They regard themselves as Muslim only in terms of national or cultural identity. Some of them completely break away from any Islamic connection. Reasons for leaving Islam include disillusionment, resentment, and supernatural intervention. A growing number of Muslims feel they have been deceived by the promises of the religious reformers who spoke of

Islamic laws leading the way to peace and prosperity. Furthermore, many Muslims are disturbed by the growing trend of militancy and want no part of an Islam that tolerates, or even promotes, terrorism. In some cases, a Muslim may have been physically punished as a teenager for refusing to say his prayers and attend the mosque. As a result, resentment led him to hate Islam and reject it altogether. Other Muslims are leaving the fold of Islam because of visions or dreams of Jesus. Whatever the reason, these Muslims are open to change and may even want to embrace a culture that is completely void of any resemblance to Islam. In most cases they would not be adverse to the typical Western evangelistic approach.

Nominal: Most Muslims are simply nominal Muslims who may attend the mosque on rare occasions, or at least for the Muslim holiday prayers. They resemble the many nominal Christians who attend church only on Easter Sunday and Christmas Eve. Though they may not observe the regular daily prayers and keep the religious fast, they pride themselves in being Muslim and are keen to preserve their distinct Islamic identity. For them, if for no other reason, it's the traditional thing to do. They may tolerate the occasional visit of a foreign culture, but they are happy to keep their own. These people hold tightly to tradition.

Sufis: Unknown to most Christians, among the many facets of Islam is its mystical side known as Sufism. Sufism focuses on the internal aspect of religion and attempts to guide a Muslim on a spiritual journey to God. Those who embrace the teachings of Sufism are Sufis. They become a part of the Sufi (pronounced "Soo-fee") system that includes saints, shrines, spiritual guides, and disciples. Generally, the teachings of the various Sufi orders reflect a tolerant view of other religious persuasions with the understanding that there are many paths that lead to the same God. Many of these teachings have found their way into the New Age movement. Since Sufi teaching reflects much about what Jesus had to say regarding organized religion and tradition, Sufi Muslims are attracted to people claiming to be followers of Jesus. They are open to dialogue but opposed to any view that would promote one approach to God to the exclusion of all others.

Most of the Muslims in the preceding categories are open to a variety of approaches of Christian ministry and outreach, especially if it includes some supernatural manifestation of the power of the gospel. Though the intrusion of a foreign culture may arouse their suspicion, these Muslims are generally tolerant, as long as there is no appearance of belligerence or disrespect toward their religion, their scripture, and their prophet.

Orthodox: This group represents the kind of Muslims who are initially most resistant to the gospel, and are therefore the least targeted by Christian evangelists. These are the conservative Orthodox Muslims who practice their faith with utmost devotion. They perform their prayers daily; they read their scriptures regularly; and they observe their yearly 30-day fast. The men are recognizable by their beards, and the women by their veils. These are Muslims determined to live according to the example of their prophet and under the guidelines of their Islamic tradition. Though concerned about their religion, they are not overly concerned about their political system as long as they are allowed to carry out their Islamic practices. For example, many Orthodox Muslims live under a Western form of government without any major problem. For some Orthodox Muslims, however, it is a major problem! That brings us to the category of *fundamentalist Muslims.*

Fundamentalist: Within the orthodox community, a minority of Muslims are extremely concerned about government and political ideology. Like their orthodox peers, they too are serious about fulfilling their religious duties such as prayer and fasting. But they believe that to be true Muslims, they must live under a government that is completely and strictly administered on the basis of Islamic law, which, they allege, comes from God. These Muslims are known as fundamentalists. They are zealous advocates for the return of pristine or fundamental Islam as it was lived and practiced in the seventh century by their prophet, Muhammad.. Fundamentalist Muslims aim to remove and replace all non-Islamic forms of government with Islam as the rule of law, both at home and abroad. They are determined to use whatever means necessary, including terrorism, to strip away from their social fabric all vestiges of non-Islamic influence for the purpose of achieving their worldwide objective. These Muslims represent the fanatical element of Islam.

From this list of profiles, it is clear that ministry to Muslim people requires a variety of approaches and concerns. In this book, we want to focus especially on the concerns that relate to Orthodox Muslims. In general, Orthodox Muslims are very careful to protect the Islamic community from the corruption of foreign ways, and are opposed to any suggestion of change. Consequently, they are suspicious of Western Christianity and react adversely to any form of Christian outreach. In most cases, Orthodox Muslims simply prefer to avoid interaction with Christian people. Because Orthodox Islam is considered the standard-bearer for the Muslim community at large, its influence reaches into all the other categories of Muslim people. Even though Orthodox Muslims represent only a small percentage of the total Muslim population, they speak the loudest. In particular, when fundamentalist Muslims carry out drastic measures to achieve their goals, their voices reverberate throughout the Islamic world.

For these reasons, it is important that we consider the matter of Christian ministry in an Islamic context that reflects Islamic orthodoxy. An examination of Orthodox Islamic culture will provide a standard for measuring our own cultural relevancy, especially if we want the Muslim community to respect and perceive us as people of God who are involved in the work of God.

Reflection

When American Christians begin to perceive the goal of fundamentalist Islam and the rapid growth of the Muslim community in the USA, they become increasingly alarmed. They begin to view these Muslims as a threat to national security and personal freedom. They resent the intrusion of bearded men and veiled women, and want absolutely nothing to do with them.

Sadly, prejudice and fear cloud their vision of the overall picture of what is happening in the world, especially as it relates to Christian evangelism in America.

Most Muslims are here because they wanted a change in life. They were dissatisfied with their past and determined to search for a better future. The countries they left are increasingly difficult for American Christian missionaries to enter. Missionaries cannot legally go there without entry visas issued by the host country. Because of growing anti-American sentiment across the Muslim world, doors for American missionaries are closing. But God, who knows all things, is already at work. If Christian missionaries cannot go to Muslim countries, then God will bring Muslims from those countries right here to our doorsteps. God is bringing them to us! Christians in America should not view this as a threat. We should view it as an unprecedented opportunity for sharing the gospel.

It is imperative that we be willing to act as good hosts. Yes, it is important for us to understand the potential dangers of Islam. But we must look beyond this religious system and focus on its people, the Muslims— fellow human beings in need of God's intervention and in need of a faithful friend. As Christians we must be willing to embrace these visitors with open arms of God's grace. Remember, God is not willing that any one of these Muslims should perish. He cares for each of them. We likewise must care. We must care to such an extent that we are willing to find a way to serve the bread of life in a manner that is both appealing and relevant, following God's example of coming to us as flesh and blood and dwelling among us. That endeavor will require a sympathetic understanding of Muslim people that will include their worldview and cultural practices.

With God's help, this book will address these vital issues. The hearts of many Muslim people remain hopeless and empty. We want to see that void filled with the gift of God's love.

2

Islam: A Religion of Peace Or A Religion of War?

Again Jesus said, "Peace be with you! As the Father has sent me, I am sending you."

John 20:21

As we try to understand Islam, we struggle with the rising incidence of atrocities committed by people who claim to be devout followers of Islam. For example, the tragedy of 9-11, the bombing of US embassies abroad, and the beheading of American hostages have ignited a fireball of anger and resentment toward Muslims as a whole. These acts of terror have cast a dark, suspicious shadow over Islam and created negative stereotypes of Muslims living in the United States. More and more, Americans are viewing Islam as an enemy to America and everything she stands for. An epidemic of Islamophobia is gripping the country and the Christian church.

In the midst of growing anti-Islam sentiment, Muslim leaders here in America are going out of their way to try to convince the American public that Islam is a religion of peace. They speak on behalf of the many Muslims who seek a better life here in the United States. Most of the Muslims among us simply want to fit into the mainstream of society. Aside from wanting to live out their faith, they want to be accepted by their communities, colleagues, and peers as fellow Americans. For this to happen, they recognize the need for friendly relations and mutual respect. They know that to be heard and respected, they need to promote a peaceful image of Islam. In pursuit of that image, moderate Muslims try to explain that atrocities committed in the name of Islam come only from misguided religious fanatics who represent the "fringe elements" of the Islamic community, and who fail to reflect the true teachings of Islam. One of the major organizations that represent the Muslim community is the Islamic Society of North America. Here is what they have said in their publication, *Islamic Horizons*, in an attempt to allay the growing concerns about Islam in our country:

> The Qur'an reminds us that there is no compulsion in religion. No overt or covert force should be used to bring people to Islam . . . (September/October 2002)

Allah sent His Prophets and Messengers to

establish peace, justice, and morality. Muslims must work and cooperate with others to establish peace and justice for themselves and for humanity. (September/October 2002)

Islam envisions a peaceful world. ...Islam asserts each person's basic freedom and equality. (September/October 2002)

Not only does the Qur'an speak of human brotherhood, but it also teaches more than tolerance; it teaches acceptance. (July/August 2003)

As the Qur'an established the sanctity of human life, it called upon Muslims to seek peace. (September/October 2004)

In contrast to such statements made by Muslims who project Islam as a religion of peace, tolerance, and brotherhood, the press prints other statements, also made by Muslims, that carry an entirely different message. The following statements come from leaders of two major fundamentalist groups, the Salafi and Al-Qaeda. These Muslims speak not of peace and acceptance, but of war and extermination:

The conflict in the world today is a conflict between belief and unbelief. The war in Palestine, in Afghanistan, in Iraq, in Algeria, in Chechnya, and in the Philippines is one war. This war is between the camp of Islam and the camp of the cross, to which the Americans, Zionists, Jews, their apostate allies, and others belong.

Every Muslim must know that defending Islam and the Muslims in this war is an obligation incumbent upon him, with his soul, his money, and his tongue. Support for Muslims is an obligation. The Islamic state will not arise through means of slogans, demonstrations, parties, and elections, but through blood, body parts, and [sacrifice of] lives.
(MEMRI [Middle East Media Research Institute]; Special Dispatch Series—No. 642; January 13, 2004)

Our number one enemy is the Jews and the Christians, and we must free ourselves to invest all our efforts until we annihilate them.

And may Allah [God] lengthen our days to allow us to infuriate the enemies of Allah, kill them, and strike them by the sword until they either join the religion of Allah or we kill every last one of them.
(MEMRI; Special Dispatch Series—No. 601; October 31, 2003)

With blood-curdling statements like these, how

can our Muslim friends in America expect us to believe that Islam is a religion of peace?

The matter becomes even more perplexing when we see that those Muslims who profess a faith of peace don't speak out against the militant Muslims. Why?

Because there is an understanding within the Islamic community that Muslims must never publicly denounce other Muslims in defense of non-Muslims. There is also the fear of possible reprisal. So instead, Muslims in America open their book of scriptures, the Qur'an, and show us that their religion does indeed teach peaceful coexistence with other religious communities. Here are some of the verses they use:

> *Invite (all) to the way of thy Lord with wisdom and beautiful preaching; and argue with them in ways that are best and most gracious, for thy Lord knoweth best, who have strayed from his path, and who receive guidance (16:125).*

> *Let there be no compulsion in religion. Truth stands out clear from error. Whoever rejects evil and believes in Allah hath grasped the most trustworthy hand-hold that never breaks (2:256).*

> *It may be that Allah will grant love (and friendship) between you and those whom ye (now) hold as enemies. ...Allah forbids you not, with regard to those who fight you not for (your) faith nor drive you out of your homes, from dealing kindly and justly with them.*

(60:7–8).

Had not Allah checked one set of people by means of another, there would surely have been pulled down monasteries, churches, synagogues, and mosques, in which the name of Allah is commemorated in abundant measure (22:40).

These scriptures are indeed from the Qur'an, as our American Muslim friends are so quick to point out, and they do speak of religious tolerance and brotherhood, but they don't explain why we hear about terrorist acts committed by people calling themselves devout Muslims. If Islam is a religion of peace, then how can militant Muslims engage in acts of terror also in the name of Islam? This brings us to the other side of the story.

Militant Muslims are the fundamentalist Muslims who aspire after a worldwide Islamic state ruled by Islamic law. They perceive themselves as God's agents for the establishment of this Islamic state, and feel duty bound to eliminate any and all obstacles that stand in the way, even at the expense of violence and destruction. We will have more to say on this subject in the next chapter. What concerns us now is this: Just as pacifist Muslims have used the Qur'an to support their view, militant Muslims do the same. Here are some of the more common Qur'anic verses that the fundamentalists use to justify their war against the "unbelievers" who refuse to submit to Islam.

18

And why should ye not fight in the cause of Allah and of those who, being weak, are ill-treated (and oppressed)? —men, women, and children, whose cry is, "Our Lord! Rescue us from this town, whose people are oppressors; and raise for us from Thee one who will protect; and raise for us from Thee one who will help!" (4:75)

Let not the unbelievers think that they can get the better (of the godly); they will never frustrate (them). Against them make ready your strength to the utmost of your power, including steeds of war, to strike terror into (the hearts of) the enemies of Allah and your enemies, and others besides, whom ye may not know, but whom Allah doth know. Whatever ye shall spend in the cause of Allah shall be repaid unto you, and ye shall not be treated unjustly (8:59–60).

But when the forbidden months are past, then fight and slay the pagans wherever ye find them, and seize them, beleaguer them, and lie in wait for them in every stratagem (of war). But if they repent, and establish regular prayers and practice regular charity, then open the way for them, for Allah is Oft-forgiving, Most Merciful (9:5).

Fight those who believe not in Allah nor the Last Day, nor hold that forbidden which hath been forbidden by Allah and His Messenger, nor acknowledge the Religion of Truth, (even if they are) of the People of the Book [Jews and Christians], until they pay the jizya [tax] with willing submission, and feel themselves subdued (9:29).

These verses encourage physical violence against anyone who rejects or even refuses to submit to Islam and the teachings of its prophet. Thus we see clearly that there are two opposing views espoused; one for tolerance and the other for intolerance. So how do Muslims reconcile these differences, especially when verses supporting both views come from the same book of scripture, the Qur'an?

Muslims who prefer to speak about Islam's tolerance argue that the verses that encourage warlike aggression must be taken in their historical context. In other words, for establishing and protecting the newly formed community of Islam back in the seventh century, it was necessary for the new Muslim community to carry out drastic measures against enemy forces or impediments that stood in the way. But now that Islam is a firmly established religion recognized the world over, many Muslims see no further need for militant aggression. They argue that times have changed. There are no longer expanding empires ruled by tyrants. The world is of a different order, composed of independent countries held together by the charter of the United Nations. For these Muslims, the verses that promote fighting are no longer relevant. They applied only to the days and circumstances of their prophet. Thus, on the basis of historical context and contemporary irrelevance, many Muslims feel these verses can be bypassed.

In contrast to this view, fundamentalist Muslims argue that the verses that prescribe fighting are indeed relevant. On the basis of a particular religious theory, they hold these verses to be binding on all Muslims for all time. This religious theory is the "theory of abrogation," which derives from the following Qur'anic verse:

> None of Our revelations do We abrogate or cause to be forgotten, but We substitute something better or similar; knowest thou not that Allah hath power over all things? (2:106)

According to the general interpretation of this verse, God at times chose to send revelations to replace or cancel previous revelations because of changing circumstances in the quickly expanding Islamic community of the seventh century. The application of this theory helps to explain away apparent contradictions, but requires a knowledge of the chronological order of Qur'anic verses. This is complicated, however, by the fact that the chapters and verses of the Qur'an are not in chronological order. For example, the verse that most Islamic scholars regard as the first words revealed to their prophet is not found in verse 1 of chapter1; instead, it is found in verse 1 of chapter 96, which is nearly at the end of the Qur'an.

With a few exceptions, these Muslim scholars have a good idea which verses chronologically follow others. Because most of the verses advocating aggression were revealed after the verses advocating tolerance, the fundamentalists argue that all the verses supporting tolerance have been canceled and are no longer binding. Thus the verses on intolerance have taken precedence.

And the result of applying this theory of abrogation is a world scene that is far from peaceful.

Reflection

Because of these contrasting views reflected in the Qur'an, it is evident that there will always be a divided camp in Islam when it comes to religious plurality. There will always be an Islam of peace and an Islam of war. There will always be Muslims who prefer tolerance to intolerance, and coexistence to extermination.

Thus it is important to remember that despite the loud voice of radical Islam that rages in the world today, there are significant numbers of Muslim people who are peace-loving people. They do not want to identify with the extreme tactics of terrorists. They want to live in harmony with their neighbors and enjoy the good things in life common to all humankind. They want to earn a respectable living. They want to feed and educate their children. They want to enjoy a secure and peaceful environment.

Some of these Muslims are so frustrated with militant Islam that they have become secretly disenchanted with their religion and are ready for a change. And some of them live right in our neighborhoods. This presents us with an opportunity. We can seek them out, approach them in love, and offer them an alternative. Through the power of the Holy Spirit, we can lead them to something greater than a "religion of peace." We can lead them to Him who is the *Prince of Peace*!

Through the Eyes of Christ

3

Why They Hate Us

Love your enemies, do good to those who hate you,
bless those who curse you, pray for those who mistreat you.

Luke 6:27–28

Three years prior to the tragedy of 9-11, rumors began to stir about a religious ruling issued by Shaykh Usamah Bin Ladin and his associates. In part, it reads as follows:

> The ruling to kill the Americans and their allies—civilians and military—is an individual duty for every Muslim who can do it in any country in which it is possible to do it, in order to liberate the al-Aqsa Mosque and the holy mosque [Mecca] from their grip, and in order for their armies to move out of all the lands of Islam, defeated and unable to threaten any Muslim. This is in

accordance with the words of Almighty Allah,
"and fight the pagans all together as they fight
you all together," and "fight them until there is no
more tumult or oppression, and there prevail
justice and faith in Allah."

... We—with Allah's help—call on every Muslim
who believes in Allah and wishes to be rewarded
to comply with Allah's order to kill the Americans
and plunder their money wherever and whenever
they find it.
(News Hour with Jim Lehrer transcript, "Al
Qaeda's Fatwa," 1998)

Most Muslims in this country tell us they love
America and her people. But as we discussed in chapter
2, not all Muslims in the world share that sentiment. The
chilling words above are those of Muslims who hate us
and want to eliminate us.

In 1998, Usamah Bin Ladin and his sympathizers
formed a militant umbrella organization named the
International Islamic Front for the War against the Jews
and Crusaders. The Crusaders are the Christians of the
West. Fundamentalist Muslims view American presence
in the Middle East, and more seriously, American
military bases on the Arabian Peninsula, as a provocation
against the regional community of Islam. Furthermore,
Muslims have resented the long-term alliance between

Israel and the United States, which they see as a conspiracy against Islam. Muslims view these developments as acts of aggression that call for war. It is on this pretext that the International Islamic Front issued its religious directive (fatwa as cited above) to kill all Americans. This fatwa began with the invocation of God's name and the name of Islam's supreme prophet:

> Praise be to Allah, who revealed the Book, controls the clouds, defeats factionalism, and says in His Book, "But when the forbidden months are past, then fight and slay the pagans wherever ye find them, seize them, beleaguer them, and lie in wait for them in every stratagem (of war);" and peace be upon our Prophet, Muhammad Bin Abdallah, who said, "I have been sent with the sword between my hands to ensure that no one but Allah is worshipped, Allah who put my livelihood under the shadow of my spear and who inflicts humiliation and scorn on those who disobey my orders."

These Muslims, whom we talked about in chapter 2, aim to establish a global Islamic State at all costs, even at the price of violence and indiscriminate killings. Though we deeply resent the turmoil that has erupted worldwide as a result of Islamic terrorism, we need to try to understand the source of this anti-West sentiment and why these Muslims hate Christian America in particular.

In the early centuries of Islam, Muslims began to

see the world divided into two communities—the House of Islam (Dar al-Islam; also known as the House of Peace) and the House of War (Dar al-Harb). This is similar to the New Testament idea of Jew vs. Gentile. The inhabitants of the House of Islam are Muslims who are ideally ruled by Islamic laws (this is what defines an Islamic State). These laws are supposed to guarantee peace, thus the expression, "House of Peace." The inhabitants in the House of War are people who live in non-Islamic communities governed by non-Islamic laws. Their fate is the opposite of peace; it is one of disharmony and chaos leading to injustice and war. Muslims perceive this war to be an ongoing struggle by which the justice of God (as defined by Islam) prevails over the injustices of the world.

Note the accompanying illustration to visualize this aspect of Islamic ideology.

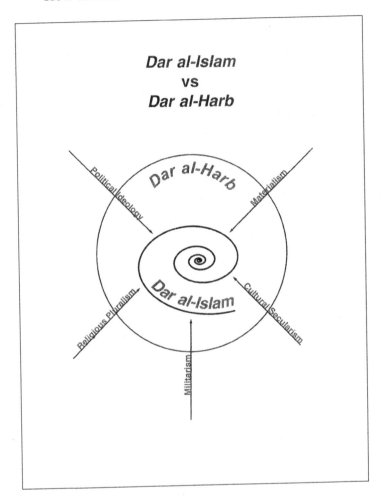

The area of the inner spiral represents the growing House of Islam. The area of the outer circle represents the House of War. As fundamentalist Muslims attempt to expand the House of Islam, they meet up with certain influences in the world today that resist their efforts. These obstructive forces are represented by the arrows that impede the spiraling growth of the Islamic State.

These arrows represent the forces of materialism, cultural secularism, militarism, religious pluralism, and political ideology. As we examine these more closely, we discover that Muslims share many of the concerns devout Christians have for the preservation of their faith and religious community.

Materialism: Orthodox Muslims realize the danger of material wealth and understand how an obsession for worldly gain can erode one's devotion toward spiritual gain. Securing greater material possessions requires more money, which requires more hours of work, which means less time for prayer, reading the Qur'an, and attending religious gatherings.

Cultural secularism: As Muslims become more educated and enter higher institutes of learning, their beliefs and dependency upon God are challenged by a Western secular mindset that denies the existence of God and depends entirely upon human ingenuity and achievement. As God is removed from center stage, the distinction between right and wrong is no longer an issue of absolute authority. Moral standards are compromised and indecent lifestyles are promoted through uncensored television, videos, cinemas, and magazines. This kind of cultural intrusion into the Islamic community is seen by Orthodox Muslims as one of the greatest threats to the cultivation of family values and moral integrity.

Militarism: As Muslims look around the world, they are aware that superpowers exist whose military might and expertise far exceed Islamic resources. This physical strength and resistance presents a major obstacle for those Muslims who feel it is their utmost obligation to spread Islam at all costs.

Religious pluralism: A growing trend throughout the world is the idea of religious pluralism. It encourages people of all religious faiths to be tolerant and accepting of one another; to respect each other's beliefs and allow each other to practice those beliefs without infringing on the freedom of other people. Such an idea is unacceptable to Orthodox Muslims because Orthodox Islam claims to be the only legitimate religion in the world, and Muslims the only true *people of God*. All other religions are viewed as rivals that must ultimately be eliminated. Opening the door to religious pluralism would open the door for Muslims to convert to other religions. In Orthodox Islam, conversion to another religion is an act of apostasy punishable by death. Christianity is Islam's greatest rival.

Political ideology: Because Muslims recognize the need to live according to the laws of God, they are very concerned about the nature of government. Fundamentalist Muslims are committed to the ideology that the Muslim community be ruled by a government that centers on God—a theocracy. Muslims can identify with Isaiah's prophecy of divine rule:

> For the LORD is our judge, the LORD is our lawgiver, the LORD is our king; it is he who will save us (Isaiah 33:22).

Notice the three branches of government outlined in this verse: the judicial, the legislative, and the executive. And God is in charge of all three of them, because God is the only one who can save us. This is what Muslims have in mind in their zeal to establish their version of a worldwide Islamic theocracy. To the fundamentalist Muslim, it makes no sense to speak in terms of separation of church and state or religion and politics. In his thinking, the survival of the community requires that religion (the laws of God) dictate the role of politics, not that politics dictate the role of religion. And for the Muslim, that religion can be only Islam.

Much to the growing frustration of these Islamic fundamentalists, a system of government standing in sharp conflict to the idea of an Islamic theocracy has been gaining momentum in the world. This political system focuses on separation of church and state, individual freedom, and majority rule. It is the system of government called democracy. A democracy is a government of the people, by the people, and for the people. It is a government that ideally functions to serve the people. Not only do people vote other people into office to serve as elected officials, but once elected, these public officials are expected to represent and fulfill the will of the people who elected them. Government leaders are expected to submit to the will of the people, which is not always the will of God.

It is on this point that Orthodox Muslims voice their loudest objection, for it raises the issue of human will vs. divine will, especially when a political system becomes a purely secular democracy. The Qur'an teaches that man is weak (4:28) and forgetful (20:115). Therefore, claim the Muslims, humans are subject to error. They are unable always to discern which laws are best for them. Only God has this perfection and therefore He alone knows which laws are needed to save the world from failure and self-destruction. Furthermore, Muslims fear that, if free to rule themselves according to self-will, humans will become prideful and godless. They will sense no need for God. They will become a completely humanistic secular society. By majority rule, they will eventually vote for laws that clearly violate God's laws.

Look again at the illustration. Review the major forces Muslims must struggle against to achieve the goal of an Islamic world community. There is struggle and turmoil wherever the arrows touch the spiral. These are the basic points of contention. For Muslims, this struggle is a religious struggle. It is their jihad in the cause of Allah.

After reviewing these forces of conflict, we now need to ask ourselves some critical questions. The answers will help to clarify why fundamentalist Muslims hate Americans.

Which country do you think Muslims view as the most materialistic—where people have all the material goods they could wish for, ranging from stereo systems to private vehicles? The answer is the United States of America. Is it any wonder that the symbol of America's economic wealth, the World Trade Center, was one of the prime targets of the 9-11 attack?

Which country do you think most Muslims view as the largest exporter of pornographic materials and vulgar lyrics? The answer is the United States of America.

Which country do you think most Muslims view as having the strongest military with the most sophisticated weapons system? You guessed it: the United States of America. Now we know why the Pentagon was another major target of 9-11.

Which country do you think most Muslims view as the leading exporter of Christianity, sending an unlimited supply of money, literature, and personnel for the purpose of amassing conversions to her "hedonistic culture"? Right again: the United States of America.

Lastly, which country do you think most Muslims view as the greatest promoter of democracy, offering special aid packages for those who agree to implement democratic ideals? Even going to war to spread democracy. Without a doubt, the United States of America. Perhaps the reason a 9-11 plane was heading for the Capitol Building, where the laws of our democratic nation are enacted.

In every scenario, the United States is seen as the major culprit. Muslims view America as the main obstacle preventing them from fulfilling their global ambition. This is why Muslims rate the USA as Islam's greatest enemy. This is why the Ayatollah Khomenei of the 1979 Iranian Revolution called the USA "the Great Satan."

Some Muslims have become so frustrated over their inability to stem the tide of Westernism that they have vented their anger through hateful acts of terror.

Because America is seen as an enemy of Islam, it is also seen as an enemy of God and must therefore be destroyed. Some Muslims have sworn to give their lives and do whatever is necessary to accomplish this destruction. Since Muslims regard such a mission as "for the sake of God," any means is permissible, no matter how ghastly and inhumane. The end justifies the means; thus the rise of fanatical, militant Islam.

This brings us to an obvious but critical key point in this discussion. What religion do most Muslims in the world associate with the United States of America? It isn't Hinduism, Buddhism, or Shintoism. It is Christianity. And Muslims regard everything about the USA as a by-product of Christianity. Now you know the reason these Muslims despise Christian America. The opposing forces to Islam are seen as the outgrowth of Western Christianity.

It is clear that Islamic militancy targets Christian Americans as today's Crusaders (bearers of the cross) bent on destroying the Islamic faith. This Islamic militancy also targets the Jews, whose lobbying power in the inner circles of American government wields great influence over U.S. foreign policy in the Middle East. Following are statements from radical Islamic groups that reflect these hostile attitudes:

> America is the head of heresy in our modern world, and it leads an infidel democratic regime that is based upon separation of religion and state and on ruling the people by the people via

legislating laws that contradict the way of Allah and permit what Allah has prohibited. This compels the other countries to act in accordance with the same laws in the same ways... and punishes any country [that rebels against these laws] by besieging it, and then by boycotting it. By so doing, [America] seeks to impose on the world a religion that is not Allah's..."

America, with the collaboration of the Jews, is the leader of corruption and the breakdown [of values], whether moral, ideological, political, or economic corruption. It disseminates abomination and licentiousness among the people via the cheap media and the vile curricula"

(MEMRI [The Middle East Media Research Institute] Special Dispatch Series—No. 388; June 12, 2002).

The goal of this war, which they falsely called a war on terror, is to prevent the Muslims from establishing an Islamic state whose regime will be in accordance with the Qur'an and the *sunnah* [example] of the Prophet, and which will constitute a source of pride and strength for the Muslims. America and its allies, the Jews, the Christians, and the apostates, will not cease their war on Islam before they remove the last Muslim from his religion and bring him into apostasy. We must be wary of this terrible plot that the enemies of Islam aspire to realize (MEMRI [The Middle East Media Research Institute] Special Dispatch Series—No. 642; January 13, 2004).

Let all know, near and far, let all the Muslims know, that we have done this deed [of 9-11] for the sake of [the belief that] "there is no god but Allah and Muhammad is his Prophet," so that the Muslims will benefit from the Shari'a [law] of Islam, and so that all the regimes that rule not according to the law of Allah, and all the regimes that rule by means of laws made by man, will be removed from them (MEMRI [The Middle East Media Research Institute] Special Dispatch Series—No. 597; October 27, 2003).

Reflection

Militant Islamic extremists have declared war on the United States.

The radical Islamic fundamentalists are on fire for their God and their faith and have committed themselves unto death to see their brand of Islam spread throughout the world. As these jihadists pursue their ambitious and terrifying goals, most American Christians feel powerless to respond.

What should the body of Christ do? How can we respond in a way that will make a difference? Should we initiate an all-out war with them?

The answer is yes.

But it will not be by forecasting victory through

any military or political solution. The struggle is spiritual. And the American Christian church has been given a strategy that is God ordained. It begins with looking at our enemy through a prism of compassion. Seeing the Muslim people as misguided and lost, and meeting that reality with the love of Jesus Christ. We must equip every fellow believer with the information he or she needs to reach out to moderate Muslims, establish relationships with them, and through the power of the Holy Spirit, share the Gospel with them.

This can't be accomplished with a confrontational approach, slamming Islam, focusing primarily on its faults and failures, and promoting the Christian religion as superior to the Islamic religion. But it can be done with a *relational* approach, whereby the dedicated lay Christian primarily promotes "Christ in him" by establishing a mutual relationship that will allow the love of God to flow from his heart and touch that of the Muslim. "By their fruit will you recognize them." "But the fruit of the Spirit is love. . . ."

Establishing that kind of relationship will require empathy on the part of the Christian, a sincere desire to know the Muslims as human beings. It will require a servant-hood mindset modeled after Christ, who descended to identify culturally with humanity. That is the heart of this book: encouraging and helping the Christian to share in the humanity of the Muslim so that the love of Christ and the gift of salvation in Christ become relevant and accessible to the Muslim people.

How many times have you heard that we are in a

"new kind of war"? It's true. We must beat our swords into plowshares and take up the cause of Christ. We must clothe ourselves with compassion and kindness (Col. 3:12) and boldly march forward in the power of love.

4

By Our Love They Will Know Us

There is no fear in love; but perfect love casts out fear . . .
1 John 4:18

Chapters two and three addressed some of the radical positions that disturb Americans today about Muslims and Islam. It is natural for us to boil over with rage when we see the atrocities committed by militant Muslims—especially when they are committed against us. This anger may cause us to want to call fire down from heaven to destroy them.

Unfortunately, we allow this anger to spill over onto all Muslims, including the Muslims living among us. Yet now we realize that many Muslims in America want peace just as much as we do. They want to be hospitable neighbors, upright citizens, and community servants. Yes, they too want to spread their religion, but not by suicide bombings and hostage beheadings. If we let our anger get the best of us, it will be extremely difficult for us to find any common ground with these people. And more importantly, deep down we know that revenge is not in the message of Jesus. His words grip us: *Love your neighbor as yourself* (Matt.22:39). Jesus commands us to live life above our natural tendencies.

Certainly Christ is concerned about the tragedies taking place in the world today, particularly as they relate to fundamentalist Islam and the West. He is deeply concerned about the root causes of this prejudice, hatred, and violence. If we truly are followers of Christ, then we too must be concerned. But the degree of our concern will depend greatly on the tone of attitude we have toward Muslims. Attitude is such an important ingredient in what we do in life, and is often shaped by what we perceive to be our purpose for being. Many of us may respond that our purpose for being centers on God's purpose for the world. Which brings us to an important question. What are God's plans and purposes? What is the underlying reason for all that He does? Let's look at Hebrews 6:13-17 to help us think through this.

When God made his promise to Abraham, since there was no one greater for him to swear by, he swore by himself, saying, "I will surely bless you and give you many descendents." And so after waiting patiently, Abraham received what was promised.

Men swear by someone greater than themselves, and the oath confirms what is said and puts an end to all argument. Because God wanted to make the unchanging nature of his purpose very clear to the heirs of what was promised, he confirmed it with an oath.

In this passage, God's purpose is linked to God's promise made to Abraham centuries before. But before examining this promise, notice that the passage speaks in terms of the unchanging nature of God's purpose. What is the unchanging nature of God's purpose? It is found in the unchanging nature of God Himself. The New Testament gives us three simple statements that address this matter: *God is spirit* (Jn.4:24); *God is light* (1 Jn.1:5); and *God is love* (1 Jn.4:8). It is this third statement that is especially important to our discussion. It helps us to understand that God's purpose revolves around the unchanging nature of His love. Whatever God does is an outflow of love, and this principle is eternal—it will never change.

Now we are ready to see how this relates to the promise of Abraham. The author of Hebrews refers us only to the first part of the promise so that we can understand what he is writing about. But in order to fully understand the impact of this passage, we need to review the whole promise as recorded in Genesis 22:17-18:

> *I will surely bless you and make your descendents as numerous as the stars in the sky and as the sand on the seashore. Your descendents will take possession of the cities of their enemies, and through your offspring, all nations on earth will be blessed because you have obeyed me."*

This passage makes it clear that God's purpose is to bless people, not only Abraham and his descendents, but more importantly, the whole world. Furthermore, from the inference of Acts 3:25, the phrase "through your offspring" refers to Jesus. The obvious conclusion, then, is that God's purpose is to bless the people of the world through Christ. It is very critical that we understand that God's blessings are just as much for the unbelievers as for the believers. Jesus said, *"He causes his sun to rise on the evil and the good, and sends rain on the righteous and the unrighteous"* (Matt.5:45). God's desire to bless comes from His unchanging nature to love. By loving and blessing others we allow God to use us to carry out his divine covenant with Abraham and fulfill His divine purpose. Unfortunately, some Christians choose not to join God in His ministry of love. Even the Bible records for us accounts of some of God's people who failed to understand the significance of the unchanging nature of God's purpose.

One of those people was Sarah. As Abraham's wife, Sarah should have had a better understanding of God's purpose for the human race. (Remember, God wanted to bless people of all backgrounds.) Nevertheless, Sarah harbored resentment toward one of the outsiders in her household who was an Egyptian servant. Her name was Hagar. Hagar was the one who bore a son for Abraham named Ishmael. On one occasion Sarah abused Hagar, causing her to run away. On another occasion, she ordered Abraham to get rid of Hagar and in a fit of rage declared, *that slave woman's son will never share in the inheritance with my son Isaac* (Gen.21:10). In one respect, this was true. Ishmael did not share in the physical property of the inheritance. But as for the inheritance of God's blessings, Sarah was wrong. God's blessings are for everyone, even for Ishmael. In fact, God promised Abraham, *And as for Ishmael, I have heard you: I will surely bless him; I will make him fruitful and will greatly increase his numbers. He will be the father of twelve rulers, and I will make him into a great nation* (Gen.17:20).

This promise of blessing is especially significant for our discussion because the 1.3 billion Muslims of the world regard themselves as spiritual kinsmen to the family of Abraham, Hagar and Ishmael. According to Islamic tradition, the lineage of Muhammad (the supreme prophet of Islam) traces back to the firstborn of Ishmael, Nebaioth. Unfortunately, like Sarah, there are many Christians today who have the idea that Muslim people will never share in the inheritance of God's blessings that are in Christ. They think it is impossible for Muslims to embrace Jesus as Lord and Savior of their lives. Some Christians believe that God has forever cursed the community of Islam and has reserved His blessings for the church only. Sadly, they fail to understand the purpose of God and its eternal nature.

Another member of God's community of believers who lacked spiritual insight was Jonah. God commissioned Jonah to go to the great city of Nineveh to preach a message of warning to the enemies of Israel, the Ninevites. God was ready to destroy the city for its wickedness. After trying to run away, Jonah finally agreed to go. His message must have been compelling. Not only did the Ninevites repent, but the king himself declared a citywide fast. As a result, God looked upon the people with mercy and spared the city. You would expect that Jonah rejoiced along with the city. But Jonah 4:1 tells us otherwise: *Jonah was greatly displeased and became angry.* We eventually learn in the story the real reason he tried to run away from his assignment. He knew that if the people repented, God would respond with mercy and compassion. In no way did he want to see God bless his enemies. He wanted to see God condemn them and destroy them.

Jonah did everything he was expected to do. He traveled to the right place; he said the right words; and he preached with zeal. He went through all the motions of being a worker for God; he did all the *right* things. But something was missing. He lacked a genuine burden for the people. He did not have a love for them. He hated them.

Today, as a result of historical conflicts and contemporary events, some Christians continue to look at Muslims as archrivals and bitter enemies. Like Jonah, they keep their hearts closed, and when they do interact with Muslims, it is often in a spirit of condemnation and retribution. For them, the issue is clear. God is poised to curse Muslims, not to bless them. Again, such people are blind to the concept of the unchanging nature of God's purpose.

Lastly, let's look at an example from the New Testament, the disciple John. John and his brother James were known as the Sons of Thunder. No doubt their tempers flared in times of conflict. Toward the end of his ministry, Jesus began to lead his disciples on one more trip to Jerusalem. It was necessary to spend a night in a Samaritan village on the way. Even though Jews and Samaritans despised each other, Jesus sent messengers ahead into the village to make lodging arrangements. When word came back that the Samaritans refused to help, John and his brother exploded in anger and asked, "Lord, do you want us to call fire down from heaven to destroy them?" John was ready to destroy these Samaritans completely! Notice that Jesus "turned and rebuked them" (Luke 9:55). Though John was a close disciple, he too failed to understand the ultimate purpose of God.

There are still followers of Jesus who would like to call fire down from heaven if they could, especially upon the people of Islam. In many areas of the world, like the Jews and Samaritans, Christians and Muslims have harbored bitter resentments. They recognize the invisible barrier of separation and are careful not to trespass each other's domain. When conflict does spark, however, long held prejudices and animosities explode into eruptions of atrocities and communal violence. Despite the tumult that still rages today in many parts of the world, the voice of Jesus continues to rebuke his people for failing to understand the purpose of God. Of course the purpose of God is embodied in the life and mission of Jesus. John 3:17 is clear: *For God did not send his son into the world to condemn the world, but to save the world through him.* Jesus did not come to condemn people and to destroy them. He came to save and to bless them. In line with God's purpose, this was the purpose of Jesus' ministry. This should also be the purpose of his body, the church. The mission of the church is never to prepare military soldiers for military combat. Instead, it is to prepare ambassadors of Christ for proclaiming to the world a message of love, forgiveness, and reconciliation in the name of Jesus. God wants to bless everyone everywhere and touch them with the life of His Spirit, regardless of their background. That includes the Muslim people in America.

God's Purpose in Action in the Ministry of John

The fact that God's blessings in Christ are for everyone is confirmed by a wonderful miracle that occurred in a most unlikely place following the resurrection of Christ. It all began when persecution broke out against the believers in Jerusalem and scattered them to neighboring regions. According to Acts 8:4-8:

> *Those who had been scattered preached the word*
> *wherever they went. Philip went down to a city in*
> *Samaria and proclaimed the Christ there. When the*
> *crowds heard Philip and saw the miraculous signs he*
> *did, they all paid close attention to what he said. With*
> *shrieks, evil spirits came out of many, and many*
> *paralytics and cripples were healed. So there was great*

joy in that city.

From this description, it is obvious that God was blessing people through Christ in a marvelous way. *There was great joy in that city.* Note who these people were. God was blessing the despised Samaritans. When news reached Jerusalem, the church leaders sent two disciples to investigate the matter. They discovered it was true and remained in Samaria to pray that the new Samaritan believers receive the blessing of the Holy Spirit. In fact they even laid hands on the Samaritans as they prayed. Imagine it—Jews touching Samaritans!

Who were these disciples? One was named Peter and the other was named John. Is it possible this is the same John we read about in Luke 9? Could this be the same disciple who hated Samaritans and wanted to destroy them with fire? It is. How is it possible that before, he wanted God to kill them, and now he wanted God to bless them? How is it possible that he was actually placing his hand on the Samaritans and perhaps even pleading in tears that God fill them with the Holy Spirit? What happened between Luke 9 and Acts 8 that brought about such a transformation in attitude? The answer is the outpouring of the Holy Spirit of Acts 2 on the Day of Pentecost. The disciple John was there when "they were all together in one place" and John was there when "all of them were filled with the Holy Spirit." When John was filled with the Holy Spirit, not only was he filled with the power of the Spirit, he was filled with the fruit of the Spirit, the first being love. It was God's love poured out in God's Spirit that changed the life and attitude of John. It was this indwelling love that aligned John's purpose with God's purpose. Peter, John's partner in Samaria, gives us an extremely important insight regarding the connection between God's Spirit and the attitude of the believer. From 2 Peter 1:3-8, we read the following:

> *His divine power has given us everything we need for life and godliness through our knowledge of him who called us by his own glory and goodness. Through these he has given us his very great and precious promises, so that through them you may participate in the divine nature and escape the corruption in the world caused by evil desires.*
>
> *For this very reason, make every effort to add to your faith goodness, and to goodness, knowledge; and to knowledge, self-control; and to self-control, perseverance; and to perseverance, godliness; and to godliness, brotherly kindness; and to brotherly kindness, love. For if you possess these qualities in increasing measure, they will keep you from being ineffective and unproductive in your knowledge of our Lord Jesus Christ.*

According to what we read, because Christ possessed inherent power and authority, he was able to make special promises to his followers, knowing that he could fulfill those promises. One of those promises was the gift of the Holy Spirit. It was through this gift in particular that the disciples would be able to "participate in the divine nature." Note the impact of those words. This does not mean we become divine beings, but it does mean that we have the capacity to wonderfully and supernaturally connect with God. Through the union of divine Spirit with human spirit, God lives in us. His divine nature in some measure becomes a part of our nature, and therefore, His divine purpose seeks to become our purpose. And notice the outcome of such a union. We become transformed and take on the qualities of the Kingdom of God—goodness, knowledge, self-control, perseverance, godliness, brotherly kindness, and love. Once again we encounter the indispensable ingredient of love.

Reflection

If we want our outreach to Muslim people to be effective and productive, then whatever we do must be characterized by love. And when we truly love Muslims, then we will truly want God to bless them. When we truly love Muslims, then we will be in tune with God's divine purpose for the Islamic world. But this divine love is not something that can be taught in a book or in a classroom. It is not something that an author or an instructor can place into the heart of a believer. This is something that only God can do, but it is so critical. Without a sincere desire to love and reach Muslims, it would be useless to continue reading this book. The chapters that follow will make some demands on the follower of Christ that may be difficult. It will cause you to stretch beyond the normal and traditional way of doing outreach ministry. It will challenge you to walk the way of sacrifice and self-denial. Unless love leads the way, this path is hard, if not impossible, to follow.

If you sense at this moment even the slightest prejudice and dislike toward Muslim people, ask the Lord to fill you with an added measure of the Holy Spirit. Sometimes we are not even aware of an unChrist-like spirit until we are brought into a situation of confrontation. All too often, Christians unintentionally explode during an encounter with Muslims and destroy any possibility for follow-up ministry. In a time of sudden or unexpected confrontation, hidden hatred can erupt into anger, and we may actually misuse the zeal within us to call fire down from heaven. By some unguarded word or action, we could destroy any opportunity for credible witness among Muslims. How much better it is for us to deal with this issue first in a secret chamber with God.

Because of years and years of bitter hostility between Muslims and Christians, it is so easy to be drawn into conflict. That is why it is so important for the Holy Spirit to fill us with self-control and love, and a forgiving spirit. Remember, "love is patient; love is kind. It does not envy, it does not boast, it is not proud. It is not rude, it is not self-seeking, it is not easily angered," and more importantly, "it keeps no record of wrong" (1 Cor.13:4-5).

If the Holy Spirit is prompting you about negative feelings toward the Muslims that you are hiding in your heart, you can offer this simple prayer:

"Lord, fill me with Your love that I might truly have a genuine burden for Muslims; that I might touch them with divine compassion; and that I might be a channel of Your blessing for their lives. Help me to lead them into a salvation experience in Christ. Amen"

5

Cultivating a Sincere Understanding about Muslim People

My food is to do the will of him who sent me and to finish his work. Do you not say, "Four months more and then the harvest"? I tell you, open your eyes and look at the fields! They are ripe for harvest.

John 4:34–35

Now that we see how important it is for us to reach out to Muslims in love, let's begin this endeavor by trying to better understand their religion. Today, as never before, we have access to a growing volume of material on Islam, and most of this material comes from a Christian perspective. However, in order to be balanced and fair in our approach, it is critical that we make the effort to look at Islam through Muslim eyes to truly understand Muslims. In this chapter we will discuss four major components of their thinking: How Islam is more than a religion, how a relationship with God is not

52

established by intimacy with Him, but by harmony within creation, how Islam is a religious system in which God's laws are revealed through prophets, and why Muslims must spread Islam throughout the world.

To the ordinary Christian observer, Islam is simply another religion among the major world religions. If asked, "Who founded Islam?" most of us would answer, "Muhammad." But for Orthodox Muslims, that would be the wrong answer. Because for them, Islam isn't just another religion—it is a divine principle, a way of life mandated by God for all mankind. Thus, they believe God founded Islam and that Islam embodies fundamental truths and standards for guiding, regulating, and assessing the conduct and practices of all people, everywhere.

The fundamental principle embedded in Islam is this: submission to God's will is the prerequisite to peace. Notice the two words which compose the literal meaning of the Arabic word *islam*—submission and peace. According to Muslims, if people want peace in their world, their country, their families, and their hearts, they must submit to God's will. And God's will is known through His revelation of rules and regulations to humankind. These rules and regulations comprise the divine law known to Muslims as the *Shari'ah*. Thus, for Muslims, it is the keeping of the law that brings peace . . . it is the keeping of the law that is the way to salvation for the world.

To Muslims, it is impossible to understand the nature of God because He is divine, but it is imperative to understand the will of God, which God revealed through Islam and the *Shari'ah*. Muslims insist that global salvation and peace do not come by some great prophet shamefully hanging on a pagan cross, but by people living according to God's will. This supports the Qur'an's teaching that the ultimate purpose for humans in life is to serve God by following His laws. For the Muslim, this is true worship.

As Christians, we know we are under grace. But we can identify with the premise that peace comes from submission to God's laws because it is reflected in the Bible. For example, Psalm 119 uses several words to refer to the law—statute, precept, decree, and command. These words, along with *law*, are found 131 times in the NIV translation of that one chapter. What was so important about the Law for it to be mentioned so many times? Verse 165 gives us the answer: "Great peace have they who love Your law." That's exactly the message the Muslim wants us to hear when he tries to explain to us the virtue of Islam. Peace and salvation come through the keeping of God's law.

The next matter the Muslim wants us to understand is that Islam speaks of a relationship of working order. Notice the following Qur'anic references:

> *Glorify the name of thy Guardian-Lord Most High, who hath created, and further, given order and proportion, who hath ordained laws, and granted guidance.* (87:1–3)

Do they not look at God's creation, (even) among (inanimate) things how their (very) shadows turn around, from the right and the left, prostrating themselves to God, and that in the humblest manner? And to God doth obeisance all that is in the heavens and on the earth, whether moving (living) creatures, or the angels, for none are arrogant (before their Lord). They all revere their Lord, high above them, and they do all that they are commanded. (16:48–50)

These verses show that connection with God is not established by having a personal relationship with Him, but instead, by living in harmony with creation. This harmony results when that which is created functions according to the laws of the Creator. For example, the Orthodox Muslim speaks of even the solar system embracing Islam. The planets revolving around the sun, the earth spinning on its axis, the moon revolving around the earth, and the force of gravity keeping each planet in its proper place—everything functions in harmony according to God's laws. If anything were to violate the laws of God's creation, this harmony would be disrupted. Clearly, if the earth were to leave its orbit and travel toward the sun, it would be annihilated by the heat of the sun.

Sometimes Muslims will use this understanding of Islam to try to urge you to become a Muslim. They will try to persuade you that you were born a Muslim. In other words, you were born with the inclination of submitting to the laws of God's creation. They will ask you, "At the time of birth, who taught you how to cry; who taught your lungs to pump air and your heart to pump blood; who taught you how to close your eyes and sleep?" According to Muslims, as a baby you automatically functioned according to the laws of your Creator. You functioned and slept in peace by submitting to the Law of God. But since birth, you have been influenced by your environment to live according to the law of man. As a result, you will experience disharmony in your life. "So return to your roots," says the Muslim. "Become what you were born to be—become a follower of Islam and return to the Divine Law."

Thirdly, Muslims want us to understand Islam as a religious system in which God's laws are revealed through human agents known as prophets. This system also provides the means to have these laws propagated, interpreted, administered, and preserved. In this understanding, Islam is an evolving religion in which God's laws are revealed in stages. According to Muslims, to reveal everything at once would have been too much for humans to absorb. So, little by little, God revealed His will through the prophets. Twenty-eight prophets are mentioned by name in the Qur'an. They include Adam, Noah, Enoch, Job, Abraham, Ishmael, Isaac, Jacob, Joseph, Moses, Aaron, David, Solomon, Elijah, Elisha, Jonah, John the Baptist, and Jesus. Of course, these names are especially significant to us because they all mentioned in our Bible. But in the Qur'an, these are the names of exemplary prophets, every one a "muslim." The literal meaning of *muslim* is "one who embraces

Islam," the divine principle of peace through submission to God's will.

According to the teachings of Islam, Adam was a good Muslim, and the revelation he received from God was good, but it was only the beginning. Noah was a good Muslim, and the revelation he received was even better, but not enough. Abraham was a good Muslim, and what he received from God was also very important, but there was more revelation to come. Moses was a good Muslim who received even more laws for the people of God, but more guidance for humankind was needed. Jesus was also a good Muslim who surrendered to God's will. The Qur'an even gives him the title *Abdullah* (servant of God). The teaching Jesus gave was essential, but the whole revelation from God for humankind was not yet complete. Muhammad was a good Muslim, and he too received revelation from God. According to the Qur'an, all these prophets embraced the same divine principle of Islam and therefore embraced the same religion. Thus was Muhammad told:

> *The same religion has He established for you as that which He enjoined on Noah—that which We have sent by inspiration to thee—and that which We enjoined on Abraham, Moses, and Jesus: namely, that ye should remain steadfast in religion, and make no division therein. To those who worship other things than Allah, hard is the (way) to which thou callest them. (42:13)*

Not only is Muhammad seen as a very important

link in this chain of evolving revelation, but he is seen as the last link in the list of prophets. During Muhammad's tenure, God said something to him that He said to no other:

> . . . This day have I perfected your religion for you, completed my favor upon you, and have chosen for you Islam as your religion. (5:3)

This is a critical verse. It is because of this verse Muslims believe Muhammad was the prophet who received the last installment, the last phase, of the divine revelation for humankind. For this reason, the Qur'an refers to Muhammad as the Seal of the Prophets (khatam-un nabiyin; 33:40). To the Muslim, this means two things. First, since Muhammad is the last of the prophets, anyone after his time claiming to be a prophet is an imposter. Secondly, because Muhammad received the latest and most up-to-date revelation from God, his teaching supersedes the teachings of all previous prophets. "Yes," says the Muslim, "what Moses received was good, and what Jesus received was better, but what Muhammad received was the best!" This makes it difficult for Muslims to think in terms of becoming followers of Jesus. In their thinking, it would require them to exchange the teaching of Muhammad for an earlier, incomplete teaching. In this mindset of progressive revelation, to leave the teaching of Muhammad to follow the teaching of Jesus is like taking a step backward. Surely, no one wants to go backward in his or her spiritual journey when dealing with the revelations of Almighty God.

According to Islamic teaching, Islam incorporates the contributions of all the prophets, including Jesus, but is not complete until it fully embraces, as the culmination of all revelation, the teachings of Muhammad. With Muhammad viewed as the final prophet, Muslims regard Islam as the only valid religion of God for today's world. People who follow any other religion fall short of God's complete revelation and therefore fall short of God's requirements for salvation. Muslims strongly support this position with the following Qur'anic references:

It is He who hath sent His messenger with guidance and the religion of truth, to prevail it over all religion; and enough is Allah for a witness. (48:28)

If anyone desires a religion other than Islam (submission to Allah), never will it be accepted of him; and in the hereafter, he will be in the ranks of those who have lost (all spiritual good) (3:85)

Orthodox Muslims believe it is God's will for Islam to rule over humankind. They see the teachings of Islam and its laws to be the only solution to global unrest and human injustice. As a result, Muslims believe it is God's plan to bring about world peace by establishing a worldwide Islamic State with Islam prevailing over all other religions. In fact, the Qur'an instructs its followers to invite all non-Muslims to embrace Islam.

Invite (all) to the way of thy Lord with wisdom and beautiful preaching; and argue with them in ways that are best and most gracious. For thy Lord knoweth best who have strayed from His path and who receive guidance. (16:125)

This invitation is known in Arabic as *dawah*. This is the same word used by Muslims for Islamic propagation. This injunction to invite others is why Islam, like Christianity, is a spreading religion that is fueled with missionary fervor. Most Muslims are content to see Islam disseminated and established through non-violent means. For example, here in America, they are happy to model their faith in public and engage in social venues such as interfaith dialogues. With time on their side, they believe that Christianity will eventually lose its influence in the world, and that through the example of good works and godly lifestyle, Muslims will attract non-Muslims to Islam.

Another factor on the side of Muslims in America is the petrodollars we pump into the oil kingdoms of the Middle East. Much of that money is reinvested in the USA to promote Islamic causes. For example, Harvard University and Georgetown University both received grants of twenty million dollars for introducing Islamic studies into their academic programs. Petrodollars are also used to build beautiful mosques and Islamic study centers in the major cities of our country.

Another more subtle factor on the side of Muslims

is their birth rate. Muslims are confident that in time, the Muslim population of the world will far exceed the Christian population. They believe the same will hold true for the USA. This is a real possibility when you realize that Muslim couples continue to have six to ten children while many Westerners limit the size of their families to two children. (See "Welcome to Christianville" population growth comparisons in appendix A).

With regard to the spread of Islam in the world, fundamentalist militant Muslims are not as patient as their Orthodox brothers are. They see the world in a severe crisis that demands immediate attention. They truly believe Islam is the sole repository of God's laws and is thus the only answer to human woes. They also believe the Qur'an obligates them to take whatever measures necessary to insure the establishment of Islam worldwide. Therefore, they take on a more proactive and aggressive approach that includes terrorist attacks.

Muslims believe they are the only ones in the world today who qualify to administer God's rule over the earth. The Qur'an speaks of the Jews as once the chosen people of God; but according to Muslims, Jews are apostates who not only rejected the prophet of Islam, but also lost their special status with God because of their sin of idolatry centuries earlier. The followers of Jesus, according to the Qur'an, were also God's people, but they likewise fell into divine disfavor. Muslims think Christians believe in a trinity of three separate gods, and that they too have succumbed to idolatry. What many

Christians do not realize is that in various parts of the Muslim world, Christianity is represented by a massive following whose members bow down to statues. It is noteworthy that idolatry, which was the abominable sin of the Old Testament, is the worst sin in Islam—the sin called *shirk*. It is the sin of worshiping any other thing or being besides God.

Muslims see no other religion today that acknowledges the one true God of Abraham and seeks to establish a community completely ruled by the laws of that God. They regard Islam as the only world religion that has preserved the divine law, in both its holy book, the Qur'an, and in its holy prophet, Muhammad. As far as Muslims are concerned, even though Christians and Jews claim to worship the God of Abraham, they have rejected God's laws in favor of manmade laws.

We can agree that the principle linking peace with submission to God's will reflects biblical teaching, and that the Law of God is a vital concern. But we do not agree that all the laws of Islam are the laws of God, a part of Islamic ideology critical to Orthodox Muslims. And, in fact, the efforts of Islamic fundamentalists to impose what they believe to be divine law, even upon their own people, has not produced the results they desired. It all sounds like a noble idea, but it doesn't work.

The Islamic country of Iran is a prime example. During the Iranian Revolution of the 1970s, the Muslim fundamentalists insisted that the establishment of an Islamic government administered by the Muslim clergy, the experts on Islamic law, would ensure the formation of an ideal Islamic community. The objectives of the fundamentalists were to depose the Shah, whom they regarded as a Western puppet, and rid the country of all Western influences. They would implement a constitution that centered on the teaching of the Qur'an and the example of Islam's prophet, Muhammad.

The fundamentalists expected that as soon as the people became subject to an Islamic government, Iran would become a peaceful society, free of corruption and turmoil.

But to the contrary, decades later, thousands of Iranians have become disillusioned. From time to time, university students have filled the streets of Tehran in mass protests against government corruption—and this while the government is run by the clergy, who know all about Islamic law!

To strive for the imposition of God's Law may appear to be a commendable mission, but why doesn't it work? The Bible gives us the answer. In regard to the Law, Romans 8:3 declares, "For what the law was powerless to do in that it was weakened by the sinful nature, God did by sending his own Son in the likeness of sinful man to be a sin offering." The intention of the Law of God, as found in the Old Testament, was to provide guidance to humankind. But according to biblical teaching, the Law was made ineffective by the fallen and sinful nature of man. The carnal nature within each of us rebels against the will of God to fulfill the will of self. As long as Satan exists in the world, people will always be affected by sinful tendencies. As a result, no descendent of fallen Adam can claim to have the moral perfection needed to interpret and legislate God's Law with perfect equity.

A theocracy centered on divine law can be administered only by a divine order of government. But this will not fully take place until Christ returns to the world to eliminate Satan and establish world peace. Until that time, before we can talk about the administration of the Law, we must first focus on the transformation of the heart. Without this transformation, good intentions can easily turn into evil results. For example, zeal can turn into fanaticism. Justice can turn into uncontrolled revenge. Anger can turn into hatred. Piety can turn into religious legalism and hypocrisy. The soul that is not transformed by the Spirit of God can become the control center of ungodly spirits. And then power turns into tyranny that wields terror and atrocity. The heart of fallen humanity must be transformed no matter what the religious background—Christian, Muslim, Hindu, Buddhist; this truth applies to all of us. Thus we must return to the work of the cross, and bring along our Muslim peers. We must return to the critical message of the Gospel that speaks of spiritual transformation.

This chapter was not meant to be a discourse on political science. There will be no perfect government until the return of Christ. Still, our democracy gives us the freedom we cherish, the freedom to worship God in peace and proclaim the Gospel openly. But we can't deny that as Christians we are beginning to see the dangers of our own democratic system. The legal struggles over abortion, same-sex marriages, school prayer, nativity scenes, and even the pledge of allegiance to the national flag are indications of how laws made and interpreted by man can delete God first from the public square, and if left unchecked, from our culture.

It is important for us to see this aspect of Westernism through Muslim eyes. It helps us to understand where these fundamentalists are coming from. Many of their concerns for justice, morality, and godliness reflect our own. We can in some measure empathize with their concerns. This empathy, if we let it, can open the door to sincere prayer on their behalf as we find common ground. For those Muslims who seek true righteousness, God can fulfill their yearning through the heart-changing, righteous work of Christ—if we will be His vessels.

Reflection

It is imperative that, as Christians, we help Muslims realize not all Americans are the American they see in uncensored magazines and movies of the West. We must live holy lives and exemplify love and service to both God and fellow beings so it can be said, when they have seen us, they have seen Jesus Christ.

Are you thinking ". . . *four months more and then the harvest?*" (John 4:35) Are you reading this book and learning about Muslims and Islam, but in your heart you aren't sure if God is really calling you to reach out to these lost people?

Jesus lived out God's will. Remember His words:

"My food is to do the will of him who sent me and to finish his work." As the body of Christ, let us recommit ourselves at this critical time in history to take up God's cause and further His kingdom by viewing the Muslims "through the eyes of Christ" and seeing that the fields are ripe for harvest at this very moment.

6

The Major Beliefs and Religious Practices of Muslims

The work of God is this: to believe in the one he has sent.

John 6:29

At times, you may have wondered, "What is it about these Muslims who so easily get swept into the frenzy of 'Death to America' chants? Have they no common decency? Have they no restraints? Don't they have any spiritual leaning? Don't they believe in anything good?" When Christians focus on only the fanatical elements of Islam, they are quick to judge Muslims as godless people who have no religious bearing.

But just the opposite is true. So far, you have learned that Muslims speak of Islam as not only a principle, but also a religious system. In this chapter, you

67

will see how this religious system obligates its people to both beliefs and practices. For Muslims to be good Muslims, they must believe in certain things and they must do certain things.

Muslims have a special Arabic word to speak of their faith. It is *iman*. For Muslims, *iman* refers to a rote acceptance of a statement of beliefs. From early childhood, a Muslim repeats the words, "I believe in God, and in His angels, and in His books, and in His messengers, and in the Last Day (see Qur'an 4:136), and in His decree over good and evil." This is the Muslim's *iman*, which is classically known as The Articles of Faith. But what exactly does he believe in regard to these tenets of faith?

God

Muslims believe there is only one God, and they call him Allah. The oneness of God is the central belief in Islam, around which all its teachings revolve. Muslims regard this oneness of God as absolute. In other words, He is not divisible into a number of divine persons that make up a godhead. He is uniquely one. He was never born from another, nor does He give birth to another. He is unlike any other in the universe. There is nothing that can even remotely compare to Him. He rules from a heavenly throne as Lord of heaven and earth. He is the Creator of all things and admonishes the human race to worship neither the sun nor the moon, but their creator (Qur'an 41:37). He commands the worship of all people and called Abraham out of idolatry to begin the community of faith. He is the Master of the Day of Judgment. From Him come all things, and to Him shall all things return. His most common descriptions are "the Merciful One, the Compassionate One." He is God Almighty, who reigns supreme over all.

God's Angels

Surrounding the throne of God are the angels of God. According to Muslims, angels are spirit beings whom God created from light. They dwell in the heavenly realm and carry out God's wishes. They play an important role in Islam because they act as intermediaries between God and humans. Islam teaches that God is so highly exalted and holy that He is beyond the reach of earthly beings. Because God is totally other than human flesh, He has no direct connection with people. However, the angels provide the link between God and humans. They convey God's message to the prophets; they intercede on behalf of the needy; and they shower God's blessings upon the faithful. Here are some of the important angels and what Muslims believe about them:

Jibril. He is the angel who brings down God's messages for the human race. It was Jibril who delivered from God the teachings of Islam to their prophet Muhammad in the seventh century. Muslims also believe he is the same angel who informed the Virgin Mary that she would have a son named Jesus. Christians recognize Jibril as

Gabriel.

Mikail. This angel is known to have great power. Muslims involved in witchcraft often invoke his name for cures and protection. Christians recognize Mikail as Michael.

Azrail. This is the angel of death, who separates the soul from the body when a person dies. The sighting of Azrail is a sure sign for Muslims of impending death.

Israfil. He is the angel who will blow the trumpet on the Day of Resurrection.

Munkar and Nakir. These are two dreaded angels. According to Muslims, immediately after death and burial, Munkar and Nakir visit the bodies of the deceased and interrogate them concerning their religious faith. If the deceased prove to be unbelievers, then these two angels continually beat their bodies in the grave until the resurrection.

Malik. This angel is the gatekeeper of hell.

Harut and Marut. These are the two angels who brought to earth the knowledge of magic and secret arts.

Recording Angels. These are angels who sit on the shoulders of every human being. One angel sits on the right shoulder and records a person's good deeds. Another angel sits on the left shoulder and records the person's evil deeds. This information is kept in a book, which, according to Muslims, God will open on the Day of Judgment.

God's Books

Muslims believe God provides guidance to humankind by sending special messages to the world. These messages represent the words of God, which supposedly have been preserved from eternity in a heavenly book known as the *umm-ul kitab* or the "mother of the book," and the source of divine revelations. At certain times in human history, God sent down these messages to the world and conveyed them to human prophets through the agency of Jibril (Gabriel). Muslims regard four of these messages as major revelations that comprise four major holy books. They are known as the *Tawrat*, the *Jabur*, the *Injil*, and the *Qur'an*. Many Christians recognize these as the Torah, the Psalms, the Gospel, and the Qur'an of Islam.

When Muslims speak of their holy book, they speak of God sending down the Qur'an to the lowest heaven. From there, over a period of 22 years in the seventh century, the angel Jibril revealed its verses to Muhammad. The Qur'an instructs Muslims to believe in all the previous revelations. But because Muslims believe that the Qur'an was the last revelation, they regard it as the most up-to-date version of God's guidance to humankind, thus superseding all previous messages. Muslims use this claim to argue that the other books, the Scriptures of the Jews and Christians, are obsolete.

The word *qur'an* literally means "that which is recited." On the basis of this definition, Muslims claim that every word Muhammad communicated to his people was the exact word of God. According to Muslims, Jibril revealed the message exactly as it came from God; Muhammad memorized it, and then spoke it in turn to his scribes so they could record it. In this way, Muslims claim, Muhammad had no human input into the delivery of the message. It was conveyed word for word as it came from God through Jibril. It was a word-for-word dictation and recitation. Muhammad memorized it as he heard it from Jibril and then recited it word for word to his people. Muslims often use this claim to argue the superiority of the Qur'an over the Bible. Christians speak of biblical authors divinely inspired yet free to use their own personal style such as prose or poetry. Muslims insist that because there was no such human element in the revelation of the Qur'an, it is above any charge of human error.

The Qur'an is divided into 114 chapters or *surahs*, and each *surah* has its own title. For example, chapter 19 bears the title *Mary* (the mother of Jesus). Some chapters are very long, the longest having 286 verses; and some are very short, the shortest having 3 verses. The larger chapters tend to be in the beginning of the Qur'an, and the shorter chapters toward the end. The Qur'an is also divided into 30 equal sections, each having a different title. The purpose of this arrangement is to facilitate the reading of the whole Qur'an during the fasting month of Ramadhan. Thus a Muslim can read the entire Qur'an by the end of the month by reading one section per day.

The Qur'an is difficult to read for two main reasons. First, the verses are not in chronological order. For example, one would expect to find a description of the creation of man in the beginning of the Qur'an, but it is in chapter 96. Secondly, bits and pieces of certain narratives are scattered throughout the Qur'an, making it difficult to get a cohesive picture.

Muslims believe the Qur'an was revealed initially in Arabic. They are loath to translate the Qur'an into another language for fear of losing anything of the original meaning. Because Muslims view the Qur'an as the word of God, they take the matter of preserving and protecting its original form very seriously. It is important to know that most Muslims live outside the Middle East and therefore most Muslims do not speak Arabic. That is why many of them at a young age go to a local religious school to learn to read Arabic. It is so they can read the Qur'an. Not only is the Qur'an in Arabic, it is also in poetic verse. Thus the chanting of the Qur'an is melodious and captivating. Some Muslims, even those whose mother tongue is not Arabic, train to memorize and chant the entire Qur'an as a religious duty. That would be equivalent to Christians memorizing and reciting the entire New Testament in Greek!

God's Messengers

Muslims believe that God appointed special people on earth to be His messengers. They were the ones God chose to reveal His will to the people and to call people to repentance. Four of these messengers are special because they are the ones associated with the major revelations of God. They are Moses and the Tawrat (Torah); David and the Jabur (Psalms); Jesus and the Injil (Gospel or New Testament); and Muhammad and the Qur'an. The Arabic expression for "messenger of God" is *rasulullah*. Thus each of these major prophets bears the title *rasulullah*; however, Muslims generally reserve this special title for Muhammad because he was the last in line of their prophets. The Qur'an mentions many of these prophets by name. Surprisingly, these names resemble many of the names of famous figures in the Bible, especially the Old Testament. Here is a list of these prophets with their Arabic names and English counterparts:

Adam	*Yaqub* (Jacob)	*Sulaiman* (Solomon)
Idris (Enoch)	*Yusuf* (Joseph)	*Yunus* (Jonah)
Nuh (Noah)	*Shu'aib* (Jethro)	*Ilyas* (Elijah)
Ayub (Job)	*Musa* (Moses)	*Al-Yasa* (Elisha)
Ibrahim(Abraham)	*Harun* (Aaron)	*Zakariah* (Zechariah)
Ishaq (Isaac)	*Talut* (Saul)	*Yahya* (John the Baptist)
Ismail (Ishmael)	*Daud* (David)	*Isa al-Masih* (Jesus the Messiah)

The Last Day

Muslims believe that time on earth will some day come to an end. The Qur'an refers to this finality of earthly existence as the Hour or the Last Day. No one knows when this last day will take place, but it will be marked by two major events—the resurrection and the judgment. Muslims believe that on this momentous day, God will raise the dead to life. All who ever lived will stand before Him to account for their lives. God will judge all human beings according to their deeds and according to His mercy. The Qur'an does not provide the details as to how this will take place. What is clear, however, is that God will reward some people by admitting them into a place called Paradise, and He will punish others by consigning them to hell.

The Qur'an describes Paradise as a beautiful place of eternal reward for those who pass God's judgment. It is a joyful garden (*jannah*) in heaven, filled with trees of luscious fruit and rivers of pure drink. It is a place where beautiful heavenly companions wait on both men and women to fulfill their wants. Humans will finally get to enjoy in Paradise all the pleasures God intended for them on earth and even more. They will dress in fine silks, recline on soft couches, and feast upon sensuous delights for all eternity.

In contrast, the Qur'an describes hell (*jahannam*) as a terrible place of eternal punishment for those who fail God's judgment. It is a place of fire and everlasting torment. The condemned will be bound in heavy chains. They will suffer the pain of boiling water on their heads and hooked irons in their flesh. Muslims take these descriptions literally. They dread the possibility of such a horrible fate.

God's Decree

Muslims believe that everything that happens, whether good or bad, occurs by the will of God. God, in His sovereign power, is in control of everything. Nothing in turn controls Him. From this premise, most Muslims believe God predetermines both the actions of people and the conditions of people. He even predestines them to an eternity in Paradise or an eternity in hell. Despite this belief, Muslims believe God will still hold people accountable on Judgment Day for their earthly deeds.

Works

Although a Muslim embraces a belief system in which he expresses faith regarding the spiritual realm, his religious works and rituals are seen as the critical pillars that uphold his religious system and provide it strength, meaning, and preservation. Being a good Muslim is determined more by works than by what is simply believed. One's inner beliefs can remain hidden in the private realm of reasoning and uncertainty, but religious works provide a public display of evidence that expresses both religious identity and religious devotion. In addition, religious works are seen as a prerequisite to salvation. Because these works are viewed as prescribed by Almighty God, to fail to fully observe them is to disobey God and incur His punishment. Conversely, to fulfill these obligations is to merit heavenly reward. Thus, such works become a means of hope for eternal salvation.

Consequently, the observance of religious works plays a critical role in the daily application of Islam. These religious works are headed by a traditional list of requirements that have become known as The Pillars of Islam. Let's look at each requirement to gain a better insight into a Muslim's religious practice.

Confession of Faith

Every Muslim is obligated to make a verbal confession of his faith by reciting what is known as the *shahada*. He does this by uttering the words, "I bear witness that there is no God but Allah and I bear witness that Muhammad is the messenger of Allah." By reciting this declaration of faith, one identifies himself as a Muslim who subscribes to the religion and community of Islam. The words of this declaration are often the first words a person hears. They are actually whispered into his ears at birth. And the last words he hears when whispered into his ears at death.

Prayer

Every Muslim is obligated to pray five times daily. These prayers, known as the *salat*, must be performed at dawn, noon, afternoon, sunset, and evening. Prayer time is announced through loudspeakers from the minarets or towers of local mosques. This prayer call summons Muslims with the words, "Come to prayer; come to prayer. Come to fulfillment; come to fulfillment." Though Muslims can choose to pray in their homes, their traditions speak of greater rewards for those who pray in the mosque.

It is important to understand that for the Orthodox Muslim, prayer is more of a required ritual than a time of personal, communion with Almighty God. As a result, great stress is given to methodology. If a Muslim performs his prayer exactly according to religious specifications, his prayer is received by God and qualifies for religious merit There are many requirements that make a prayer valid.

For example, before entering the prayer hall of the mosque, the Muslim must remove his shoes and perform a meticulous ceremonial washing of face, hands, and feet. When ready to pray, the Muslim must place himself in line with fellow worshippers, face the direction of the city of Mecca, and then proceed through the prescribed postures of the prayer. These include standing, bowing, kneeling, and prostrating. While going through these postures, the Muslim recites from memory the words of the prayer, which must be spoken in Arabic. These memorized portions of the prayer are, according to Islamic tradition, the very words which Muhammad, the prophet of Islam, uttered centuries ago. An Orthodox Muslim dare not pray his own words lest he say the wrong thing and unknowingly incur the wrath of God. Seeing hundreds of Muslims bowing and prostrating in unison is indeed an impressive sight and one in which Muslims pride themselves when talking about the unity of the Islamic community.

Fasting

Muslims are also required to fast, which is known as *saum*. Specifically, they are required to fast during the whole month of Ramadhan, which is the ninth month of the Muslim lunar calendar. According to Islamic teaching, the month of Ramadhan is a holy month because that is the month when the angel Jibril began to deliver the scriptural revelation from God to the prophet of Islam, Muhammad. Upon the sighting of the new moon, marking the beginning of the month of Ramadhan, Muslims are to begin the fast from dawn until sunset of each day, abstaining from food or liquid. Some Muslims are so strict about not drinking any liquid that they spit out their saliva all day long rather than swallow it and risk divine disapproval. This fast of Ramadhan lasts twenty-nine or thirty days, depending on the sighting of the next new moon.

For most Muslims who happen to live in third world conditions and tropical climates, the fasting of Ramadhan is an extremely rigorous exercise. However, it is an exercise that seeks to unite the world community of Islam, as Muslims the world over bear this hardship together as an act of religious devotion.

Almsgiving

Every Muslim is obligated to contribute toward the social and religious needs of the community by means of almsgiving known as *zakat*. His religious teachings are clear in terms of helping the needy such as the poor, the orphan, and the widow. As a result, Muslims are required to give 2½ percent of their earnings. In many cases, this amount is collected by the government and distributed under government supervision toward humanitarian causes, such as orphanages and hospitals, as well as toward religious causes, such as the maintenance of mosques and religious schools.

Pilgrimage

Every Muslim is obligated, at least once in his lifetime if he is financially able, to perform a pilgrimage to Mecca, Saudi Arabia. This pilgrimage, known as the *hajj*, lasts the first ten days of the twelfth month of the Muslim calendar. It enables the Muslim to visit the birthplace of the prophet of Islam as well as the greatest of all holy sites, the *Al-Masjid Al-Haram* (the Sacred Mosque) complex, which encloses the cubical shrine known as the Kaaba. Like the Tabernacle of the Old Testament, the Kaaba is viewed symbolically as the House of God where Muslims congregate annually to celebrate His praises. According to Islamic tradition, Abraham and Ishmael laid the foundation of the Kaaba, and from that time, the rite of pilgrimage was instituted to be a lasting ordinance.

Today, as many as two million Muslims converge in Mecca each year to perform the many rituals associated with the pilgrimage. These ceremonies center on the traditions of Abraham, Hagar, and Ishmael, and climax with the most important ritual of all, the slaughter of an animal sacrifice. This rite takes place on the tenth day of the pilgrimage and marks the most important of all Muslim holidays, the Celebration of the Sacrifice (*Eid-ul Adha* or *Eid-ul Qurban*).

Perseverance

Some Muslims add to this list of religious obligations the matter of perseverance or struggle, which is known as jihad. Jihad is often translated by Western authors as "holy war." Muslims, however, want us to know that the word *jihad* has a much broader meaning and refers to a variety of personal experiences that involve perseverance or struggle. For example, some Muslims speak in terms of jihad of the soul; jihad of the hand; jihad of the tongue; and jihad of the sword. Jihad of the soul is seen as the most important in the list and refers to the spiritual struggle of overcoming the temptations of Satan. Jihad of the hand refers to perseverance against the physical hardships of life. Jihad of the tongue refers to the perseverance a Muslim must exert when trying to share his Islamic faith through dialogue and debate. Jihad of the sword speaks of the Muslim's obligation to defend and spread his faith at all costs, even if it means by the sword of physical combat.

Reflection

As Bible-believing Christians consider the "religious works" aspect of Islam, they may be quick to condemn Islam as a religious system whose salvation is based on works. They reinforce their assessment with the teaching of Ephesians 2:8–9: *For it is by grace you have been saved, through faith—and this not from yourselves, it is the* *gift of God—**not by works**, so that no one can boast.* (Emphasis is the authors'.)

In all fairness, the complete view of salvation by Orthodox Muslims can be represented by the following equation:

$$\text{Faith} + \textit{Works} + \text{Divine Mercy} = \text{Salvation}$$

Notice that Muslims do see the need for God's mercy in the picture, but that works are a major focus. What we need to consider, however, is that even for Christians, works are not removed from the equation. They are simply shifted, because the biblical equation regarding salvation also includes works. That equation looks like this:

$$\text{Faith} + \text{Divine Mercy} = \text{Salvation} + \textit{Works}$$

Remember that works is an important part of the Christian experience as well. It's just that works are not the input of salvation, but the output of salvation. In other words, the true Christian does not perform works to earn salvation; rather he performs works as a result of salvation and the indwelling love of Christ. This love compels him to want to become involved in tangible expressions of loyalty and devotion to both God and fellowman. As James wrote: . . . *faith, if it hath not works, is dead* . . . (James 2:14 NKJV). With that in mind, we can allow ourselves to appreciate a Muslim's devotion to his religious works.

Though the Islamic theology regarding salvation is not scriptural, we can still find common ground with Muslims by noting the surprising similarities between Christians and Muslims. For example, Christians also believe in one creator God who is merciful, compassionate, and all-powerful. They too believe in angels, holy books, and prophets. Christians likewise pray, fast, and give to the poor. And some Christians even perform a pilgrimage to Jerusalem.

In finding common ground, we have something solid to step out on as we seek friendship with moderate Muslims. Focusing on our differences only polarizes us. Jesus covets the hearts of the unsaved no matter what their ethnicity, culture, or traditions. He loves them. And if we are open vessels, we too can love them with His love.

7

The Dark Side of Islam—Folk Islam

All authority in heaven and on earth has been given to me.
Matthew 28:18

In the previous chapter, we took a close look at orthodox Islam—the official version of Islam with its conventional beliefs and requirements. However, it is important to know that most Muslims in the world are not orthodox Muslims. They are nominal Muslims who tend to be lax in their religious duties and may go to the mosque only on Fridays or holidays. Many of them are still religious, but the Islam they adhere to reveals to us an entirely different side of Islam—often the dark side of Islam—which we commonly refer to as Folk Islam and which speaks of good spirits and evil spirits, white magic and black magic, the evil eye, amulets and charms, love potions and incense, astrology charts and fortune tellers, witchdoctors, Muslim saints and Muslim shrines. Though most Muslims in America tend to be moderate or nominal, there are still those who migrate to this country from marginalized communities, such as refugees, who represent this version of Islam. That is why we need to take a closer look at Folk Islam.

The religious beliefs and practices of Folk Islam are a product of religious syncretism that developed during the initial spread of Islam. The early Muslim rulers were intolerant of pagan religion with its witchcraft and gave the local people only one option— convert to Islam, or be put to the sword. In many cases the people converted to Islam but they managed to retain their traditional practices simply by superimposing upon their witchcraft Islamic names, phrases, and motifs. This was enough to appease their Muslim rulers. And so the outer form of their new religion looked and sounded Islamic, but its substance was still to a great degree local witchcraft.

This seemingly easy transition of Islam into religious syncretism was facilitated by the fact that both the Qur'an and Islamic traditions keep the door open to activity in the spirit realm. For example, the Qur'an teaches that before God created a race of human beings, he created a race of spirit beings, known as the jinn, to inhabit the earth. These jinn are believed to be created from pure fire and possess supernatural power. In the beginning, the jinn were all good spirits. But when God created Adam as the best of His creation, one of the influential jinn named *Iblis* became jealous and rebelled, at which time God cursed him. From that time on, *Iblis* became known as *Ash-Shaitan*—"the Rebel." Many of his companions sided with him and together vowed to become enemies of God and to inflict harm upon the human race as an affront to God. This then explains for the Muslim the origin of the evil jinn or evil spirits. According to Islamic teaching, there are now both good jinn and evil jinn (good spirits and evil spirits) who not only inhabit the earth with humans, but interact with humans to bring either benefit or harm.

Not only does the Qur'an introduce the idea of the jinn, but also conveys the idea that certain individuals endowed with secret knowledge can tame the jinn to their advantage, especially the good jinn. For example, King Solomon is cited in the Qur'an as one who had the power to subjugate the jinn and make them his slaves.

In day-to-day life, most Muslims are fearful of the jinn and the mischief they can create for human beings. And so they have a variety of customs which they practice on a daily basis to provide special protection. For example, Muslims invoke sacred words and names that are believed to be infused with power to ward off the jinn. Of course, the one word most commonly invoked is Allah, along with His ninety-nine names. Muslims can often be seen reciting these ninety-nine names with the help of their prayer beads. Other names include those of the angels and prophets.

Muslims also use certain verses of the Qur'an which likewise are believed to possess special power of protection. Examples are the first chapter of the Qur'an known as *Surat-ul Fatiha* and the so-called "Throne Verse" of chapter two which speaks of God's greatness. Verses like these are decoratively displayed in homes, shops, and vehicles.

Another common practice is to burn sweet smelling incense inside the home. According to Muslim tradition, the evil jinn are attracted to bad smells, and so Muslims conversely believe that the evil jinn are repelled by good smells.

Some Muslims even try to use trickery. For example, Muslims believe that their babies and small children are especially vulnerable to the jinn. And so mothers will call their children by nicknames to conceal their real identity. And because they believe that the jinn specifically target baby boys, mothers will dress their little boys to look like girls in order to confuse the jinn.

Whenever Muslims feel that they are under grave danger or that a jinn has already attacked them, then they seek the services of professionals who are reputed to have special power over the jinn. These practitioners are known by a variety of names, such as *shaman, marabout,* and *faqir,* depending on their location in the Muslim world. Their expertise includes protection and cures against the jinn, as well as divination. Whatever their specialty, they enter the spirit realm through occult rituals that include fasting, ablution, incantation, and even drugs. It is in the altered state of consciousness that they supposedly become empowered to interpret dreams, tell fortunes, and prepare amulets and charms which are then worn by the client on the body, or on the clothing, or placed somewhere in the home. Though these practitioners participate in a variety of forms of witchcraft, their activity for the most part is tolerated by

Orthodox Islam because it falls under the category of white magic, as opposed to black magic. For Muslims, black magic is magic that involves pagan forms and evil jinn, and is therefore forbidden. However, white magic involves only Islamic forms and good jinn, and is therefore permitted.

Aside from the local spirit practitioner, throughout Islamic history, there were certain individuals who became widely celebrated for their religious teaching, charisma, and extraordinary miracles, like the miracles of Jesus such as walking on water and healing the sick. These individuals were known to possess special power to bestow upon their followers divine blessing called *baraka*. When these unique individuals died, their followers elevated them to sainthood and transformed their tombs into beautiful shrines. Though the saint may be long dead, Muslims believe that not only does his power to bless reside at the tomb, but it is even more potent because he is nearer to God. The shrine of a Muslim saint for many Muslims becomes a destination of pilgrimage and serves as a convenient substitute for the conventional hajj to Mecca.

Muslims by the thousands flock to these shrines in hope of some miracle to help them in their time of crisis. A wife may be barren. A child may be fatally ill or demon-possessed. A businessman may be worried about a future transaction. A woman may suspect infidelity on the part of her husband. A government official may suspect a curse on him by a political rival. Orthodox Islam has no answer for these kinds of pressing problems except to fully submit to whatever fate God has decreed. But most people are not ready to simply submit to their difficulty. They want to rise above their difficulty. They want to exert some measure of control over their fate. They want to find a source of power that can change their situation for the perceived good. Furthermore, their hearts yearn for a mediator to act on their behalf. That is why they visit the shrine of the Muslim saint. They believe he has a special connection to God and look to him for intercession and special favors. Muslims pray to the saint, unloading the cares of their hearts and hoping for a miracle—an outflow of *baraka*. Shrines are especially frequented by Muslim women. Though they are usually discouraged from attending the mosque, they are free to visit the shrine. This is one place where Muslim women can seek to fulfill their desire for some spiritual connection and for some sense of self-worth.

Orthodox Muslims have tried to eliminate Muslim shrines and saint worship, but without success. They object that praying to saints is a form of polytheism—only God is to be the recipient of worship and prayer. However the thousands of Muslims who visit the shrines justify the practice with evidence of answered prayers. For them, that can mean only one thing; it is sanctioned by God.

As we come to grips with the reality of Folk Islam, we learn two very important lessons. First of all, many Muslims sense a dire need for a mediator, an intercessor. This yearning reflects one of the deepest cries of the heart which is echoed in perhaps the oldest book of the

Bible.—Job 9:32-34:

> *He [God] is not a man like me that I might
> answer him, that we might confront each other in court.
> If only there were someone to arbitrate between us, to
> lay his hand upon us both, someone to remove God's
> rod from me so that His terror would frighten me no
> more.*

This is the epitome of the universal plea for a mediator between God and man and it is so prevalent in the Muslim world.

The second lesson we learn is that Muslims all over the world constantly feel the need for a source of power to deliver them from evil. Unfortunately the teaching of the Qur'an, which has led Muslims to believe that there are good spirits on earth as well as evil spirits, and that they can be tamed for the good of humankind, is a falsehood. It is a deception that has led millions of Muslims down the wrong road. It has propelled them into the spirit realm of counterfeit powers and counterfeit deliverers. It has lured them into the snare of witchcraft which may offer a temporary cure, but ultimately produces a life of dependency on that which is evil and fearfully wretched. According to the Bible, the spirits here on earth are fallen angels; they are evil spirits. Not one of them is good. And so there is no such thing as white magic. It is all black magic. The objective of these evil spirits is to harm people and corrupt their souls. It is to destroy the glory of the kingdom of God and the glory of its King.

But in all this darkness, there is good news for these Folk Muslims. Remember that in the beginning of this chapter, we learned how they invoke sacred names for protection against evil. Now we begin to understand the significance of Phil. 2:9 that proclaims:

> ... God exalted him [Jesus] to the highest place
> and gave him the name that is above every name.

The name Jesus. The name that is above all other names on earth and in heaven. The name of him who can do far more than tame spirits or appease spirits. He can fully destroy the very work of the devil and set people free from the curse of witchcraft.

Reflection

The dark side of Islam should not be viewed as a problem, but as an opportunity. Because of this component of Islam, most Muslims are more open to the spirit realm than are Westerners who sometimes quickly label such things as superstition. Because of their openness we don't have to be shy about declaring the power in Jesus' name as revealed in the scriptures.

The group of Christians that are most prepared to deal with this side of Islam, the dark side, are those who believe in the power of Jesus' name and who are endued with this power to advance against the strongholds of evil. Those who are familiar and armed for spiritual warfare—the war in which the Light penetrates the

Darkness to set the captives free. Remember Jesus' words to the apostle Paul in Acts 26: "I am sending you to them to open their eyes and turn them from darkness to light, and from the power of Satan to God." In the same way, perhaps the Lord may send you to a Muslim friend or neighbor, to lovingly turn him or her from the power of Satan to the power of God.

For many Muslims who may in some way or another be influenced by Folk Islam, Jesus is the mediator for whom they sincerely yearn, the one and only mediator who can fully represent them before God. Jesus is the source of power for which they desperately seek, the one and only source of power which can completely deliver them from the Evil One. With your prayerful intercession and complete submission to the Holy Spirit, Jesus will set the captives free.

8

How Muslims View God and Sin

*. . . no one knows who the Father is except the Son and
those to whom the Son chooses to reveal him.*

Luke 10:22

Who is your father and what is he like? If you are
one of the fortunate ones who lived with a great dad,
then you will be able to answer these questions easily
because you know his intentions for you were always
lofty and good. And much of what you became in
character and deed was a result of his influence. Your
perspective of your dad helped to steer the direction of
your life. The same can be said about our relationship
with the Heavenly Father. We know His intentions for us
are always good. And our perspective of God shapes our
actions and our overall outlook on life.

This brings us to the question, "How do Muslims
view God?" The answer will lead us to a Muslim's view
of life, and more importantly, to his view of sin and the

remedy for sin. It will help us understand why the Muslim cannot accept the biblical remedy for sin—the cross.

We learned in the last chapter that the fundamental tenet of Islam is the absolute oneness of God. Although He is the one and only God, Allah, He is the God of many names. In fact, Islamic tradition claims that God has ninety-nine names. The Qur'an instructs Muslims to invoke God by His names, but neither the Qur'an nor the traditions provide an orderly and complete list. In the early centuries of Islam, Muslims attempted to collect as many of these names as possible and found them scattered throughout the Qur'an and Islamic traditions. These names are actual words for attributes, such as *As-Salam*, the Peaceful One, and *Al-Quddus*, the Holy One. Today, throughout the Muslim world, there are several versions of the ninety-nine names of God (see the appendix for an example).

Muslims divide these names into two categories: names that refer to God's terrifying attributes and names that refer to God's gentle attributes. The Bible reflects a similar delineation. Romans 11:22 introduces us to the two faces of God when it invites us to "consider therefore the kindness and sternness of God." For the Muslim, God's kindness is represented by His gentle attributes and God's sternness is represented by God's terrifying attributes. And he sees these terrifying attributes as the ultimate manifestation of God's power. This brings us now to a very important observation.

For most Muslims, God is supremely a God of

power. It is no secret that the carnal nature of people is attracted to power. Power implies protection, stability, victory, conquest, supremacy. For this reason, Muslims are very familiar with the names that relate to God's terrifying power, such as *Al-Jabbar* , the Mighty One; *Al-Muzil*, the Destroyer; *Al-Ali*, the High One; *Al-Qahhar*, the Victorious One; *Al-Kabir*, the Great One; *Al-Qawi*, the Strong One; and *Al-Muntaqim*, the Avenger. In addition to these names, the rallying cry of Muslims worldwide is *Allahu Akbar, Allahu Akbar*, God is greater, God is greater! No matter how great a source of power you can imagine—water energy, solar energy, or nuclear energy—Almighty God is far greater and more powerful.

To help us in this discussion, let's look at a typical Semitic view of God found in the Book of Job.

> *But he stands alone, and who can oppose him?*
> *He does whatever he pleases.*
> *He carries out his decree against me,*
>   *and many such plans he still has in store.*
> *That is why I am terrified before him;*
>   *when I think of all this, I fear him.* (23:13–15)

> *God is exalted in his power.*
>   *Who is a teacher like him?*
> *Who has prescribed his ways for him,*
>   *or said to him, 'You have done wrong'?*
> *How great is God—beyond our understanding!*
>   *The number of his years is past finding out.*

(36:22–26)

The Almighty is beyond our reach
and exalted in power . . . (37:23)

Notice the expressions that describe this view of God: He is a God who "stands alone"; is "beyond our understanding"; is "beyond our reach"; is "exalted in power"; and "does whatever he pleases." This is exactly how most Muslims view God.

The phrase "exalted in power" is particularly significant. The common Islamic reference for God, *Allah Ta'ala*, literally means "God the Exalted." According to Orthodox Islam, God is so exalted that He resides completely outside the realm of humankind, far beyond the reach and understanding of mortal beings. God's complete otherness and majestic grandeur is what makes Him so distant and aloof. Furthermore, God's exalted position fits the Muslim view that God's most dominant attribute is power to which all other attributes are subject. Muslims believe nothing at all can limit God or dictate His actions. Not even a code of ethics defining right from wrong. In other words, God can do anything He wants to do and not be answerable to any other entity. If God were limited or constrained in any way for His actions, then He would be less than a God who is powerful over all. The belief that nothing can restrain or constrain God is what makes Him unpredictable. And it is this unpredictability that makes God so fearsome in the lives of countless Muslim people. For whatever reason

God chooses, He can admit people into heaven or He can cast them into hell.

Muslims have their own interpretation for a verse like Hebrews 12:29: "For our 'God is a consuming fire.'" A fire is unpredictable; no one knows which direction it will turn. It can quickly inflict damage without warning. Remember the story of the Israelites of Exodus 20 when they were at the foot of Mount Sinai. They heard the thunder and saw the lightning, and they trembled with fear. Instead of wanting to approach the mountain of God's glory, they wanted to keep their distance. That is the way it is with many Muslims. Because of the fear that derives from a prevailing "God is Power" view, Muslims think in terms of remaining distant from God rather than getting close to Him. And in this fear, they are careful to revere God in visible ways. They must never offend Him. No Muslim dares to incite the anger of God and incur the fury of His power.

Coupled with this idea of fear and respect is the Muslim's perception of his relationship to God. Because God is Lord of the universe and exalted over all, Orthodox Muslims view their relationship to God as that of slave to master. The Qur'an warns that no one can approach God except as a slave (19:93). For a Muslim, to speak of becoming "children of God" is an insult to the majesty of God, for it suggests a horizontal relationship in which deity is dragged down to the level of humanity. This is impossible, according to the Muslim, for God who is the God of power is always Master, and therefore, there can never be a time when He is any less.

A slave must always obey his master. Any lapse in obedience is deemed an offense subject to punishment. The same holds true for the Muslims and their relationship to God. Any violation is viewed as an act of disobedience and reckoned a sin. Muslims believe, as we do, that people can commit certain acts worthy of God's punishment. The Qur'an mentions some of these, such as the consumption of carrion, blood, and swine (2:173); gambling and the consumption of wine (2:219); miserliness (4:37); murder (4:93); theft (5:38); dishonor to parents (17:23); adultery (17:32); and the failure to pray and feed the hungry (74:43–44). Muslims tend to classify these acts as major sins that will lead them to hell unless they repent and fulfill the requirement of atonement. But there is one sin that is unpardonable; it is called *shirk*. It is the sin of idolatry, the sin of worshiping any other entity either alongside God or in place of God.

There are other sins which Muslims classify as minor. These are sins that are excusable. They are seen as ordinary mistakes that result from the imperfect nature of humans. Most Muslims are not in agreement as to which sins fall into which category (major or minor), but it is easy to see how Muslims can excuse their shortcomings as simply human lapses that are necessitated by the natures of God and humanity. This is their line of reasoning: if God is truly perfect, and if there is none comparable to God, then it follows that humans could never be similarly perfect. For Muslims, it is only logical that human beings are marked with defects. To be less than God necessitates being imperfect. With this reasoning, sin is not such a grievous matter; it is the expected norm.

Because humans are created with the capacity to worship God, Muslims insist that everyone is born good. However, the fact that people are born imperfect underlines their "weakness" and propensity to yield to temptation and commit sin. It is important to understand that for Orthodox Muslims, sin is not a condition but a commission. In other words, it is not that we are born sinners; rather, we become sinners—because of our human imperfections. And because we are born good, there is no need for any spiritual transformation. According to Muslims, what we need is the willingness to obey God to the best of our human ability. What is critical for the Muslim is to atone for the major sins when he succumbs to temptation. The description of suffering in hellfire is vivid in the Qur'an, and the Muslim will do everything possible to avoid it.

When Muslims commit sins, even major sins, they do not experience the sense of personal transgression against God, as expressed in the anguish of Psalm 51:1–3: "O God . . . against you, you only, have I sinned." To the Muslim, because God is predominantly powerful and far removed, He is immune to human sin. God is not affected by the Muslim's shortcomings, and neither is the Muslim's relationship with God. The Muslim remains a servant, and God remains the Master, aloof in His royal realm of power and majesty. This wide gap of separation is not seen as a result of sin; it is seen simply as the obvious reality that exists because of who God is and who man is. That is why a Christian's explanation about sin separating man from God makes no sense to a Muslim.

In Islam, God is not only powerful, He is just. Thus, He has set in place a system of justice for His subjects whereby any wrong can be rectified by payment of a penalty. According to Muslim belief, God in His mercy provides a means by which Muslims can fulfill the requirement of justice and atone for their sins. This means of atonement is basically good works such as saying extra prayers, fasting extra days, feeding the poor, and giving to charity.

In regard to good works, the Qur'an declares:

For those things that are good remove those things that are evil (11:114).
He that doeth good shall have ten times as much to his credit (6:160).

With this idea of accumulated good works and atonement for sin comes the imagery in the Qur'an of a balance that holds both good deeds and bad deeds.

The balance that day [Day of Judgment] will be true (to a nicety). Those whose scale (of good) will be heavy will prosper. Those whose scale will be light will find their souls in perdition, for they wrongfully treated Our signs (7:7–9).

It is now clear why an Orthodox Muslim is

100

obsessed with good works. They are the means of his salvation. His objective is to accumulate as much credit as possible on the good side to offset any weight on the bad side. As a result of this obsession, Muslims have devised a system to categorize human acts on the basis of merit, demerit, and neutrality. The following table helps to visualize this kind of system.

Deed	Credit(+) vs. Debit(-)	
	Commission	Omission
Obligatory	+	-
Desirable	+	0
Neutral	0	0
Undesirable	0	+
Forbidden (*haram*)	-	+

(Note : + credit;   - debit;   0 no bearing)

With the above table in mind, if a Muslim says his prayer, he earns credit. If he fails to perform his prayer, his ledger is debited because prayer is obligatory. Failing to pray is a sin. If a Muslim eats pork, his ledger is debited because eating pork is forbidden (*haram*); it is a sin. If he refuses to eat pork when tempted, he earns credit. Between deeds that are clearly obligatory and forbidden, there are issues classified as either desirable or undesirable. For example, performing extra prayers during the night hours is desirable and will earn the Muslim credit. But if he doesn't perform them, his ledger is not debited. Similarly, smoking cigarettes is undesirable. If a Muslim refrains, then he earns credit. If he smokes, there is no loss. Many of his deeds are assessed as neutral, neither increasing nor decreasing his credit.

From this system and the mindset it creates, it is understandable how a Muslim can indulge in some desirable sin on the basis of accumulated good credit. He can actually plan for a night of pleasurable sin by accumulating enough credit beforehand to compensate for his weakness. It is especially helpful for him to know that some religious deeds qualify for multiplied credit. For example, according to Islamic tradition, a Muslim can earn twenty-five more credits by saying his prayer in the congregation of the mosque instead of praying alone at home. Furthermore, he can earn seventy-five additional credits if he cleans his teeth before prayer.

By now it should be clear why Orthodox Islam is so works oriented, and why knowledge of the Law (what is permissible and what is not) is so critical. The Muslim's salvation depends on it. What is especially important is that believing in their capability to atone for personal sin, Muslims see no need for the Christian cross. Not only do they dismiss any need for the cross, they adamantly reject it.

Muslims find it repugnant that Christians would stoop to such a level of ignorance as to believe in a ridiculous story which features Prophet Jesus (Islam's second-greatest prophet) abandoned by God and left in the hands of pagan soldiers to be humiliated on a cross.

For Muslims, the cross speaks of a weak God who was not powerful enough to rescue one of His own. For a Muslim whose God is all-powerful, such a story is unthinkable. In fact, it is demeaning to the exalted majesty of the Almighty; it is blasphemy.

This rejection on the part of Muslims brings us to a great divide. Though we can find common ground with Muslims regarding God the Creator and moral teaching, we are separated by eternity when it comes to the most critical issue of all—the remedy for sin. The Muslim contends for atonement through the merit of human works. The Christian contends for atonement through the blood of the cross. One adamantly rejects the cross. The other gives his life for it.

It is the Christian concept of God that brings us to this impasse. Though we acknowledge God's omnipotence, the Gospel reveals a far more profound truth— God's predominant attribute is love, not power. This is what accounts for the vast difference between the Muslim and Christian worldviews. For example, because God is love (1 John 4:8), Christians do not see Him residing in some aloof corner of the universe. Instead, He is found in the garden calling out to Adam, "Where are you?" Because His love dominates, all that He does is constrained by love. In this way, He is predictable. We can be sure His power will serve only for the good of creation, and whatever He does will be born of His mercy and compassion. His kindness will always predominate over His sternness. And because God is love, because He is near, and because He deeply cares, our sins do affect Him. This is clearly revealed in the story of Noah. God was deeply concerned about the affairs of the world, and as He looked upon humankind, He saw the depravity of sin. Notice now how the Scriptures vividly describe God's reaction:

> The LORD saw how great man's wickedness on the earth had become, and that every inclination of the thoughts of his heart was only evil all the time. The LORD was grieved that he had made man on the earth, and his heart was filled with pain (Gen 6:5-6).

For the Muslim whose God is Power, the idea that God could suffer pain is both unthinkable and insulting. But the Scriptures reveal to us the truth that God is first a God of love. Any loving parent can identify to some degree with this pain, especially when a child rebels. Yes, because God is lovingly near, our sins are not committed only against one another; more tragically, they are committed against God. We dishonor His righteousness. We violate His holiness. We pierce and break the heart of a loving God who yearns for our worship and adoration. This is what makes sin so terrible. Can we really believe there is something we mortal beings can do to heal the broken heart of God? Of course not. There is no way we could atone for such a grievous and horrendous crime. All we can do is rely on God's mercy. And God is merciful. His mercy devised a way for this penalty to be paid, a penalty that we could never pay. In God's sovereign wisdom, Christ's suffering on the cross fulfilled the requirement of divine justice. This is God's gift to the world—Jesus the Savior, in whose blood there is atonement, forgiveness, and remission of sin.

This brings us to a crucial aspect of this discussion. In most cases, the only way Muslims will come to accept the message of the cross is by perceiving God as a God of love. Unless they see *this* face of God, the cross will remain a stumbling block. It is this face that Jesus came to reveal, the face of the father, Yahweh, who is described in Exodus 33 by the twin attributes of mercy and compassion. These are the very components of love that describe the traits of an affectionate father. But Jesus is no longer here on earth revealing this face of His Father. Where will Muslims find this divine love? Where will they see this mercy and compassion revealed? How ironic that the Qur'an of the Muslims has the answer.

> *We sent after them [previous prophets] Jesus the son of Mary and bestowed on him the Gospel; and We ordained in the hearts of those who followed him compassion and mercy (57:27).*

This is where Muslims will find the love of God—in the hearts of those who follow Jesus! The Qur'an is not our Bible, but these words contain a surprising glimmer of truth. We will never know how these words found their way into the Scriptures of Islam, but we can be sure it was not by coincidence. Remember, God's desire is that none should perish. He will do everything possible to bring people to the Light. The question is, will we?

Reflection

Sadly, many Muslims have failed to understand the salvation message of the cross because the followers of Jesus have not always shown them hearts of mercy and compassion. History reveals a scathing commentary on past injustices and atrocities. The Great Crusades that began in the eleventh century witnessed the slaughter of thousands of Muslims in the name of the Christian Church of Rome, which seemed more interested in power and wealth than in the spiritual harvest of souls. The Crusaders were esteemed bearers of the cross, but the cross they carried conveyed a message radically different from that of the Gospel.

The Christian colonial empires of the Middle Ages fared no better in proclaiming the message of the cross. For countless Muslims who were forced to bow to Christian kings, the cross spoke only of subjugation, humiliation, and exploitation. The Christian cross was meant to represent a message of love. Instead, for many Muslims, the cross has delivered a message of hate.

You may be thinking, "Wait. What about all the things the Muslims have done to Christians throughout history and even today?" Does it matter? Will we decide what we will do based on what others do? Will we only offer God's love to those who have never harmed us? Will we refuse to love our enemies?

Today, as never before, we have the unprecedented opportunity to correct the mistakes of the past and to reveal the true message of the cross. But making the best of this opportunity will require Christians who are willing to live the message instead of just speaking the message. So many times we try to preach about the cross to Muslims. We try to explain it as clearly as possible to people who vehemently oppose it. But remember, most Muslims will not be ready to embrace the cross until they begin to experience God's greatest attribute—His love. And that divine love will have to be demonstrated by us through the power of the Holy Spirit. Muslims will be impacted far more by what they feel coming from our hearts than by what they hear coming from our lips.

9

What I Need to Know Before I Witness

Go into all the world and preach the gospel to every creature.
Mark 15:16

God has commissioned us, as Christians, to share the gospel of Jesus Christ with everyone. "Everyone" includes the Muslim community, and what greater joy in Christian ministry could there be than to present the gift of salvation to the people of Islam. It is a love-gift that derives from the love of God (for God so loved the world that He gave... John 3:16), and it is available to all who reach out to embrace it in faith.

It is extremely critical that we understand clearly what this gift is. It is not a gift of money or material gain; nor is it a philosophy or even a religion. It is simply and wonderfully the person of Jesus, the Savior of the world, in whose name there is forgiveness and remission of sin. Jesus Christ is the gift!

However, as is true in many parts of the world, we

108

have a practice of enhancing gifts by decorating them with colorful paper, ribbons, bows, and flowers. Often the greater the value of the gift, the more concerned we become about its wrapping. The decorative wrapping is also an expression of our desire and joy to present the gift. And so we try to make it as beautiful as possible. What we deliver then is a package that not only contains the gift, but reflects the sentiments of the giver.

In the same way, in our effort to deliver the gift, Jesus, to the Muslims, we place this gift in a package. Of course, the wrapping paper we use is Christian wrapping paper that includes such things as hymns, instruments, terminology, visual aids, worship patterns, church furniture, church buildings, and holidays. All this represents our Christian culture, and this is what we use to enhance the gift. We are extremely proud of our wrapping paper. Some Christians have worked very hard to design the wrapping and some have even given their lives to preserve it. We do our very best to ensure that the gift is delivered in a package that is as attractive as we can make it. That package becomes what is called Christianity.

The Package of Christianity

After all of our effort in preparing the package, we are appalled when people refuse to reach out to receive it. This is especially true in ministry to Muslim people. In fact for centuries, Christians have found the adherents of Islam to be among the people most resistant to the gospel. Christians have tried their best and have even given their lives in order to deliver the gift. But not only have Muslims refused it, they have hurled it to the ground, vowing to kill any Christian daring to enter their community with the package again. Needless to say, we become deeply hurt and insulted.

Unfortunately, some Christians react in scornful anger and threaten the Muslims with God's wrath. Then they target Muslims of another area, only to be rejected again. Eventually, utter frustration leads them to conclude that this hardhearted rejection is a divine curse making it impossible for any Muslim to enter the Kingdom of God. With total disgust and despair, they take their package to another people group and abandon the followers of Islam to waste away in their wretched unbelief.

At this point it is important to examine the primary reason for a Muslim's rejection of the gospel. It is the same one Paul the Apostle encountered two thousand years ago. In regard to preaching the gospel, Paul declared: *The god of this age has blinded the minds of unbelievers, so that they cannot see the light of the gospel of the glory of Christ, who is the image of God* (2 Co.4:4). Satan has cleverly deceived Muslims, and people of other religious backgrounds, into thinking that good works will get them into heaven. And any religious system that bases salvation on good works has no need of a savior and a cross. The cross becomes a stumbling block and the object of ridicule by Muslims.

But there is another major reason that accounts for a Muslim's rejection of the gift. It has to do with the package. Not everybody likes the same wrapping paper. For different reasons, people have different likes and dislikes. Not all people have the same favorite food, color, song, or book. We are all different because our backgrounds and our cultures are so different. When it comes to the gift of the gospel, that beautiful wrapping paper we're so proud of may be unappealing to others. In fact, there may be something about the wrapping paper that for some reason unknown to us could be objectionable and extremely offensive. As we learn more about the culture of Islamic people, we will understand this to be true. We will see that in many cases, what Muslim people reject is not the gift, but the wrapping of foreign culture that accompanies the gift. Muslims may become so enraged about the wrapping that they throw out the whole package. Tragically, when this happens, Muslims never get to see the actual gift, because they never get to open the package.

As we begin to learn and understand more about the culture of Muslim people, we begin to see how different they are, and why our Western culture can be so offensive. In fact, we will be surprised to see that Islamic culture is far more similar to biblical culture than our contemporary Western culture. Even as true believing Christians, there are many things we do and say that negatively affect Muslims. For example, if Orthodox Muslims ever walked into a typical Sunday morning church service, there would be many things they would be shocked to see and not to see.

One of the first things Orthodox Muslims would notice upon entering a church is that there are no greetings of, "Peace be unto you." Though this is a typical Islamic greeting, notice the instruction of Luke 10:5 that Jesus gives to his followers: "When you enter a house, first say, 'peace to this house.'" Next, they would notice the absence of any facility for ritual washing. When Muslims enter the mosque to pray, they remove their shoes and stop at the water fountain to wash their hands and feet. This reminds us of Aaron of the Old Testament who had to first wash his hands and feet before entering the Tabernacle. The Muslim guests would be even more surprised to see everyone with their shoes on, singing the chorus, "Standing on Holy Ground." Muslims have a similar story of God speaking to Moses from a burning bush telling him to remove his shoes while standing on holy ground. The Muslims would also notice Christians sitting in pews. In the mosque, Muslims sit on the floor because only God Almighty is King and therefore only He deserves to sit on anything resembling a throne or chair. All others sit on the ground in obeisance to Him.

Muslims would be surprised to see men and attractively dressed ladies sitting side by side. In most mosque settings, only men are allowed into the main worship hall lest a woman distract a man from performing his prayer. Also in most mosque settings, singing and instruments are forbidden lest the format of worship take on a worldly appearance. When Muslims hear the lively music of guitars, keyboards, and drums in a church, they cannot fathom how Christians allow "disco music" into their place of worship. Muslims would be shocked to see Christians place their Bibles on the floor. For Muslims, any book viewed as God's word is most sacred and must never be placed on the ground where the soles of men's feet touch. The Muslims would hear the choir sing and the preacher speak; but would be troubled to hear joking and laughter in the same setting. For them, the worship room is no place for frivolous behavior; it is the place for utmost reverence. It is the place where one fearfully submits himself in humility and homage to Almighty God.

After the church service, the Muslim visitors would think to themselves what a well-planned performance this all was: the singing of a choir; the speech of a minister, and the special music of talented individuals, just like television. But the one thing they expected to see never took place. The congregation as a whole never bowed down to the floor as an expression of submission and reverence to Almighty God. The Muslims would ask, "Christians, do you really believe with all your heart that God is the sovereign king of the universe, and if you do, why don't you bow to Him as you would to an earthly king?" Perhaps now you can see why Muslims regard us Christians as terribly irreverent, and why they would prefer to remain within their own community where people show far more respect to God.

If we truly want the people of Islam to experience the gift, then we are going to have to think deeply about the issue of the wrapping paper. We may even have to think about adjusting it or removing it altogether. "But," you may argue, "we worked hard to wrap the gift. The wrapping paper is our identity; it represents our Christian heritage. Our people gave their lives to protect that heritage. We cannot simply tear it off. It would be too painful." Yes, it would be painful. And this is the kind of suffering that Jesus may have meant when He told his followers that they would have to take up their crosses daily and follow him. Our commitment to Christ demands self-denial—the dying of self to that which means so much to us. It may mean sacrificing what is familiar and dear to us for the sake of ministering more effectively to others.

If our cultural wrapping paper is in any way offensive and indeed becomes a stumbling block, then as servants of God, we are obligated to remove it. But this does not change our human attachment to culture. Remember, culture is something we cannot eliminate completely. We can change culture, but we can never fully remove it. It is something that is inherent in the daily lives of all people. Thus, if our own cultural wrapping paper has to be removed, then it will have to be replaced with something else. But what will that wrapping paper look like? Surely, we will want to decorate the gift so it is attractive to Muslims. We want them to not only reach for the package, but to open it and find the true gift inside, Jesus the Savior of the world. At the same time, we will need to be careful not to distort nor dilute the truth of the gift inside. And remember, the gift is Christ, not a denomination, or dogma, or our personal views.

This will mean that the new wrapping paper may likely reflect Islamic culture. But can we as Bible believing Christians use anything that is culturally Islamic? If we believe that God created all humankind in His image, and that God's imprint is traceable in all cultures, then perhaps there are elements of the Islamic culture that can be retrieved for our purposes. If this is so, then out of love and concern, what adjustments can we make in the wrapping of the gift for Muslims? In coming chapters we will attempt to answer that question by first examining Islamic culture, and then by examining biblical principles that deal with cultural issues.

Reflection

We have discussed extensively how Muslims may reject the gift of Christ, because they reject the cultural wrapping paper they associate with Christianity. We see how even within our churches we may offend the Muslims, who the Holy Spirit is drawing, because the way we worship conflicts with their perception of godliness, reverence and modesty. Now, let's take our eyes off the broad view of culture and look inward, what is our individual part in all of this?

The Word says, *"Man looks at the outward appearance, but the Lord looks at the heart."* (1 Samuel 16:7), so, unfortunately, what Muslims see is the outward appearance. We must not only be mindful of our "wrapping paper" culture and the gift inside, Christ, when witnessing, but also our individual "wrapping paper." Our demeanor, attitude, and tone of voice, which wraps what is inside us, the Holy Spirit. With God's help we can become the humble, serving, loving vessels. The living "wrapping paper" of the Holy Spirit.

As we prepare to reach out to Muslims and separate ourselves from the elements of our culture that stop Muslims from seeing our faith in God, our concern for righteousness, and most importantly, our love, we can do so boldly. Knowing that it is the transformational power of the Holy Spirit Who will change the heart of the

Muslim. The Holy Spirit has no need of the cultural trappings we hold dear. He wants to draw the Muslim people to Jesus, loosening their fists into outstretched hands, waiting to accept the gift.

10

What I Need to Know About Islamic Culture

Therefore let us stop passing judgment on one another. Instead, make up your mind not to put any stumbling block or obstacle in your brother's way.

Romans 14:13

In the previous chapter, we looked at our culture and how it influences the way we are perceived by the Muslim people. Now we'll take a look at the Islamic culture.

There are many factors that shape the culture of a community. Some of the more common ones are geographic location, weather, history, language, and neighboring cultures. But as for the community of Orthodox Islam, the major factor that has influenced the lifestyle and practices of its people is the collection of religious traditions dating back to the sixth century AD. To understand the impact of this material, we must first understand the value Muslims place on time, honor, and reverence for the sacred.

One significant difference between Muslim people in general and Western Christians in particular is the direction of focus given to time. Westerners are future oriented. Not only do we dream and plan for the future, but we delight to tread where none have ventured. We pride ourselves in being great explorers, inventors, and innovators who lead to new discoveries, new methods, and new fashions. We learn to live in a flux of constant change because change has become for us a mark of progress, and progress is viewed as good and necessary for human survival and improvement. The past lies buried in the pages of history books and is eventually forgotten. After all, who cares about the past—what's done is done. It cannot be changed. On now to the future. We glory in the future, which represents for us an unlimited reservoir of untapped potential. We strive ahead for bigger and better things.

In contrast to this mindset, Muslims are past-oriented people who glory in their history. They place great importance upon events, people, and teachings that preceded them. With their deep regard for the past comes the necessity to preserve its heritage. That is why tradition plays such an important role in the lives of Muslims. Their honor for the past is intricately interwoven with honor for parents, elders, and ancestors.

This honor is exhibited by each generation living life as it was lived by its predecessors. Thus, the possibility for change from one generation to the next is minimal. In fact, change is frowned upon as an undesirable intruder.

This obsession with preserving the past becomes even more significant when we understand that for devout Muslims, more important than honor for parents and ancestors is honor for God and prophet. We know now how Muslims believe that as Lord of the universe, God has instituted laws to govern the working order of everything that exists, from the huge planets of the solar system to the minutest particles of the atom—how every existing body must function in strict accordance with these laws, including the body of the human being. This premise leads to the belief that God has prescribed divine laws for every aspect of human activity. And to honor God means to honor those laws.

That is why the life of a devout Muslim is so deeply intertwined with his religion. It is his religion that provides these regulations that cover the whole gamut of human experience, such as rules for human conduct, interpersonal relationships, bodily functions, body care, and ritual worship. A devout Muslim interprets the phrase "surrender to God" in a very comprehensive and literal sense. For him, every single act related to human behavior must be surrendered to God's will, which is revealed by God's laws. Therefore, details become critical because they serve as divine guidance that represents for the Muslim the only means of salvation and universal peace.

One would think that Muslims look to the Qur'an for these detailed instructions. But the Qur'an speaks mainly in general terms covering broad principles. For example, the Qur'an instructs Muslims to establish regular prayers, but offers very little detail regarding ablution, posture, and wording. The Qur'an talks about giving to the poor, but doesn't specify how much. The Qur'an prescribes the pilgrimage to Mecca, but says little about its ceremonies. There are so many other issues that beg for details. For example, how should a Muslim eat? What clothes and ornaments may a Muslim wear? How should he keep his body clean and healthy? What are the rules for interaction with the opposite gender? The questions are endless. Though the Qur'an is limited in its responses, it does point the Muslim to the source that provides him the answers. The Qur'an declares: *You have indeed in the Apostle of God [Prophet Muhammad] a beautiful pattern (of conduct) for anyone whose hope is in God and the Final Day, and who engages much in the praise of God* (33:21).

Coupled with other verses admonishing Muslims to obey and follow Muhammad, Muslims have taken this verse to mean that the life of Muhammad (AD 570–632) is the one and only perfect model for human conduct and therefore the one to be fully emulated. Muslims refer to this idea as following the *sunnah* (the example of Muhammad). They believe that by imitating their prophet in every detail of human activity, they are in actuality following the laws of God. That is why, during his lifetime, Muhammad's loyal companions were very careful to remember his deeds and memorize his words.

In the passing away of Muhammad, and the eventual passing away of his companions, this information became crucial. It became an important supplement to the Qur'an and provided the major repository of divine prescriptions for the religious community and the Islamic world at large. Consequently, certain individuals (later referred to as traditionists) took on the task of collecting every iota of information about Muhammad from wherever and whomever they could, and recording it for the sake of preservation. Each written compilation is known as a *hadith* (narration) and contains thousands of entries. Because there was more than one individual involved in this undertaking, there are several official *hadiths* throughout the world that Muslims turn to.

Besides recording the deeds of Muhammad, the *hadiths* record the sayings of Muhammad. It is these sayings, thousands of them, and not the Qur'an, that provide the information found in Islamic folklore, history, and beliefs. These components of Islamic tradition provide the missing pieces about the past and the present that are not found in the Qur'an. For example, who was the mother of Ishmael? Who were Muhammad's wives, and how did he treat them? What are the details of Muhammad's night journey into heaven? The Qur'an speaks of Jesus as "the Sign of the Hour," but what will Jesus do when He returns to the world? The Qur'an says that God will punish the apostate from Islam, but should he be punished by Islamic authorities as well? Why do Orthodox Muslims avoid pictures and refuse to keep pet dogs in their homes? Why do Muslims practice circumcision when the Qur'an is silent on this issue? What do Muslims recite when they finger their string of prayer beads? What should be the Muslim's views regarding abortion and homosexuality? Why do Muslims blow into their hands and rub their faces when they pray? What is so significant about the braying of a donkey and the crowing of a rooster? Why should wedding invitations never be turned down? The answers to these questions, and many more, are not in the Qur'an, but in the literature of the *hadiths*.

In order to examine more closely some of the practices that reflect Islamic culture, it will be helpful to look at selections from the *hadith* material that particularly relate to social etiquette and religious ritual. These selections are from two widely used *hadiths*, one entitled *As-Sahih*, by Imam al-Bukhari (AD 9th cent.), and the other entitled *Mishkat-ul Masabih* by Sheikh Wali ud-Din (AD 14th cent.).

Listed below are some selections that deal with issues you will encounter in your growing involvement with Muslim people—issues related to hospitality, food, gender, and prayer. In each of the examples, you will notice the names of individuals from whom the traditionist gathered his information. For example, Abu Bakr (Muhammad's closest friend) heard from Aisha (Muhammad's young wife and Abu Bakr's daughter) that Muhammad said such and such. Muslim scholars use these names to determine the reliability of the tradition. Names of people of Muhammad's household and closest friends render the material trustworthy.

Hadith Selections
Hospitality

Narrated Abu Shuraih al-Adawi: My ears heard and my eyes saw the Prophet when he spoke, "Anybody who believes in Allah and the Last Day, should serve his neighbor generously, and anybody who believes in Allah and the Last Day should serve his guest generously by giving him his reward." It was asked, "What is his reward, O Allah's Apostle?" He said, "(To be entertained generously) for a day and a night with high quality of food; and the guest has the right to be entertained for three days (with ordinary food), and if he stays longer, what he will be provided with will be regarded as *sadaqa* (a charitable gift).

Abu Hurairah reported that the Messenger of Allah said, "It is a part of sunnah that a man should go with his guest up to the door of the house" [when the guest is leaving].

Eating and Drinking

Narrated Umar bin Abi Salama, "I was a boy under the care of Allah's Apostle and my hand used to go around the dish while I was eating. So Allah's Apostle said to me, 'O boy! Mention the name of Allah [as in the invocation, *bismillah*] and eat with your right hand, and eat of the dish what is nearer to you.'"

Ibn Omar reported that the Messenger of Allah said, "None of you shall ever take food with his left hand, nor shall he drink therewith, because the devil eats with his left hand and drinks therewith."

Ayesha [Aisha] reported that the Messenger of Allah said, "Don't cut meat with a knife, because it is an act of the foreigners, but bite it because it is more beneficial and wholesome."

Anas-b-Malek reported that the Messenger of Allah said, "When food is served, take off your shoes, because it is more solacing to your feet."

Narrated Abu Umama, "Whenever the dining sheet of the Prophet was taken away (whenever he finished his meal), he used to say, '*Al-hamdulillah. . . .*'" (Praise be to Allah…)

The Prophet said, "When you eat, do not wipe your hand till you have licked it [clean of food particles]…"

Narrated Suwaid bin An Numan, "We went out with Allah's Apostle to Khaibar, and when we reached As-Sahba, the Prophet asked for food.... We ate, and then Allah's Apostle stood up for the prayer. He rinsed his mouth with water, and we too, rinsed our mouths."

Narrated Hudhaifa, "The Prophet forbade us to drink out of gold and silver vessels, or eat in them."

Ibn Abbas reported that the Messenger of Allah said, "Don't take drink in one breath like the drinking of a camel, but take drink twice or thrice and utter *'Bismillah'* (in the name of God) when you drink and utter *'Alhamdulillah'* (praise be to God) when you finish."

Narrated Ibn Umar, "Umar stood up on the pulpit and said, 'Now then, prohibition of alcoholic drinks have been revealed, and these drinks are prepared from five things: grapes, dates, honey, wheat or barley. And an alcoholic drink is that which disturbs the mind.'"

Gender issues

Narrated Ibn Abbas, "The Prophet cursed effeminate men (those men who are in the similitude or assume the manners of women) and those women who assume the manners of men, and he said, 'Turn them out of your houses.' The Prophet turned out such-and-such men, and Umar turned out such-and-such women."

Narrated Aisha, "The Prophet used to take the

Pledge of Allegiance from the women by words only after reciting this Holy Verse, '. . . that they will not associate anything in worship with Allah' (60:12). And the hand of Allah's Apostle did not touch any woman's hand except the hand of that woman his right hand possessed (his captives or his lady slaves)."

Omar reported from the Prophet who said, "A man shall never keep alone with a woman except that the third between them is the devil."

Jaber reported from the Prophet who said, "Don't visit women whose husbands are absent, because the devil runs through you like the circulation of blood."

Worship
Ayesha [Aisha] reported that the Messenger of Allah said, "The prayer of a grown-up woman is not accepted without a veil."

Ibn Omar reported that the Messenger of Allah said, "Don't prevent your women from going to the mosque, but their houses are better for them."

Abu Hurairah reported, "I heard my beloved Abu'l Qasim [Muhammad] say, 'The prayer of a woman may not be accepted who perfumes herself to go to the mosque, till she washes (it with a washing from impurity).'"

Abu Darda'a reported that the Messenger of Allah said, "Verily the best dress with which you can meet Allah in your graves and mosques is of white color."

Ali reported that the Prophet said, "O Ali, There are three things about which you shall not make delay. Prayer when it comes, a dead body when it presents itself for burial, and marriage of an unmarried woman when you find a match for her."

Jaber reported that the Messenger of Allah said, "The key to Paradise is prayer, and the key to prayer is cleanliness."

Ibn Omar reported that the Messenger of Allah said, "Prayer without ablution is not accepted, nor charity from unlawful wealth."

When it comes to worship, Orthodox Muslims view their religious rituals as holy acts directed toward a holy God. The idea of holiness includes not only inner holiness, but also outer holiness, which is expressed in terms of ritual purity. As in the Old Testament, there are certain conditions and certain acts that render Muslims ritually unclean or impure. For example, body waste and fluids such as sweat, menses, urine, semen, and pus are all polluting agents that must be removed. Before Muslims can engage in any act of religious worship, such as prayer, fasting, and Qur'anic reading, they must undergo a ceremonial ablution or cleansing. Failing to do so nullifies any religious act. Notice the following description regarding the general ablution for the daily *salat* prayers. Though extremely meticulous, Orthodox Muslims are very careful to wash in this exact manner because this prescription is seen as the example of Muhammad and the law of God.

> Narrated Humran (the slave of Uthman): I saw Uthman bin Affan asking for a tumbler of water (and when it was brought) he poured water over his hands and washed them thrice; and then put his right hand in the water container and rinsed his mouth, washed his nose by putting water in it and then blowing it out. Then he washed his face and forearms up to the elbows thrice, passed his wet hands over his head and washed his feet up to the ankles thrice. Then he said, "Allah's Apostle said 'If anyone performs ablution like that of mine and offers a two-*rakat* prayer during which he does not think of anything else (not related to the present prayer), then his past sins will be forgiven.'" After performing the ablution, Uthman said, "...I heard the Prophet saying, 'If a man performs ablution perfectly and then offers the compulsory congregational prayer,

Allah will forgive his sins committed between that (prayer) and the (next) prayer till he offers it.'"

By now we are beginning to develop a better understanding about the mindset of Orthodox Muslims and the way they live and practice their religion. By examining some of these important aspects of their culture, we begin to understand the reasons why Muslims are offended by many of our customs and practices. In regard to sensitive matters like modesty, mixed gender relations, and reverence for the sacred, it is obvious that the culture of Orthodox Islam is in stark contrast to Western culture. For example, after learning about all that Muslims go through to ensure the efficacy of their prayers, imagine what they think when they see Christians slumped in their chairs with eyes closed, and doing what they call prayer. We can begin to empathize with our Muslim neighbors as we realize some of the obstacles they must overcome to feel comfortable with us American Christians.

Some of us are quick to retort, "That's their problem. This is America, and if they're going to live here, then they'd better adjust to the American way. Otherwise they can just return to where they came from. And besides, we are the ones sanctified in Christ, and so they need to adjust to our Christian culture, not we to theirs." But that attitude will only widen the gap between "them" and "us." As long as there are these cultural stumbling blocks, we will not be able to get close to the Muslim people. God will not be able to use us.

Reflection

You may be thinking, I don't want to be a stumbling block to anyone, but to what extremes should I be willing to go to relate culturally with Muslims?

It will be easier to answer that question if you ask this one: To what extremes am I willing to go for the opportunity to tell people about Jesus?

The apostle Paul left us an example when he passed through southern Galatia on his second missionary journey. Paul, the chief spokesperson of salvation by grace alone, had Timothy circumcised so he could take Timothy into the Jewish synagogues (Acts 16:3). "So the churches were strengthened in the faith and grew daily in numbers" (Acts 16:5).

So we must be willing to allow a circumcision of our hearts by the Holy Spirit. A cutting away of that fleshy part of us that insists on keeping God in the context of *our* culture. It is not that we are giving up American culture and now identifying with Muslim culture, it is that we are giving up our identity with all lifestyles, customs, and practices that are of this world. Whether they be American, Muslim, or any other. And instead, embracing the culture of Jesus, a wrapping paper of love, service, and humility. One He designed to appeal to all cultures.

131

11

How to Respond to Islamic Culture

. . . the Son of Man did not come to be served, but to serve . . .
Matthew 20:28

When a follower of Jesus feels compelled by the love of God to leave his own cultural zone to minister to people of a different culture, that person engages in what is known as cross-cultural ministry. One of the greatest examples of cross-cultural ministers was the apostle Paul. Because Paul came from a strict Pharisaic Jewish background, it must have been extremely difficult for him to adjust to the Gentile cultures of Asia and Europe. Surely there were many aspects of the idolatrous Gentile culture that greatly disturbed Paul and caused him to feel a sense of superiority about his own Jewish culture. But Paul recognized the importance of cultural diversity and the strong hold culture has on each of its bearers. In his effort to evangelize the Gentiles, he had to understand the problem of the wrapping paper and the need for appropriate adjustments.

We are often perplexed when we meet up with people of a different culture, like the Muslims. We surely don't want to be rude, but if we are "free in Christ," then we don't like the idea of belittling ourselves by submitting to someone else's culture. It seems only fitting that others be the ones to submit to our culture since we are on God's side. We are concerned about the danger of compromising our biblical standards by associating with a culture that is heavily influenced by non-Christian practices. And yet we know that unless we associate with Muslims, we will make little headway in leading them to Christ. To help us work through this issue of cultural conflict, Paul offers us some important scriptural principles in his first letter to the Corinthians. First of all, in 8:9, Paul admonishes us, "Be careful, however, that the exercise of your freedom does not become a stumbling block to the weak." Then in 9:1, he asks, "Am I not free?" Later, in 9:19–23, we find this revolutionary teaching:

> *Though I am free and belong to no man, I make myself a slave to everyone, to win as many as possible. To the Jews I became like a Jew, to win the Jews. To those under the law I became like one under the law (though I myself am not under the law), so as to win those under the law. To those not having the law I became like one not having the law (though I am not free from God's law but am under Christ's law), so as to win those not having the law. To the weak, I became weak, to win the weak. I have become all things to all men so that by all*

possible means I might save some. I do all this for the sake of the gospel, that I may share in its blessings.

Further on we read in 10:23–24:

"Everything is permissible"—but not everything is beneficial. "Everything is permissible"—but not everything is constructive. Nobody should seek his own good, but the good of others.

Let's take a closer look at what Paul is saying. He mentions the freedom we have in Christ. This does not mean the freedom to do absolutely anything we want. No, Paul is referring here to the freedom we have in Christ from a legalistic system that bases salvation on what a person does or doesn't do. For example, in Christ, our salvation is not based on the things we eat or the things we wear. We are free from that kind of religious bondage. But then Paul warns us to be careful in how we apply this freedom, because in some cases, what we eat or wear can be offensive to people of another culture. It can even create a stumbling block for future ministry. That's why Paul says, "Everything is permissible, but not everything is constructive." What we do can sometimes actually be destructive. Here is an example:

Most American Christians live in a culture where eating pork is permissible and common. If you are in the habit of eating eggs and bacon, then pork consumption has become a part of your wrapping paper. Suppose God leads you to a Muslim family to share His gift of salvation. You begin to establish a relationship with them, and now you're ready to invite them to a lovely meal in your home. But they refuse your invitation because they know you eat pork. According to Paul's teaching, you are free to eat as much pork as you want. Your salvation is not based on abstention from pork. And you can criticize your Muslim friends for living in such meaningless bondage. You can continue to enjoy your pork as a demonstration of your freedom in Christ. It's permissible, but as far as getting closer to your Muslim friends, it's not going to happen. And because of what they see in the wrapping paper, they will throw out the whole package. They might remain somewhat cordial, but as for your religion and Savior, they won't be the least bit interested. This is how your insistence on eating pork in your home can be destructive. It can become a stumbling block.

Notice Paul says, "Nobody should seek his own good, but the good of others." Truly this is a mark of a servant—denying self for the good of others. Elsewhere, Paul said, "Though I am free and belong to no man, I make myself a slave to everyone, to win as many as possible." This leads us to an interesting paradox. On one hand we are free, and on the other we are not. We are free from one law, but subject to another. We are free from the law of religious legalism, but we are subject to the law of Christ—the law of love. If we truly identify with Christ, then we must identify with his law—the law to love God, which leads us to love fellow beings; thus the role of servanthood. Paul said in effect that even though he was not bound to any man or culture, he purposely subjected himself to others and their culture so that he could serve them more effectively. Though he was free to keep his own wrapping paper, he was willing, as a servant, to deny himself that right, and replace his own with the wrapping paper of others. Thus, for the Jew, he took on Jewish culture, and for the Gentile, he took on Gentile culture. He was willing to sacrifice his own cultural identity in order to identify with others of a different culture. We see in all of this Paul's passion for lost souls. He said, "I have become all things to all men so that by all possible means, I might save some." We need to find the source of this passion that moved Paul to such radical thinking. In 2 Corinthians 5:14, he speaks of being compelled by the love of Christ. Not only was Paul compelled by the love of Christ, he was most certainly stirred by the example of Christ. This is clearly seen in 1 Corinthians 10:32–11:1:

> Do not cause anyone to stumble, whether Jews, Greeks or the church of God—even as I try to please everybody in every way. For I am not seeking my own good but the good of many, so that they may be saved. Follow my example, as I follow the example of Christ.

First, notice the purpose of all of this: "That they may be saved." In other words, that they get to open the package and embrace the gift. But now notice the admonition of Paul, "Follow my example, as I follow the example of Christ." Not only are we instructed to follow this approach, but we are also told to consider the example of Christ Himself—the true Servant of God who came to serve.

Of course, Jesus was the greatest messenger who ever lived, bringing to the world the good news of hope and eternal salvation. The words He spoke brought healing and newness of life to many. We are aware of the influential ministry of Christ, but what we often fail to realize is that Jesus Christ was also involved in cross-cultural ministry. Notice His initial culture. According to the Scriptures, Christ as the eternal Word of God, was of a heavenly nature—in the form of God. He was full of glory and full of splendor. He was clothed in divine wrapping paper. But when He came to earth to live and minister among humankind, He changed his wrapping paper for another. *The Word became flesh and made his dwelling among us* (John 1:14). Not only did the divine Word of God take on flesh, but He took on culture. In fact, He submitted Himself to Jewish culture. Romans 15:8–9 reveals this amazing truth: *Christ has become a servant of the Jews on behalf of God's truth, to confirm the promises made to the patriarchs so that the Gentiles may glorify God for his mercy . . .* Think about this for a moment. Jesus, the eternal Son of God, could have chosen to keep His heavenly form of divine splendor. He could have lived in a royal palace. He could have chosen to intermingle with only the angels of heaven and communicate solely in their language. He could have traveled from one place to another in a golden chariot. He could have adorned Himself in silk and jewels. He could have fed on daily banquets fit for a king. Instead, He chose to become a servant of fallen humanity.

The fact that Christ became a servant of the Jews and willingly subjected Himself to their culture leads to some astonishing observations. For example, we read in Luke 2:21–22:

> *On the eighth day, when it was time to circumcise him, he was named Jesus. . . . When the time of their purification according to the Law of Moses had been completed, Joseph and Mary took him to Jerusalem to present him to the Lord. . . . and to offer a sacrifice. . . . .*

From this account, Jesus' submission to Jewish culture not only necessitated circumcision, but more shockingly, a purification offering. The condition of his birth, (i.e. the flow of the water and blood of the womb), was rendered ritually impure according to Old Testament law (Lev.12:2). Think of it; Jesus was willing to be born in a state of ritual impurity. This is unbelievable. The angels must have wondered what would cause this Jesus, full of divine glory and purity, to stoop to such depths. Look again at Romans 15:8–9. Jesus was willing to take on human culture in order to effectively relate to humankind and confirm the promise that God made centuries ago. It was the promise of a blessing (Gen. 22:18) for all nations through the offspring of Abraham. Of course, Jesus was the offspring and the blessing—the gift for all humankind. Jesus truly sought to identify Himself on human terms so that people could adequately understand Him and wholeheartedly embrace Him.

Jesus became a servant, not only willing to change, but also willing to suffer. Paul speaks of this truth in his description of Jesus in Philippians 2:6–9:

> *Who, being in very nature God, did not consider equality with God something to be grasped, but made himself nothing, taking the very nature of a servant, being made in human likeness. And being found in appearance as a man, he humbled himself and became obedient to death—even death on a cross!*

Two extremely important considerations emerge from this passage. First, notice the *two* natures that represent the two wrapping papers. He who was the *divine* took on the *physical*. This is known as the incarnation—the divine nature taking on the embodiment of human nature for the sake of identification and relevance. From this model of Christ, we get the phrase "incarnational ministry," meaning the willingness to identify culturally with others for the sake of identification and relevance. This is precisely the principle that Paul expresses in his teaching of 1 Corinthians chapter 9. Let's look again at verses 19–23:

> *Though I am free and belong to no man, I make myself a slave to everyone, to win as many as possible. To the Jews I became like a Jew, to win the Jews. To those under the law I became like one under the law (though I myself am not under the law), so as to win those under*

*the law. To those not having the law I became like one
not having the law (though I am not free from God's
law but am under Christ's law), so as to win those not
having the law. To the weak, I became weak, to win the
weak. I have become all things to all men so that by all
possible means I might save some. I do all this for the
sake of the gospel, that I may share in its blessings.*

Notice the number of times you see the word
become or *became*—five times. This word speaks of
flexibility. It speaks of a willingness to change for the
sake of others. It speaks of identifying with others who
are different. It points to the greatest example of
incarnational ministry—the Word *became* flesh. In the
footsteps of Jesus our Lord, and in the footsteps of Paul
our mentor, we ourselves need to consider what we are
willing to "become" in order to identify with Muslim
people. This brings us to the second important point of
the passage—the issue of suffering.

Truly Christ Jesus was the ultimate example of
death to self. He was the living lesson of the kernel of
wheat described in John 12:24: "Unless a kernel of wheat
falls to the ground and dies, it remains only a single seed.
But if it dies, it produces many seeds."

Jesus vividly personified this principle. He was
the seed of divine glory, majesty, and life. Yet He fell
from the splendor of heaven to the cursed ground of the
earth. He identified with fallen humanity, suffered an
ignoble death, and lay buried in the sin-stained bowels of
the earth. Yet it was because of that willingness to

condescend that there is living fruit today—fruit that continues to produce life-bearing seeds. These seeds constitute the body of Christ, which lives and continues to send forth servants willing to exemplify the principle of death to life.

Incarnational ministry calls for dying—dying to self and living for others. It calls at times for nailing our cultural preferences to the cross and taking on the culture of others. It calls for the role of servanthood. More profoundly, it calls for the role of priesthood.

On the subject of Jesus' priestly role, the writer of Hebrews points back to the prophecy of Isaiah 8:18 by picturing Jesus before God, saying, *"Here am I, and the children God has given me."* (Heb. 2:13). The author uses this picture to speak of Jesus and the people whom He came to save. Then he continues with this imagery to speak of Jesus taking on human flesh:

> *Since the children have flesh and blood, he too shared in their humanity so that by his death he might destroy him who holds the power of death—that is, the devil—and free those who all their lives were held in slavery by their fear of death. ...*
>
> *For this reason he had to be made like his brothers in every way, in order that he might become a merciful and faithful high priest in service to God, and that he might make atonement for the sins of the people.*
>
> *Because he himself suffered when he was tempted, he is able to help those who are being tempted.*
>
> (Heb. 2:14–18)

In the first part of this passage, we find again the two elements of incarnational ministry that we found in Philippians chapter 2. First, Jesus took on the culture of His earthly ministry: "He too shared in their humanity." Secondly, He suffered. Jesus suffered not only at the climax of His ministry, but all along the path of His ministry, as Satan continually tried to discredit and destroy Him. But this passage in Hebrews offers further enlightenment. We begin to understand why Jesus chose this approach to ministry. He took on the identity of humanity so that He could serve not only as prophet, but also as priest. Remember that a prophet speaks on behalf of God to the people, but a priest speaks on behalf of the people to God. Jesus came to represent the human race and to minister for its deliverance from sin and misery. Of course, being the greatest in authority under God, Jesus serves as the high priest. But in order for the people to recognize and appreciate Him, He had to meet them at their level so that they could feel His empathy. To become one with them, He became one of them. He lived with them; He cried with them. He suffered with them and genuinely sympathized with their weaknesses (Heb. 5:13). And because He was willing to come in human form, they could feel His tender love and compassion. They could say, "Yes, He really does understand what we are going through; yes, He really does care." Jesus not only served people, but in His office of high priest, He empathized with them.

There can be no greater ministry than that of

priesthood. For that reason, Peter reminds us: *You are a chosen people, a royal priesthood* (1 Pet. 2:9). Nothing will touch a Muslim's heart more than someone who will meet him at the level of his circumstances, identify with his suffering, and pray for mutual deliverance. The voice of a prophet prays, "O God, have mercy on him." The voice of a priest prays, "O God, have mercy on us." As a Christian ministers in an Islamic context, it is helpful for him to ask these questions: "Can Muslim people say that I really want to understand what they are going through?" and "Can they say that I really care about them?" The answers to these questions will determine the measure of priesthood in ministry.

It is the ministry of priesthood that returns us to the issue of the suffering of the cross. The priest offers the sacrifice up to God as a sweet-smelling incense. The sacrifice we offer up to God is our lives, our desires, our cultural preferences, our safety, our conveniences, our status, our financial security. In the fact that we have been crucified with Christ, we have put to death the "old man" and have been resurrected to new life. But though we have been raised to newness of life, we still bear the marks of the crucified life. In our identity with Christ, who bore the scars on His hands and feet, we likewise bear the scars of the cross. This is what Paul meant when he said, "*I bear on my body the marks of Jesus*" (Gal. 6:17). In Paul's identification with Christ, the pleasures and preferences of the world died in his life. He was consumed with the ministry of priesthood. But in that ministry of identifying with the suffering of others, Paul bore the marks of the cross. He knew what it was to take up his cross daily and follow Christ. In his epistle to the Corinthian church, Paul shares with us some of those marks of suffering:

> *Five times I received from the Jews the forty lashes minus one. Three times I was beaten with rods, once I was stoned, three times I was shipwrecked, I spent a night and a day in the open sea, I have been constantly on the move. I have been in danger from rivers, in danger from bandits, in danger from my own countrymen, in danger from Gentiles; in danger in the city, in danger in the country, in danger at sea; and in danger from false brothers. I have labored and toiled and have often gone without sleep. I have known hunger and thirst and have often gone without food; I have been cold and naked.* (2 Cor. 11:24–27)

It is obvious that Paul bore the marks of the cross by ministering among the people. He shared their humanity, their weakness, their suffering. Paul did not keep his distance from the masses. He did not remain resident in a comfortable setting and risk-free environment. A priest mingles among the people and identifies with their cultural context. This is how he can genuinely represent the people and empathize with them. We need to remember that incarnational ministry requires a bodily presence. It is noteworthy that the emphasis of John chapter 1 is not that the Word spoke to us, but that the Word lived among us. He became accessible to human sight, human sound, human touch, and human emotion. Jesus took the initiative to enter the human frame of reference. Jesus made the Word all the more relevant and empathetic by appearing in person. In the same way, Christ in us will become all the more relevant when we take the initiative to appear in person and serve as priests—establishing relationships with Muslims, suffering with Muslims, praying with Muslims.

Reflection

This teaching of cross-cultural ministry is critical if you truly desire to touch the people of Islam. If you do not serve as a priest, you will find yourself acting as a judge. You will be quick to condemn Muhammad and the Qur'an. You will focus on the wives of Muhammad, the descriptions of Paradise, and the call to slay infidels. You will find yourself bogged down in debates about the nature of Jesus, the mystery of the trinity, and the need for the cross. You will become obsessed with winning arguments and defeating foes. But you will lose the key to effective ministry. You will stretch the mind of a Muslim, but you will turn away his heart. Remember, in most cases, spiritual illumination will come to a Muslim only when he sees God as a God of love. That love is revealed when you take up your cross daily on behalf of others.

For so long, Christians misunderstood the meaning of "boasting in the cross," particularly in their interactions with Muslim communities. At different times throughout history they used the icon of the cross, coupled with the military strength of Christendom, to say to the Muslim people, "We hate you; God wants to destroy you." But today is a new day. A day to display the marks of the cross and the love of Jesus. A new opportunity for a new generation of servants of Christ. A time to walk in the truth that *the Son of Man did not come to be served, but to serve.* And live out a priesthood ministry to the Muslims with the love and humility of Christ.

12

What Would Jesus Do?

As you sent me into the world, I have sent them into the world.

John 17:18

If the Holy Spirit is whispering to you, encouraging you to reach out in love to a Muslim you have met or know of, you're ready to take action. Perhaps there is a Muslim family in your neighborhood, or someone at church knows of a Muslim family elsewhere in town. But you are not sure where to begin. First and foremost, begin with prayer and ask the Holy Spirit for guidance and discernment. Pray for an open door for meeting this family. Make it your objective to befriend these Muslims and to be a channel of blessing. Your mission is not to convert them with an on-the-spot sermon about Christianity. It is to establish an enduring relationship that will ultimately attract them to Jesus within you.

After you have prayed through this issue, have the

courage to knock on their door and introduce yourself. Let them know that you have taken an interest in Islam because of current world events, and that you want to learn more about Islam and their culture. Let them know you feel bad about the negative stereotypes most Americans have of Muslims, and that you want to encourage them that not all Americans are the same. If they are new to the area, and maybe settling in from overseas, offer to help them. You can direct them, or even take them, to various social services that specialize in employment, education, and health care. You can help them find the post office, the grocery store, the library, the laundromat, and the motor vehicle department. If they're struggling with English, you can help them fill out complicated forms.

When you go to their door to introduce yourself, take along a gift item—preferably a fruit basket. Be careful about taking homemade food, such as bakery items. Muslims are suspicious of food that might contain pork fat (lard). Include a personal note along with your name and telephone number. The note could read something like this: "We are pleased to have you in our community. May God bless your family and keep you in His merciful care." Most likely, the Muslim will feel obligated to invite you inside his home. However, because you caught him off guard, find an excuse to politely refuse but make it a point to call him about a future visit.

Let's look at ways you can identify with the culture of the Muslim family God has put in your path so that you avoid as many stumbling blocks as possible. You may want to review the *hadith* selections in Chapter 10.This will help you to relate to the suggestions that follow. One of the first issues you may have to deal with is the way you dress. Muslims come from a culture that emphasizes modest attire. This applies to both men and women. Religious Muslim men keep their arms and legs covered. Seldom do you see them in public dressed in short-sleeved shirts and short pants. Anything between a man's waist and kneecap is regarded the private area of his body. Don't approach a Muslim's home in a T-shirt and Bermuda shorts. Wear loose-fitting trousers and preferably a long-sleeved shirt. Avoid wearing a shirt that is decorated with religious designs, such as a picture of Jesus, the name of God, or a Bible verse. Remember that sweat, like urine, is a pollutant that renders everything it touches unclean.

The issue of modesty is even more acute for women. In the Muslim community, the degree of modest dress reflects a woman's level of moral standing and piety. Of course, the concern for modesty should not be a strange concept for the followers of Jesus who live by the teachings of the New Testament. Paul speaks on this very issue by saying, *"I also want women to dress modestly, with decency and propriety . . ."* (1 Tim. 2:9). The biblical call for modest dress should encourage Christian women to observe the Muslim's concern for modesty, especially as it applies to women who profess to worship God. It is important for a Christian wife to know that the way she dresses in a Muslim setting also reflects upon the reputation of her husband.

In a conservative Islamic setting, any woman seen in public in a knee-length skirt and short-sleeved blouse with head uncovered and hair down is automatically branded a prostitute When in public, religious women wear a robe-like garment with headscarf to cover everything except the hands and face. The garment is loose fitting in order to conceal body contours and often drab in color to avoid drawing attention. It is commonly referred to as a *hijab* or *chador*. Among the very strict Orthodox Muslims, women are expected to cover their faces as well. This is done with a face veil often referred to as a *burqa*. Women wear the face veil to protect themselves from accusations of seductive eye contact or other facial expressions, such as an alluring smile. And because a woman's long hair is viewed as a major part of her beauty, many Muslim women wear their hair up and tucked behind their veil. No man is allowed to look upon a woman's feminine beauty except the male members of her family.

Surprisingly, despite the concern for modesty, Muslim women are permitted to wear their jewelry, most of which is gifted to them by their husbands. Earrings, nose rings, and bangles, all of gold, are extremely common. The woman's jewelry is significant because it is a public sign of her married status as well as a sign of her husband's favor.

In order to establish a close relationship with the Muslim family you are reaching out to, you will want to learn some simple phrases. First you'll want to learn the

Muslim greeting, *as-salamu alai kum* (peace be unto you). The return greeting is, *wa alai kum as-salam* (and unto you be peace). According to the Qur'an (4:86), if someone greets you, you should respond with an even better greeting. Thus some Muslims will respond: *wa alai kum as-salam wa rahmatullah* (and peace be unto you and the mercy of God). Some Muslims would even add the phrase: *wa barakatuh* (and His blessing). Certainly, these are things in a Muslim's culture we want to talk about: God's peace, mercy, and blessing. These are all provided in Jesus, the gift.

One important aspect of Islamic culture that Westerners often overlook is gender etiquette. This applies to both men and women. Unfortunately, one of the most common stereotypes Muslims have of Westerners is that they are terribly promiscuous. Muslims view sexual impropriety with grave concern. They strongly believe that the survival and well-being of the community depends on the survival and well-being of the family structure. In turn, the well-being of the family can be preserved only if the code for sexual conduct is strictly observed and enforced. This concept of family value is so deeply engrained that the sin most detrimental to family honor is sexual misconduct, such as adultery. In many cases, an adulterous affair can cost the life of the woman involved, and sometimes the man. Killing the violators is viewed as "honor killing" and is the sole remedy for restoring family honor.

Muslims view the urge for sexual activity as very real and powerful. Though sanctified by God, it must be carefully guarded until the time of marriage and then carefully maintained within the bond of marriage. Muslims view sexual activity outside the marriage contract as a clear violation of God's law that is punishable by death. Unfortunately, because the woman is viewed as the one possessing beauty, charm, and seductive prowess, she is the one held responsible in any illicit affair. Thus, it is incumbent upon her to take extreme precautions to avoid any appearance, act, or gesture that could be misconstrued as enticement in the presence of men. For this reason, the Muslim community holds different codes of behavior for same-gender interaction and cross-gender interaction. In Western societies, most men and women treat each other as equals. They intermingle freely and converse freely. But this is not the case among Orthodox Muslims.

For example, it is improper for a Muslim man to be in the company of a woman who is unrelated to his family. It is also improper for a man to enter the home of another woman whose husband is away. He is not even allowed to look at the woman to ask about her husband's whereabouts. When a man visits another home, he signals his approach by clearing his throat to warn any women of his arrival. And he is careful in the way he steps up to the doorway. By approaching a doorway from the side, and voicing his greeting, he avoids the risk of inadvertently looking upon a woman.

When unrelated Muslims visit one another, usually the males congregate in the sitting room, and the females congregate in the bedroom or kitchen. Some

Muslim homes even have different entryways to accommodate this segregation. Usually, a man does not extend his hand to shake the hand of a woman visitor, and never would he put his arm around her. In fact, he is careful even with his own wife. Very seldom is he seen with her in public, but when it happens, he avoids any display of affection. His relationship with her is something private, not something to be shared with the outside world. Men seldom ask other men about their wives. When they mention their wives, they refer to them in terms of the eldest son's mother, not by name. For example, an Orthodox Muslim would not say, "My wife, Fatima, is from a respectable family," but rather, "Karim's (the eldest son) mother is from a respectable family." A man would never go around showing his friends a picture of his wife; her beauty is for his eyes alone.

The issue of gender etiquette is more acute for women. In a strict Islamic setting, a Muslim woman spends most of her time in the seclusion of her home. She can never leave the privacy of her home without a male escort, who must be a relative. It is improper for a married woman to look into the eyes of a man who is not a family member. Her conversation with a man is rarely more than a few respectable words of greeting that come from behind a veil. Never must she allow herself to be alone in a secluded area with a man. In an Islamic community, it is automatically understood that the only reason a woman is alone with a man is for sexual engagement.

As a Christian woman grows in her relationship with Muslim women, she will learn even more about their lifestyle. She will learn about other matters that are very important, such as the taboos related to menstruation. Like the teachings of the Old Testament, Muslim women are regarded "unclean" during their period of menses. There are certain restrictions that apply to them during this time that relate to prayer, Scripture reading, fasting, and socializing. Knowing this helps the Christian understand why a Muslim woman is at times reluctant to hold a Bible or pray.

Most women in America view these kinds of restrictions for women's dress and social behavior as outdated and repressive. However, if Christian women can learn to respect these elements of Islamic culture and make appropriate adjustments, they will find the door to Muslim women wide open. It may require a meek and passive demeanor. It may mean ankle-length skirts, long-sleeved blouses, upswept hair, and head scarves. But it would be worth it all to reach the heart of a Muslim woman. Because of their secluded lives, Muslim women are happy for any opportunity to receive visits from the outside. They are eager to talk about women and family issues that are so important to them. This provides a Christian woman with a unique opportunity. Her husband can assist her by escorting her to a Muslim home and picking her up later at an appointed time. A single Christian woman should visit a Muslim home with a woman companion. Your ability to socialize as a woman according to proper Islamic cultural norms can lead to meaningful relationships that can bring hope and inspiration to a Muslim woman who craves acceptance. It will also ease the suspicion of Muslim men who fear that Christians want to lure their women into a decadent Western lifestyle. Removing that suspicion will help these Muslim men to respect the Christian woman. More importantly, it will help them to respect her husband. In most cases, the women are the ones to strike up a relationship first. And this often leads to a relationship between the husbands. It's important for the Christian husband to establish friendship with the Muslim husband. In Muslim societies, it is the man who makes the family decisions. And someday, you will want him to make the most important decision of all—the decision to embrace the gift of God's love.

You might be wondering why you can't just learn the intricacies of Muslim culture by interacting with your new Muslim friends—in other words, simply learn as you go along. It's an understandable question, since that's how we learn about each other here in America. In order to deal with this question, let's take a look at a scenario we might find ourselves in should we try reaching out to Muslims without first taking the time to learn about Islamic culture:

Pastor Bob and his wife Eva are doing door-to-door evangelism with another church couple. Bob is a handsome man and Eva, an attractive woman with long blond hair hanging down to her waist. Each person has a Bible and set of tracts. Wanting to relate to people on a more casual level, they are dressed in their evangelism T-shirts and matching Bermuda shorts. On the front of the T-shirt are the words, "Jesus Saves," and on the back, "God Loves You." Today is a particularly hot day, and by late afternoon, the two couples are drenched in perspiration. But there are only two more houses to visit, and one of them belongs to Mahmoud.

Pastor Bob recently met Mahmoud, a new Muslim neighbor who is married and has a daughter seven years old. Bob decides that he and Eva will visit the Muslim family. Upon reaching Mahmoud's residence, Eva, the more outgoing of the two, rings the doorbell. The young daughter opens the door, and Eva immediately introduces herself and asks if the father is home. Just then, a woman's voice from within calls out, "Fatima, who is it?" Fatima, the daughter, answers, "It is a lady and a man wanting Father." The voice calls out again, "I am sorry, but Fatima's father is out on an errand. Would you like to wait in the living room until he returns?" Not knowing that the woman was only being polite, Bob and Eva, who are now hot and tired, gladly accept the offer.

Within a few minutes, Fatima appears with a tray of lemonade and cookies. But her mother never comes out to introduce herself. Eva considers that rather rude! Finished with the lemonade, Eva wonders if the other couple has ended their visit up the road. She decides to check outside. While she is away looking for her friends, Mahmoud returns from his errand. As he is about to enter the house, a female voice calls from the sidewalk, "Hello, you must be Mahmoud." Extending her hand to shake Mahmoud's, the woman introduces herself. "I'm Eva, Pastor Bob's wife." Mahmoud is overwhelmed by Eva's forwardness and can't help noticing her T-shirt. Before he can respond, Bob calls from within the house, "Mahmoud, how are you? I wanted to bring my wife so that you could meet her."

Immediately, Mahmoud storms into the living room. He points his finger at Pastor Bob and orders him to leave and never return. Bob and Eva are completely shaken and speechless. They cannot believe anyone could be so insulting and insensitive to culture. They leave in righteous indignation, knowing that Mahmoud stands on dangerous ground for the way he just mistreated two of God's choice servants.

Prior to reading this chapter you probably would have sided with Bob and Eva. But hopefully by now you can see the problem from a Muslim's perspective. For example, Eva comes across as immodest and brazen— loose hair, shorts and T-shirt, greets Mahmoud with a handshake, and refers to him by his first name. Bob fares even worse. He too is in shorts and a T-shirt. And by the way, for Mahmoud to see the words "God" and "Jesus" drenched in smelly human perspiration is the same as seeing them drenched in a bucket of urine. Back to Bob, Bob tells Mahmoud he brought his wife to meet him and Mahmoud wonders why in the world does this man want to introduce his wife to a stranger who is already married. Of course, Bob's biggest mistake was to be left alone inside the house with Mahmoud's wife. Avoiding these kinds of cultural pitfalls will go a long way in establishing respectable relationships with Muslim people.

As you continue to build on the relationship you have started, it won't take long to notice the enthusiasm Muslims have for hospitality. This aspect of Islamic culture helps us to better understand the words of Jesus in Revelation 3:20: "Here I am! I stand at the door and knock. If anyone hears my voice and opens the door, I will come in and eat with him, and he with me." Eating together is a sign of mutual acceptance. Have no doubt that you will be invited by Muslims as a guest into their home. Out of courtesy, your Muslim host will treat you like royalty and set before you the best he has. If you are with a spouse, then both of you will be seated at the same table and left to eat together, just the two of you, while family members look on, ready and eager to serve you. Unless you are familiar with Muslim etiquette, despite your verbal pleas, they will keep your plates heaped with food and supply you with one bottle of cola after another.

As you continue to interact with your Muslim friends, you will learn the gestures and words that say, "Thank you, I have eaten enough food and am pleasantly satisfied." You will hear them say *bismillah* (in the name of God) at the onset of the meal and *alhamdulillah* (praise be to God) at the end. You will want to remember the significance of eating only with your right hand, never with the left one. The left hand is understood to be the hand that cleans the body. You will learn how to eat with your fingers and clean them. You will learn the practice of sipping a glass of water after your meal to rinse your mouth. Though you may be served together at the same table in the Muslims' home, you will learn that ordinarily, when there are guests, men eat in one room, and the ladies eat in another room   (unless they are relatives). And throughout the visit, the men and women remain segregated.

If you want this Muslim family to reciprocate your visit by coming to your home, you will need to continue to respect their social norms on your own turf. This applies to both modest dress and behavior. And even though it is your own home, you may have to make some additional concessions to make your Muslim guests feel welcomed and comfortable. For example, if you have a decorative door mat at your entryway that reads, "God Bless You," be sure to remove it. Imagine the shock when Muslims realize the function of door mats. Another shocker is when Muslims see devotionals and even Bibles in your bathroom. Remember, for Muslims, the bathroom is a place associated with human wastes and bad smells—not a place for sacred literature.

Here's another consideration. Most Muslims don't like dogs, especially black dogs. They would be aghast if your pet dog Blacky jumped on their lap to offer a hearty, tail-wagging welcome with lavish licks to the face. For many Muslims, touching a dog renders them unclean.

Initially, your Muslim guests will suspect that you cook pork. It makes no difference whether or not you serve them pork. For an Orthodox Muslim, the fact that pork is cooked in a home defiles every cooking utensil and dish, and no Muslim wants to eat or drink out of anything that is unclean. If you really want mutual acceptance from Muslim people, then you will have to offer hospitality in your home. And for that to materialize, you will have to sacrifice your pork. That aspect of the wrapping paper will have to change. In addition, no Orthodox Muslim will eat the meat of an animal unless it is *halal* (acceptable, kosher). In Islam, the slaughter of animals for food must be accompanied by the invocation, *bismillah Allahu akbar* (in the name of God; God is greater). This is the way Muslims acknowledge God as the source of human sustenance. Unless God's name is invoked, the meat is forbidden; it is *haram*. To solve this problem, ask your Muslim friends where they get their meat, and arrange to buy the meat from the same source. It will be a tremendous relief to your potential guests if you can tell them that for their visit you will not serve pork and that you will purchase any meat from a Muslim butcher.

As you have learned in this chapter, Muslim hospitality means guests are highly honored. During this first visit, plan for a two- or three-course meal. Anything less would be insulting. And you must display enough

160

food so that your guests never feel as though they are taking the last serving. That would imply that you did not consider them worthy of ample food. You must be the one to heap their plates with food and insist on more at least three times until they have given the appropriate signal that they have had enough. The signal may simply be a hand extended over their plates.

It is so important to let your Muslim family know you were honored by their visit. Hospitality can be a costly affair in a Muslim society. For many Muslim families, it is a great sacrifice, but it is a sacrifice that can reap benefits. This is equally true for the Christian who learns how to properly and generously host Muslim guests.

Reflection

As you and your family commit yourselves to getting to know a Muslim family, acquaintance, or coworker, you will begin to realize the need to apply some of the principles of cross-cultural ministry that we have been discussing. You will feel overwhelmed about possible cultural conflict and that's when you will be forced to ask, "What would Jesus do?"

Jesus, the Son of God, mingled with the people and became one of them. He spoke their language and ate their food. He socialized with them. He prayed with them. He rejoiced and mourned with them. Then the Apostle Paul showed us in his own ministry what Jesus would do. And it was Paul who said he became all things to all men. To the Jew, he became like a Jew, and to the

Gentile, he became like a Gentile. Had there been Muslims in his day, he would have become like a Muslim to the Muslim.

It is for us now to continue this incarnational approach. It is something Jesus has already prepared us for. It is the very thing He asked us to do when we first invited Him to be our Lord and Savior. He asked us to follow Him, forsake our identity with the world. To die to the flesh and become like Him. He prayed to the Father about His disciples (John 17:16-18): *They are not of the world . . . As you sent me into the world, I have sent them . . .*

And He has sent a Counselor to help us. We cannot separate ourselves from our culture and embrace the Muslims in our own strength. We can't simply say, "I will put aside what is comfortable to me and reach out to those who are different." If we try to do that, we will fail as soon as things do not go as we imagined. We will think, perhaps, "I misunderstood God and this is not His leading for me." It is always His leading to love others.

As you take those first bold steps, make that first phone call, knock on that first door, invite your first guests, remember that this is not something you are going to do. It is something He is doing. Something he began over two thousand years ago when he said "I have sent them . . ."

13

How Can I Deepen My Relationships With Muslims?

I have become all things to all men so that by all possible means I might save some.

I Corinthians 9:22

If your ministry has grown to the point where you are visiting Muslims regularly and eating in each other's homes, then you have made considerable headway in your relationships. You have gotten past the stage of exchanging pleasantries about family, food, and weather and are now entering the stage where you begin to share about the serious issues of life. The subject will eventually take a spiritual direction, and you will be talking about God. Muslims are very open in talking about God and their religion. And you will hear them repeat the Arabic word for God, Allah. As you try to relate to a Muslim and communicate in his terms, you may struggle with the idea of using this word to talk about God. No doubt you have heard repeatedly that Allah is a demon or a pagan moon god. But for Orthodox Muslims, Allah is the supreme God—Creator of the universe. In chapter six, we learned He is the God who called Abraham out of idolatry to establish a new community of faith.

It is true that most Muslims view *Allah* as a proper name for God, and this may be another reason for your reluctance to use it. For us, God's proper name is Yahweh (or Jehovah). Not all Muslims, however, view *Allah* as a proper name. Some Islamic scholars tell us that the expression *allah* is composed of the words *al ilah*, which literally mean "the god." This helps us to understand why Arab Christians (our brothers and sisters in Christ who speak Arabic) use the word Allah in their prayers and worship. This is the Arabic word for deity, just as God is our word for deity in English. It is also helpful to know that in Islamic teaching, among the ninety-nine names ascribed to Allah that speak of His divine attributes, the two most common are *Ar-Rahman* (the Merciful One) and *Ar-Rahim* (the Compassionate One). With this in mind, we can qualify our own usage of Allah to refer in general terms to the one creator-God who is full of mercy and compassion. There is a reason we are attracted to these two attributes. They are the very attributes God uses to reveal Himself as Yahweh in Exodus 33:19 (see also James 5:11). This God of mercy and compassion—this is the God whom Christ came to reveal, and this is the God we indeed want to talk about—for these are the attributes that speak of God's love. Terminology like *Ar-Rahman Ar-Rahim* is the kind of wrapping paper we definitely want to adopt in presenting the gift.

As you learn to converse about the things of God, pay particular attention to how Muslims verbally honor the mention of God whenever they utter the word Allah. In most cases they will not use the word Allah by itself but will add honorific expressions such as Allah *ta'ala* (God the exalted) or Allah *subhannahu wa ta'ala* (God, glorified is He and exalted). Learning to revere God in similar fashion will mark you as a godly person. You can do this by referring to God as "God Almighty" or "God the Most High."

As you hear Muslims engage in everyday conversation, you will constantly hear them using Arabic phrases with the mention of Allah (God) in them. Make note of how each one is used and be prepared to recognize them. Knowing that Arab Christians also use some of these phrases may encourage you to apply them in your own day-to-day interaction with Muslim people. Speaking some of their language is a part of sharing in their humanity.

Some Common Islamic Expressions:

Bismillah. "In the name of God." This phrase is commonly used to invoke God's blessing and protection. For example, it is used in the slaughter of animals as *bismillah allahu akbar* (in the name of God; God is greater). *Bismillah* is also used to begin the eating of a meal. In both cases, God is acknowledged for His provision for humankind. This phrase is often expanded to *bismillah-ir rahman-ir rahim*, which means, "in the name of God, the Merciful One, the Compassionate One." This expanded phrase is uttered or written to mark the beginning of something, such as a ceremony, a class lecture, a journey, a letter, or a book. In fact, every chapter of the Qur'an except one begins with this phrase.

Alhamdulillah. "Praise be to God." This phrase is used to express joy or thanksgiving. For example, "Christ Jesus is the Savior of the world; *alhamdulillah!*" When one Muslim asks another, "How are you?" the response is not, "I am well" or "I am sick." The response is always "*Alhamdulillah!*" When Muslims finish eating a meal, it is fitting to express thanksgiving with the phrase, "*Alhamdulillah!*"

Insha'allah. "If God wills." This phrase is simply used when speaking of some expected event or act in the future, acknowledging that anything could change since life is in God's control and not ours. For example, "Tomorrow I will arrive in the evening, *insha'allah.*" We find this idea reflected in

166

James 4:13–15: . . . *you do not even know what will* *happen. . . . Instead, you ought to say, "If it is the* *Lord's will, we will live and do this or that."*

Masha'allah. "That which God wills." This phrase is often used to acknowledge God as the provider of something good. As you begin to interact with Muslim people and begin to show them kindness in tangible ways, you will expect them to acknowledge your kindness by saying something like "thank you." Instead, you only hear, *"masha'allah."* Before being quick to judge a Muslim as utterly ungrateful, try to see things as he sees them. If the Muslim says to you, "Thank you," then you get all the credit. You receive the praise and the honor. And that could lead to self-glory. However, when the Muslim responds, *"Masha'allah,"* "that which God wills," he is acknowledging that all good things come from God and that God deserves the credit. By pointing to God, neither the giver nor the recipient risks the danger of usurping God of His rightful praise and honor for which He alone is worthy.

A'authubillah. "I seek refuge in God." This phrase is used when Muslims sense danger, especially from evil influences, to invoke God's protection. It is often expanded to *"a'authubillahi min ash-shaitan-ir* *rajim"*— "I seek refuge in God from Satan the accursed one." Using this phrase can provide us opportunity to speak about the reality of spiritual warfare and how we find refuge in God through Christ; for the *Injil* (New Testament) proclaims that the reason Christ came into the world was to destroy the works of the devil (1 John 3:8).

At this point, we need to discuss a very critical issue. As you begin to identify with Islamic culture and even use some Islamic terms, Muslims will become curious. One of the first things they will ask you is, "Are you a Muslim?" What they are really asking is, "Do you profess that there is no god but Allah and that Muhammad is His messenger?" This is not a difficult question to deal with if you have prepared for it by knowing the literal meaning of the word *muslim* and the way it is used in the Qur'an. The literal meaning of *muslim* is "one who finds peace by surrendering to the will of God." It is the very thing we are doing in order to minister to Muslims. In this way, we too are *muslims*, but we are not like those who are followers of Muhammad. We are like those described in the Qur'an who are followers of *Isa al-Masih*, Jesus the Messiah.

> Said the disciples [of Jesus]: *We are God's helpers; we believe in God, and do thou bear witness that we are Muslims. Our Lord! We believe in what thou hast revealed, and we follow the apostle (Jesus): then write us down as those who bear witness (3:52–53).*

It is *extremely* important that you clearly establish this distinction of identity. Saying, "No, I'm a Christian" can give a very wrong impression. Remember what we discussed earlier; the word "Christian" has so many negative connotations for a Muslim. It would be the same as a Muslim saying, "I believe in Allah," and you thinking he worships a moon god. It is far better to identify yourself as a believer and a follower of Jesus the Messiah. In doing so, you then provide yourself the opportunity to explain to Muslims your reason for identifying with their culture. Your explanation could go something like this:

We believe Jesus the Messiah came to the world as the great Servant of God, and that He is the example we are to follow of true servanthood. In his footsteps, our mission is to serve others by helping them, both physically and spiritually. To do this, Jesus the Messiah has taught us to sacrifice aspects of our own culture, if necessary, to better identify with people of another culture. This is our way of saying we do not consider ourselves as superior to you, but rather, as fellow human beings who also need the help of a God who is merciful and compassionate.

If you can make a statement like this in Islamic wrapping paper, then your ministry will not be seen as an incursion of Western imperialism. You have clearly clarified your identity, but in such a way that Muslims will want to know more about you and your own understanding of Jesus the Messiah. Furthermore, they will take notice when they begin to perceive that you are not the typical Westerner; you are different. When they learn that you pray and fast; you believe in God and in holiness; you are morally upright and modest; you are honest and sincere, they will become attracted to you and to the love of Christ within you. Once you break through the cultural barrier, Muslims will invite you not only into their homes, but also into their lives. One way will be to involve you in their holidays.

Like us, most Muslims are happy for any occasion that calls for celebration, such as a holiday. For Muslims, holidays are important events that provide wonderful opportunities for community interaction. Two of the most popular holidays are *Eid-ul Fitr* (Celebration of the Breaking of the Fast) and *Eid-ul Adha* (Celebration of the Sacrifice).

Eid-ul Fitr is a very joyous occasion. It marks the end of the month-long fast of Ramadhan and the beginning of a three-day holiday. The anticipation and exuberance of this special time resembles the excitement of Christmas. New clothes, gifts for loved ones and friends, toys for the children, and special foods make this a favorite holiday. To share the festivity, Muslims visit from house to house to exchange *Eid-Mubarak* (blessed celebration) greetings and sample the many delicacies specially prepared for the occasion. It does not matter whether you kept the fast during Ramadhan. This is a blessed occasion to share with everyone. *Eid-ul Fitr* provides one of the best opportunities to meet Muslim families, enter Muslim homes, and observe Muslim culture. Becoming involved will give you a greater appreciation for Muslim community life.

One important question that arises concerning *Eid-ul Fitr* is whether you should join your Muslim friends in the fast of Ramadhan that precedes the holiday. If you live in a Muslim neighborhood, you will feel awkward eating while others around you are not. You may be tempted to use this occasion to speak of your freedom in Christ, but remember that exhibiting your freedom unwisely could create a stumbling block. Again we are faced with the issue of how far should one go in identifying with the Muslim people. We are reminded of the passion of Paul who said, "*I have become all things to all men so that by all possible means I might save some. I do all this for the sake of the gospel*" (1 Cor. 9:22–23). Of course there can be no hard-and-fast rules in matters like this. According to Romans 14:5–8, each individual has to do what he or she feels to be right as *to the Lord*.

> *One man considers one day more sacred than another; another man considers every day alike. Each one should be fully convinced in his own mind. He who regards one day as special, does so to the Lord. He who eats meat, eats to the Lord, for he gives thanks to God; and he who abstains, does so to the Lord and gives thanks to God. For none of us lives to himself alone and none of us dies to himself alone. If we live, we live to the Lord; and if we die, we die to the Lord. So, whether we live or die, we belong to the Lord.*

171

Many Christians object to keeping the Muslim fast of Ramadhan under any circumstances, and if this is done out of honor for the Lord Jesus, then their convictions must be respected. On the other hand, some Christians, especially those who live among Muslims, choose to keep the fast, or at least part of it, also as a way of honoring the Lord, particularly as it relates to the incarnational example of Christ. You may even decide, because you are free in Christ, this is a sacrifice you are giving to the Lord in order to further His kingdom. Surely, such decisions are critical and require much prayer. However, after prayerful consideration, if you choose to join the Muslim community in the fast of Ramadhan, your decision will reap many important benefits.

First of all, it will encourage you to become more involved in fasting yourself, and will provide occasion for intercessory prayer for your Muslim friends and neighbors. It will give you the opportunity to fast without making a show of it since Muslims are expected to fast during the same time. When Muslims ask you why you fast, it will give you the opportunity to identify yourself as a follower of Jesus the Messiah who taught about fasting and fasted forty days Himself. In answer to the question, you can share the various examples and teachings of fasting from the Bible such as the fasting of Moses, David, and Daniel, and the teaching of Zechariah 7 and Isaiah 58. If you join the fast, you will be marked by the community as a man or woman of God. It may also provide you with about thirty extra days of interaction with the community, and it can happen in the following way:

During the month of Ramadhan, each day of fasting ends at sunset just before the sunset prayer. Immediately, Muslims will eat a quick snack before performing their prayers. This snack is called *iftar* (literally meaning "break fast" or the food that breaks the fast) and may consist of fruit, juice, and some traditional type of pastry or protein food that can be eaten quickly. Often Muslim families will send trays of these snacks to neighbors and friends or invite others to come to their home for an *iftar* gathering. If you are likewise fasting, then you do not feel guilty receiving one of these trays or invitations and you have the opportunity as well to return the favor by preparing some specialty of your own. Or this is a time when you can simply send a basket of fruit or cans of fruit juice to your Muslim friends as a friendly gesture. Perhaps the most important benefit of joining the fast is that it gives you the opportunity to identify and empathize with people whom God wants to love through you. You will find the thirty-day fast of Ramadhan to be an extremely rigorous exercise, particularly during the heat of summer. However, identifying with Muslims by participating in some way in the fast will widen the door to acceptance and mutual respect. You will see this evidenced when Muslims come to joyfully greet you on the culminating holiday, *Eid-ul Fitr*, and embrace you with the words, *Eid-Mubarak!*

The other major holiday is *Eid-ul Adha*, also known

as *Eid-ul Qurban* (Celebration of the Sacrifice) and *Eid-ul Kabir* (The Great Celebration). As indicated by this last name, this is the most important holiday in Islam. *Eid-ul Adha* falls on the tenth day of the twelfth lunar month, *Dhul Hijja*. This happens to be the tenth day of the annual Hajj as well, and this is the day when Muslims all over the world offer an animal sacrifice as do the pilgrims at Mecca during the Hajj rituals. This animal sacrifice is offered as a reminder of the story of Abraham's submission and God's (Allah's) provision of the animal sacrifice. Depending on the financial status and size of family, the animal could be a chicken, a goat, a cow, or a camel. It is important to know that in Orthodox Islam, this animal sacrifice is not viewed as an atoning sacrifice for sin. Instead, it is an act of commemoration. As a result, animals are slaughtered on this day, and the meat is cooked for consumption. Because the family is allowed to keep only a third of the meat, the remainder is given to charity and to friends and neighbors. Consequently, this is another time for visitation and eating. The meat is eaten either in homes or at the mosque.

It is very probable that on this holiday, you will either receive fresh meat from your Muslim friend or you will be invited to his home to partake of the meat in a cooked meal. You will wonder how to respond. Again, we look for scriptural principle to help us. On the issue of food sacrificed to idols, we read in 1 Corinthians 8:8, "But food does not bring us near to God; we are no worse if we do not eat, and no better if we do." It is apparent from the context of this verse that the consumption or abstention of food does not determine one's salvation. Furthermore, in Orthodox Islam, this sacrifice is by no means a sacrifice to idols. That would be *shirk*, the unpardonable sin. Refusing the meat of the sacrifice from a Muslim friend, or an invitation to eat the meat in a Muslim home, would be an insult to that Muslim. It would cause a severe setback in any attempt to establish a relationship of mutual respect and even friendship. On the other hand, responding in a positive and grateful spirit of acceptance would open the door to further opportunities. Remember that in the Muslim world, eating and talking together is a sign of mutual acceptance, and this is an important step for developing relationships. More importantly, identifying with this most important holiday provides the opportunity to talk about one of the most important stories in both Islam and Christianity, the story of Abraham and the *sacrifice*.

Weddings provide another occasion for celebration. They also provide opportunities for family interaction that leads to new acquaintances. Muslims are admonished in their traditions to never turn down an invitation to a wedding banquet, and so be prayerful in how you respond to a wedding invitation. If you choose to go, be prepared to be bombarded with questions. Asking a lot of questions is a Muslim's way of showing interest. Be ready to explain who you are, what you do, and whether or not you are a Muslim. This type of setting may give you the opportunity, as a follower of Jesus, to share your own views about marriage and the need for God's guidance, strength, and blessing for preserving family values. But be careful to avoid religious controversy. This is not the time to preach. It is the time to learn and develop close friendships.

Just as there is a time to rejoice, there is a time to mourn. The most common occasion for mourning in the Muslim community is the funeral. Funerals are extremely important for Muslim people because they offer a time to both honor the dead and pray for their salvation. Included in this prayer for salvation are prayers for the blessing of God (Allah) upon Muhammad. If you are very close to a Muslim family, you will most likely receive an invitation to a funeral. This is to both honor you and to be honored by your presence. Because this is a time of bereavement, it is very difficult to refuse such an invitation. Before attending any funeral service, you may want to inform the Muslim family that as a follower of Jesus the Messiah, it is not your practice to pray for the dead, nor is it your practice to pray for Muhammad. However, you do pray for God to comfort the bereaved family. Let them know that as much as you would want to attend the funeral to honor the deceased and sympathize with family members, you would not want to create any embarrassment by not being able to participate in the prayer ritual. You would only be able to come as a respectful observer. Then let the family decide whether you should still come. Again, this is another opportunity to meet friends and relatives of the family. It also provides opportunity for some later time to talk about death and the assurance of salvation. Most importantly, funerals give you an opportunity to empathize with Muslims in their time of grief. Remember, the priestly ministry of empathizing with others helps to create bonds of lasting and meaningful relationships. Sincerely weeping with Muslims brings you a few steps closer to them—hopefully close enough to where they begin to feel the love of God yearning to flow from your heart into theirs.

Reflection

This chapter is about sharing in the day to day lives and experiences of Muslims. You may find making cultural adjustments awkward. Using common Islamic expressions may feel uncomfortable because speaking with them is something you've never done. Carefully choosing words that allow you to avoid calling yourself a Christian might strike you as not being completely honest. There may be several times as you've read the chapters that you haven't been sure about committing to ministering to Muslims by identifying culturally with them.

It may seem that the conventional way of sharing the gospel is better suited to you. Ministering to Muslims effectively requires a lot of study, prayer and sacrifice. This can be challenging when you are already committed to your own family and church.

It will help if you remember furthering God's Kingdom by ministering to Muslims must be a labor of love.

Love suffers long and is kind; love does not parade itself, is not puffed up; does not behave rudely, does not seek its own, is not provoked, thinks no evil; does not rejoice in iniquity, but rejoices in the truth; bears all things, believes all things, hopes all things, endures all things.

And best of all . . . Love never fails.

You need only be obedient to His call, faithful to his Word, and yielded to His Holy Spirit. The rest is up to Him.

14

Leading Muslims in Prayer

For I will give you words and wisdom that none of your
adversaries will be able to resist or contradict.

Luke 21:15

Once upon a time there was a beggar who decided to beg at the palace beneath the king's window. He brought his blind friend to beg with him, hoping to receive a silver coin. When they reached the king's palace, they each lifted their voices in prayer. The one who could see faced the king's window to be sure to be heard.

"O mighty God," he began loudly. "May you bless the king. May you give him many sons. May you give him great victories. May you increase his wealth for being so generous to paupers like me"

The beggar who was blind simply lifted his face to the sky and prayed, "Praise be unto God, Lord of heaven and earth. You alone we worship and you alone we ask for help."

Of course the king was flattered by the prayer of the first beggar. Nevertheless, he ordered the cook to prepare two roast chickens, one for each man. But he instructed the cook to stuff three gold coins into one of the chickens and deliver it to the beggar who prayed especially for his success. And so it was done.

When the seeing beggar laid eyes on the chicken, he blurted out, "What is this? I came for a silver coin and all I get is this little chicken!" He turned to his beggar friend and asked, "How much will you give me for this chicken?"

The friend replied, " I only have a few small coins."

"It will be enough," said the other and the exchange was made.

The following week, the seeing beggar returned to the king's palace hoping for better results. Again he prayed, "O mighty God, May you bless the king. May you give him many sons. May you give him great victories. May you increase his wealth for being so generous to paupers like me."

The king was surprised to hear this petitioner return. He expected the blind beggar to come back, not this one. Nevertheless, he was once more flattered and gave his cook the same instructions for delivering a roast chicken stuffed with three gold coins.

When the beggar saw the chicken, he again reacted with great disappointment. He immediately went to his blind friend to see if he would buy another chicken. The blind beggar was more than happy to comply and even offered to pay twice as much as before.

The following week, the seeing beggar decided to try one more time at the king's palace. He prayed the same prayer, but even louder. This time the king was disturbed to hear the beggar back a third time. He ordered the guard to bring him into his chamber. "What is the meaning of this?" demanded the king. "I made you a wealthy man, not just once, but twice, and still you are begging for more!"

"Your majesty," pleaded the beggar. I was only hoping to get a silver coin, but all I got was chickens, and I sold them both to my blind friend. And as for my friend, somehow he managed to purchase a shop, and here I am still begging in the streets."

"Aah," sighed the king. "Truly, you are the beggar who is blind. For now I see what you failed to see. God honors those who look to the Lord of the universe for sustenance, not those who look to mere earthly kings." Then the king raised his face heavenward and prayed, "Praise be unto God,

181

Lord of heaven and earth. You alone we worship and you alone we ask for help."

As Christians, we can readily identify with this story. It relates to the biblical theme of seeking first the kingdom of God. But this story is a Middle East Islamic folk tale. It is a story Muslims use to emphasize the importance of prayer and dependence upon God. The lines of the blind beggar's prayer are verses from the first chapter of the Qur'an. This simple little story is a reminder that Muslims value prayer. We learned a little bit about Islamic prayer in chapter 6, and the emphasis Muslims place on outward form.

As you progress in your journey of identifying with Muslims, you will sense the urge to pray not only for your Muslim friends, but with your Muslim friends. As a follower of Jesus, you will already be in the habit of prayer, but the outward form of your prayer is probably totally different from that of Muslims. When we pray, we want to be sure there is nothing in our method that would distract a Muslim from the sincerity of our prayer. This is where we want to consider the idea of praying like Muslims to identify with them. Perhaps there are aspects of our wrapping paper that we can adjust for the sake of effective ministry.

When we suggest that you "pray like a Muslim," we are not advocating in any way that you memorize his prayers of the *salat* (the five obligatory prayers) and pray exactly like a follower of Muhammad. But the wording of some parts of the Muslim prayer reflect biblical themes and provide us with examples that can be adapted. For example, many of the words of the Muslim prayer focus on God's power, greatness, glory and majesty. We can relate to these attributes if we remember that Muslims address them to Him whom they believe to be the one true deity, Creator of the universe, and the God of Abraham. An example is the following portion of the *salat* known as the *Sana*

> Glory to thee, O God
> And praise be to Thee,
> And blessed is Thy name,
> And exalted is Thy majesty,
> And there is none worthy of worship except Thee.

Notice the similarity to David's prayer of 1 Chronicles 29:10 -13, which begins, "Praise be to you, O Lord," and then speaks of God exalted, His glory, His majesty, and His name.

Other parts of the *salat* prayer, however, pose a problem. Not only do they include passages from the Qur'an, but they also include a prayer for Muhammad that acknowledges him as God's messenger. An example is the following portion of the prayer known as the *Tashahhud*:

> All reverence, worship, and sanctity are due to God. Peace be upon you, O Prophet, and the mercy of God and His blessing. Peace be upon

us and all the righteous servants of God. I bear witness that there is no god but God, and I bear witness that Muhammad is His servant and His messenger.

To recite this prayer with Muslims would convey the misconception that, like them, we are followers of Muhammad who fully subscribe to the teachings of Islam. Clearly, that prevents us from joining Muslims in their ritual prayers. Remember, it is critical that we establish from the onset of ministry our identity as followers of Jesus the Messiah.

But it does not mean that we should distance ourselves from prayer with Muslims. To the contrary, they need to know that we also are a people of prayer. From the above discussion, it should be clear that the suggestion to pray like a Muslim refers more to some of the terminology and body posture and not an exact imitation of the Islamic *salat*.

On the basis of John 4:24, which speaks of worshiping God in spirit and truth, most Christians view prayer as very personal, giving little thought about matters like body posture and placement of hands. In contrast, as we have seen already, Muslims place great importance on the outward form of prayer. Thus the body gestures such as hand raising, standing, bowing, and prostrating are all seen as expressions of submission to God. From our own Christian perspective, it should not matter if we stand, sit, or bow when we pray. Neither should it matter if our eyes are opened or closed. The

New Testament really doesn't legislate restrictions in this regard. Therefore, we want to explore the possibility of adapting customs that are common to Muslims and relate to their cultural expression of prayer. This idea is not as radical as it sounds when we realize that the preparation and posture for the Muslim *salat* prayer reflect Old Testament practice. Notice the following examples:

> **Removal of shoes.** *"Do not come any closer,"* God said. *"Take off your sandals, for the place where you are standing is holy ground"* (Exodus 3:5).
>
> **Ablution.** *He [Moses] placed the basin between the Tent of Meeting and the altar and put water in it for washing, and Moses and Aaron and his sons used it to wash their hands and feet. They washed whenever they entered the Tent of Meeting or approached the altar, as the LORD commanded Moses* (Exodus 40:30–32).
>
> **Prostration.** *When all the Israelites saw the fire coming down and the glory of the LORD above the temple, they knelt on the pavement with their faces to the ground, and they worshiped and gave thanks to the Lord . . .* (2 Chronicles 7:3).

You may find it helpful to get in the habit of praying in a kneeling and prostrate position on a prayer rug. You may be amazed to experience a greater sense of humility and reverence before Almighty God. And you will be able to identify with Muslims when they speak about the awesomeness of bowing before the Lord of the universe.

One of the most common ways the power of the Gospel touches the lives of Muslims is through prayer on their behalf. It is very important that you be known not only as a person of prayer, but also as a person who is always willing to pray for others—no matter who they are. This is so important that you should make every effort to find a reason to pray for Muslim people in their presence. In this regard, two issues need to be considered: the posture of our prayer and the wording of our prayer.

Since we are free in Christ and not restricted to form when it comes to prayer, we can pray in a way that is very similar to the informal Islamic form of prayer that relates to prayers of supplication. This is known as *du'a* or *munajat*. This is different from the liturgical form of *salat*. Muslim clergy, as well as religious Muslims, lead in this type of prayer for special ceremonies such as dedications, death anniversaries, and business inaugurations. The manner is very simple. The one leading the prayer dons his prayer cap, stands with shoes removed, , raises his hands (palms upward to chin level), bows his head with opened eyes looking into the hands, and recites the words of the prayer, which in most cases is a memorized prayer. The prayer is concluded with the word *ameen* (amen), and the face is rubbed with the palms of the hand, suggesting the rubbing in of blessing. Muslims joining in the prayer likewise raise their hands, interject an occasional *ameen* in support of the prayer, and also rub their faces at the conclusion. Try practicing this form during your prayer time at home and you'll see that it can easily be adapted when you pray with Muslims.

Perhaps the best time to initiate prayer with Muslim people is in your home around the dinner table. You may all be seated at the table or the men may be in the dining room and the ladies in the kitchen. If you are all seated together, then the Christian husband can lead out in prayer. If you are segregated, the Christian husband can pray on behalf of the men, and the Christian wife on behalf of the ladies. Before leading in prayer over the food, explain to your Muslim guests that you have a similar practice. Just as they acknowledge God's provision by invoking his name with *Bismillah-ir Rahman-ir Rahim*, you acknowledge His provision by thanking him with prayer. Most likely, if Muslims enter your home and see you with shoes removed, they will leave their shoes at the door. That means everyone at the table will already have their shoes off. The Christian wife should be prepared to cover her head for the prayer by planning in advance and wearing a decorative scarf as part of her dress. It is not critical for the men to cover their heads (although it is preferable), but it is critical for the women. For this kind of prayer (*du'a or munajat*) you can remain seated in your chairs. However, it will be meaningful to raise your hands to chin level, with palms opened upward, before you pray. Keep your eyes open and fixed on your hands as you recite your prayer. When you raise your hands, don't be surprised if you see your guests joining you with raised hands. Now you are ready to utter the prayer. Let's look at the wording of that prayer.

When Muslims pray, they offer their praise to God and acknowledge Him as Lord of heaven and earth, the Merciful One, the Compassionate One. With that in mind, notice how Jesus prefaces His prayer in Matthew 11:25: "I praise you, Father, Lord of heaven and earth. . . . " Remember that the Father is Yaweh who is described in Exodus by His two prominent attributes, mercy and compassion. This is a bridge for us to someday talk about not only God the Creator, but God the Merciful One, the Compassionate One. We will cross this bridge in a later chapter. For now, we are laying the groundwork by our simple prayer at the dining table. Here is a suggested prayer that a Muslim would relate to:

> Almighty God; with hands raised, we praise you with all our hearts. We acknowledge you as not only the Lord of heaven and earth, but also the Merciful One, the Compassionate One, who provides us our daily bread. Thank you for the blessing of this food. Give us strength to serve you and the people you bring into our lives. Amen (Muslims say *ameen*).

This first prayer will break the ice for future opportunities. For example, you may want to pray after a friendly visit in a Muslim home. By the way, be sure that you remove your shoes whenever you enter. Out of politeness, Muslims will insist that you need not do so.

But this will prepare you for prayer later. When you sense that it is time for the visit to end, (often the cue is the serving of refreshments or a meal), it would not be out of place for the Christian husband to ask the head of the family for permission to lead in prayer to thank God for the wonderful hospitality and to ask for His blessing upon the host family. In most cases, your Muslim friends will consent out of courtesy. Of course if this is the first time, they will feel uneasy. Their anxiety will be more than justified if, seated on a sofa, legs crossed, and eyes closed, you pray words such as:

> Dear Jesus, the only begotten Son of God, who was crucified on the cross of Calvary and shed His blood for the sins of the world, may you deliver these people from the darkness and oppression of Islam. May they accept you into their hearts and become Christians. In Jesus' name, amen.

It should be obvious by now that this kind of prayer with its posture and wording does not reflect Islamic wrapping paper. In fact, it would be taken as an offense, not as a benediction. You would probably never again be invited to that Muslim home.

If you receive permission to pray, the Christian man should stand by the men of the family, and the Christian woman with the ladies. And the Christian wife should be wearing some kind of scarf so that she can easily cover her head for prayer. The one leading in prayer can do so standing, with hands raised to chin level, palms opened upward, and eyes fixed on the hands. As for the wording of the prayer, if the intent really is to ask for God's blessing, then this is not the time to use prayer as an opportunity to teach church doctrine or apply terminology that is completely foreign or misleading. The purpose of this prayer is to provide an opportunity for your Muslim friends to feel the peace and presence of God within you. Here is an example of how you can word such a prayer:

> Almighty God, the Lord of heaven and earth, the Merciful One, the Compassionate One. We lift our hands to praise you and to thank you for all of your goodness to us. I thank you especially for the friendship of this family and for their kind hospitality today. May you wonderfully bless them and provide for all of their needs. Almighty God, we pray that you will help us all to be good servants and to do that which is pleasing to you. Protect us from Satan and give us spiritual strength to resist all temptation. May you alone be glorified in our hearts and may your mercy and compassion be reflected in all that we do in life. Praise be to you, O Lord of heaven and earth. Amen.

This is a simple and general prayer, but you can pray it with feeling. If you can pray this in sincere love, your Muslim host will feel it. You will notice that the prayer does not end in the usual formula, "in Jesus' name, amen." Because Muslims are not Christians, they are unaware of Jesus' teaching about the use of His name in prayer. Thus, to avoid confusion, you will find it helpful to set aside this custom until later in your relationship when you can explain its significance. There is nothing in Scripture to suggest that God does not hear the prayer of people unless it ends with the words, "in Jesus' name." Think of the number of times you've recited the Lord's Prayer, and simply ended it with the words, "For yours is the kingdom and the power and the glory forever. Amen." Remember the story of Cornelius of Acts 10. Even before hearing the Gospel message about Jesus, an angel appeared to Cornelius to say, *"Cornelius, God has heard your prayer and remembered your gifts to the poor"* (Acts 10:31).

Besides this kind of general prayer to God for blessing and protection, there may be opportunities that do require you to pray specifically in the name of Jesus. For example, there may be a sick person in the home you visit, possibly a child. You will want to know a proper way to pray for that child without offending the family. The believers' prayer of Acts 4:24-30 helps us with some of the wording for such a prayer. First notice how the believers addressed God: "Sovereign Lord," they said, who "made the heaven and the earth and the sea, and everything in them." In other words, "Lord the Creator" or "Lord of the universe." Then notice how the believers refer to Jesus in their request for God's intervention: "Stretch out your hand to heal and perform miraculous signs and wonders through the name of your holy servant Jesus." Remember that one of the titles the Qur'an gives to Jesus is "Servant of God." Thus the prayer of Acts 4 is an excellent model when you sense the need to specifically pray in the name of Jesus with Muslim people. Getting back to the sick child in the Muslim home, it is only proper that you kindly ask first for permission to pray for the child. Then take the time to explain how you are going to pray. Gently remind your Muslim friends that Jesus the Messiah was the messenger whom God especially honored with power to heal the sick and raise the dead. Furthermore, God never withdrew that honor when He raised Jesus to heaven. You may want to remind them that such truths are reflected in their Qur'an. For example:

> *I [Jesus] have come to you with a Sign from your Lord. . . . And I heal those blind, and the lepers, and I quicken the dead by God's leave; . . . Surely therein is a Sign for you if ye did believe (3:49).*

> *Behold! The angels said: O Mary! God giveth thee glad tidings of a Word from Him: his name will be Christ Jesus the son of Mary, held in honor in this world and the hereafter and of (the company of) those nearest to God. (3:45)*

> *As said Jesus the son of Mary to the Disciples, "Who will be my helpers to (the work of) God?" Said the Disciples, "We are God's helpers!" Then a portion of the Children of Israel believed, and a portion*

disbelieved: But We gave power to those who believed against their enemies, and they became the ones that prevailed. (61:14)

In view of the facts that Jesus the Messiah has the power to heal, that He is still alive, and that His disciples continue in the work of God, encourage your Muslim friends to believe that the power of healing is still available today for Jesus' followers who invoke His name. Then have the child brought to you or ask to go to the child's bedside. In the standing position with hands uplifted to chin level and palms up, and with the model of Acts 4 in mind, you can lead in a simple prayer as follows:

Almighty God, Lord of heaven and earth. You alone are worthy of all our praise and worship. Thank You for all of Your blessings. Thank You for this child. In faith we humbly ask that You stretch out Your hand to touch this child and to perform a miracle. We invoke the name of Your holy servant, Jesus the Messiah, and believe for a complete healing. Amen.

After saying this prayer with complete faith, you may want to reach out to place your right hand on the child and simply speak the name of Jesus by saying, "Child, in the name of Jesus the Messiah, be healed." If the sick individual being prayed for is an adult of the opposite gender, then simply have your spouse place his or her right hand on that person when invoking the name of Jesus.

Knowing how to pray with Muslim people and taking advantage of every opportunity to pray will open many doors of communication. Since most prayers that Muslims pray are memorized, they will be amazed to hear you pray directly to God extemporaneously, from the depths of your heart. They will also be moved by the feeling of your prayer because their hearts deeply yearn for the same kind of experience. With this in mind, never hesitate to pray in the Spirit, if the Lord leads you, because it is what Muslims feel, not what they hear, that impacts them the most. You may find that as you get into the habit of praying with Muslims, they will come to you asking for prayer. They will sense that you have a special connection with Almighty God. This is important because in many cases, Muslims come to Christ through a miracle performed in his name.

Reflection

Perhaps you have felt a twinge of uncertainty as you read that you should refrain from the custom of ending a prayer, "in Jesus name, Amen." It somehow seemed spiritually dishonest and even unnecessary to plan prayers and posturing rather than speak from the comfort of common Christian practice. Nothing could be further from the truth.

You are moving in areas with which you have had little experience. Not only are you trying to identify culturally with Muslims, you are doing it on a spiritual battlefield. We are not to engage in spiritual warfare on our own. We are to be vessels through which the Holy Spirit will fight the battle and reveal truth.

As we move to take ground for the kingdom we must be ever mindful that our flesh is weak. It would be so easy, as we perceive the softening of a Muslim friend's heart, to run out before the Lord and speak things that that friend is not ready to hear. Only God knows the condition of a man's heart . . . and only His Holy Spirit can change it.

Remember, you are a bondservant to Jesus Christ. You are to walk where He directs, be patient, and instead of uncensored thought, allow His love to be the spontaneity of your prayers. At first it is best to draw on the words He has given in the Scriptures. In time, as you labor with Him, you will move into moments of discernment. And rest assured, then, too, He will give you words, other words, words *that none of your adversaries will be able to resist or contradict*. Words designed specifically for the heart He has prepared, delivered by the life-changing power of the Holy Spirit.

15

Why Are We So Often Misunderstood by Muslims?

*For by your words you will be acquitted, and
by your words you will be condemned.*

Matthew 12:37

Through the preceding chapters, we have learned a lot about the Muslim people and how to reach out to them. We have come to see how they view Christians, God, and sin. We have learned about our cultural wrapping paper, what we need to know before we witness, and how to identify with Islamic culture. We have considered the Scriptures that call us to serve Christ by serving others. Now the time has come not only to reach out, but also to speak out. We cannot avoid the mandate to go into all the world and *preach the good news*

196

to all creation.

God continues to reveal Himself and His purpose to the world through the medium of words, both oral and written. For this reason, it is imperative that we carefully consider the wording of the message that communicates the "good news" about Jesus, giving special attention to the components that give it shape and meaning. If the message is truly a matter of spiritual life and death, then we want to be absolutely sure we are delivering a message that is not only theologically correct, but also correctly understood.

Whenever we deliver any message, we deliver it in words and expressions that derive from our personal cultural context, which we will refer to as our "frame of reference." As long as we proclaim the message to an audience that shares a similar frame of reference, we can be fairly certain that the recipients understand the message as we do.

Problems arise, however, when we deliver a message to people who are outside our frame of reference. If they are completely unacquainted with our culture, such as the language we speak, the vocabulary we use, idioms and metaphors, our facial gestures, the tone of voice, and even the climate and geography we live in, then we can expect difficulty. They will interpret the message through their own personal culture, and because their frame of reference is different, the meaning they derive from what they hear will also be different. In fact, what you wanted to convey may end up completely misrepresented or distorted.

The true story that follows (names have been changed) is an illustration of how a message perceived through the lens of one culture can become totally distorted when viewed through the lens of a different culture.

Missionaries Peter and Susan were excited when they arrived in the country of their new ministry, halfway around the world. They found themselves transplanted from a beautiful countryside of pine tree forests, flowers, and dry air to an overcrowded urban center of pungent odors, bustling bazaars, and tropical heat. Peter and Susan immediately engaged in ministry and decided to teach the local congregation some of the new choruses that had become popular back home. One chorus was especially meaningful because it uplifted the name of Jesus. The words went like this:

Jesus, Jesus, Jesus, there's just
something about that name;
Jesus, Jesus, Jesus, like the fragrance
after the rain;

Peter and Susan even had the chorus translated into the national language so that the local believers could appreciate the beauty of the song. Each time Peter and Susan sang the words "like the fragrance after the rain," they closed their eyes. Their minds took them back to their frame of reference—the pine tree forests, the beautiful wildflowers, and of course the beautiful scent that followed a misty rain. What they envisioned was so beautiful; and for them, it all reflected the beauty of Jesus' name. But the local believers were visibly reluctant to join Peter and Susan in their enthusiasm for the chorus. Peter and Susan became somewhat perturbed. They realized they still had a long way to go in language study, but an occasional mispronunciation was no reason for the locals to refuse to cooperate. Besides, this was a song to glorify the Lord Jesus. How could they resist such a beautiful chorus?

The answer came a few months later, when the monsoon rains arrived. Day after day, torrents of rain flooded the city. Because the streets and narrow lanes were lined with open sewers, the waste matter began to rise with the water level. The sewage eventually overflowed onto the roadways and footpaths. When the rains finally stopped, the water receded into the sewers. But the waste matter stayed behind, fully exposed. The sun slowly broke through the clouds, spreading its sweltering heat, and producing the putrid stench of raw sewage that even the locals found nauseating. In contrast to Peter and Susan's frame of reference, this was the frame of reference most familiar to the local believers. They knew nothing about the fragrance of pine trees, wildflowers, and misty rain. All they knew was the horrid smell that follows the monsoon. And in no way could they associate that terrible smell with the precious name of Jesus. They just couldn't understand the motives of those strange missionaries.

This is an example of how the beautiful message, "There's just something about that name," became terribly distorted because of a different frame of reference, influenced by geography and climate. The choice of chorus for conveying that particular message certainly did not fit the local context. The local believers ended up with an entirely different concept. In previous lessons, we have already noted how our concepts differ from those of Muslim people with regard to God, sin, forgiveness, and prayer. In this lesson, we will look carefully at the wording of our message.

In our discussion about the wrapping paper in chapter 9, we learned that one of the components of that wrapping paper has an important link to the message. It is the component of Christian terminology. There are certain words and phrases that carry profound meaning to us as Christians, but are very misleading from the Muslims' frame of reference. In fact, some terms we use convey an entirely different message than intended. As a result, the meaning of the message becomes distorted and misunderstood, often to the point of complete rejection.

The Muslims' frame of reference is made up primarily of the Qur'an, the traditions of the *hadith*, and Islamic history. This background material contributes to their interpretation of what Christians say. To understand this more clearly, we will look at five common words or phrases we use in the delivery of the message. Then by examining the Muslims' frame of reference, we will understand the reason for their rejection. It will then be necessary to consider appropriate adjustments so that we can remove as many misunderstandings as possible.

The Phrase *Son of God*

Undoubtedly, the most common Bible verse that Christians use for world evangelism is John 3:16: "For God so loved the world that he gave his one and only Son [his only begotten Son—KJV], that whoever believes in him shall not perish but have eternal life." For most Christians, this is the most meaningful verse in the Bible because it reflects the core message of the Gospel. It speaks of God and God's love for humankind. It speaks of the Son of God, Jesus the gift. It speaks of the reward of eternal life in Heaven. On the basis of this verse, we continue to explain the Gospel and keep talking about Jesus as the Son of God. Ironically, John 3:16 is one of the most troubling verses for a Muslim. Whenever he hears the phrase "Son of God," he reacts in disgust. Let us look at his frame of reference to understand why.

One of the most common Qur'anic passages a Muslim learns to recite in his prayer of *salat* is the following:

> *He is God, the One and only; God the Eternal, the Absolute;*

He begetteth not, neither is He begotten;
And there is none comparable to Him. (112:1–4)

Notice the line "He begetteth not, neither is He begotten." In other words, God was never born, and God does not give birth to gods and goddesses. God does not have sons and daughters. This was a common pagan belief that Muhammad felt commissioned by God to stamp out. This idea was blasphemy. Here are some related passages:

To Him is due the primal origin of the heavens and the earth. How can He have a son when He hath no consort [mate]? He created all things, and He hath full knowledge of all things. That is God, your Lord! There is no god but He, the Creator of all things. (6:101–102)

And exalted is the majesty of our Lord. He has taken neither a wife nor a son. (72:3)

On the basis of this frame of reference, when a Muslim hears John 3:16, or the phrase "Son of God," he thinks that Christians believe God had a wife, and together, they had a son. After all, common sense tells him that a son cannot be born without a woman. Remember, five times a day and every day of their lives, many Muslims recite in their prayer, "He begetteth not and neither is He begotten." The moment a Muslim hears about the Son of God, he shuts his ears to whatever else the messenger has to say. He is compelled to completely reject all that he has heard because for him, the "Son of God" phrase is blasphemy.

Of course, you cannot delete "Son of God" from the Bible no matter how deeply it offends Muslim people. But as servant and priest, you must try to be sensitive to his reaction to this phrase. For even as followers of Jesus we object to any teaching that suggests God had a female companion who bore Him a son.

Let's look at how we can deal with this problem. First, it is important to explain to your Muslim friend that this phrase should not be taken literally. It does not mean that God in union with a goddess had a son. Rather, the phrase is a metaphor. Even the Qur'an makes use of metaphor. For example, the Qur'anic expression, "son of the road" (*ibnu sabil*; 2:215) is not to be taken literally. In other words, the road did not have a wife who bore for it a son. That would be ridiculous. This phrase is clearly a metaphor that is translated "wayfarer" or "traveler." Similarly, the phrase, "Son of God" is a metaphor or symbolic expression that could mean several things. It could refer to the special relationship Jesus has with God. Simply ask your Muslim friend, "Who was Jesus' father?" He will most likely know that according to the Qur'an, Jesus was miraculously born of a virgin and therefore had no earthly father. Precisely. The phrase "Son of God" reminds us that Jesus was not the son of any man. Instead, he came directly from God. We could direct the Muslim to Old Testament prophecy where God spoke of one of King David's descendents, saying, "*I will establish the throne of his kingdom forever. I will be his father and he will be my son"* (2 Samuel 13–14).

In this regard, the term "Son of God" also points to Jesus as the representative and heir of God's great power. The Scriptures tell us that God gave Jesus authority to rule over His entire Kingdom. Just as a king hands power over to the heir, the prince, so did God hand over power to the heir, Prince Jesus. And notice that the relationship between king and prince is father and son. As the Son of God, Jesus is the representative of God and the inheritor of great power and authority. For this reason, the term "Son of God" is often used in Scripture to refer to the messiahship of Jesus. As the Messiah (the Anointed One), Jesus was to come as a great ruler to overthrow the forces of darkness and deliver the people of God from evil. Thus did Peter utter his confession, *"You are the Messiah, the Son of the living God."* (Matt. 16:16)

Many Christians feel compelled to continually refer to Jesus as "Son of God" in their preaching and writing in order to uphold the deity of Jesus. However, there is a much better descriptive phrase that speaks of the deity of Christ, and that is His name in Revelation 19:13, "Word of God." Muslims also know Jesus by the name "Word of God" (*Kalimatullah*) because the Qur'an refers to Him as "His [God's] Word" (4:171). When Muslims talk in general about the word of God, many of them agree that the Word of God is not a product of creation and therefore can only be of divine essence. We will speak more about this issue in the following section.

Because of the Muslim's frame of reference that

leads to misunderstanding, try to avoid using the phrase "Son of God" in your initial contacts with Muslim people. There are so many other scriptural terms to describe Jesus. It is especially noteworthy that in the Book of Acts, which records the preaching of the Apostles, the expression "Son of God" is found only once (9:20). From the context of the passage, it is used not to address the deity of Jesus, but rather to speak of His identity as the long-awaited Messiah (9:22). Notice this varied list of expressions and titles that are found in the Book of Acts to speak of Jesus: "Lord and Christ" (2:36); "servant" (3:13); "Holy and Righteous One" (3:14); "author of life" (3:15); "holy servant" (4:27); "Prince and Savior" (5:31); "Son of Man" (7:56); "Lord of all" (10:36); "judge of the living and the dead" (10:42); "the Savior" (13:23); and "the Christ" (18:5). This list should help us understand that we are not limited solely to the title "Son of God" in our desire to share Christ with Muslim people.

The Term *Trinity*

In the course of our delivery of the message, we often try to explain the God of the Bible in terms of the Trinity or the godhead of three persons. However, the word *trinity* and related expressions only complicate and distort the issue for Muslims. In fact, they lead the Muslim to one of his strongest objections to Christianity—the objection that Christians believe in three separate gods. How ironic. We both say we believe in the one creator-God of the universe. Yet, we label

205

Muslims as blasphemous because we think they worship a moon god, and they label us as blasphemous because they think we worship a pantheon of three deities.

Let us look again at the Muslim's frame of reference, which includes influences from both the historical record and the Qur'an. Unfortunately, during the time of Muhammad, there lived in Arabia a heretical Christian sect that venerated Mary as a divine being along with Jesus. Thus, these Christians worshipped a trinity of God the Father, Mary the Mother, and Jesus the Son. Of course, such a trinity is contrary to biblical teaching. This is the trinity that the Qur'an refutes:

> *And behold! God will say, "O Jesus the son of Mary, didst thou say unto men, 'worship me and my mother as gods in derogation of God?'"* (5:116)

> *They do blaspheme who say God is one of three in a trinity; for there is no god except one God* (5:73).

Because of this misunderstanding of the true biblical Trinity and the strongly sensitive feelings Muslims have toward anything that suggests the worship of more than one god, it is best not to even use the term *trinity*. Be sure to inform your Muslim friend in the clearest terms that you also believe in just one God, and that you do not worship three separate gods. Share with him the biblical teaching that God is one, using Deuteronomy 4:35, 6:4, and Mark 12:29. However, try to explain to him that you believe this one God exists with a will, and that His will is both expressed through His Word and accomplished by His Spirit. Thus, wherever there is God, there is also His Word and His Spirit. This truth is reflected in the biblical account of creation where God spoke the Word, and by the power of His Spirit, creation came into being (Genesis 1:1–3; Psalm 33:6, 104:24, 30). Explain to your Muslim friend that you believe that both the Word and Spirit of God are inseparable from God. As long as God existed, so did His Word and His Spirit. They were never created and they will never die. In this sense they are divine.

Surprisingly, unknown to most Muslims, the Qur'an also points to three things that are divine. Of course, the first is God himself. But the Qur'an also speaks of the "Word of God." It is referred to as the "Word or Command of creation."

For to anything which We have willed, We but say the Word, "Be," and it is (16:40).

Verily when He (God) intends a thing, His Command is "Be," and it is! (36:82)

In regard to verse 36:82 above, in "The Holy Qur'an: Translation and Commentary" by A. Yusuf Ali, footnote number 4028 says this about God's Word: "The moment He (God) wills a thing, it becomes His Word or Command, and this thing forthwith comes into existence." We have already noted that the biblical accounts likewise demonstrate that things are created by the word of God. Now if creation is by the Word of God, then it is obvious that the Word itself could never be a product of creation, since it is the agent by which creation emerges. For this reason, most Muslim scholars agree that the Word of God is uncreated.

Related to this discussion is the belief in the "Mother of the Book" as described in the Qur'an :

> God doth blot out or confirm what He pleaseth. With Him is the Mother of the Book (13:39).

Many Muslims recognize this Book by the Arabic rendering, *Umm-ul Kitab*. Again, referring to a footnote by Yusuf Ali (number 1864), we discover that this *Umm-ul Kitab* is seen as "the original foundation of all revelation." Many Muslims visualize this Mother of the Book as a majestic book in heaven from which all previous holy books are descended. It is regarded as the source of all divine revelation and represents the Word of God. Muslims regard the *Umm-ul Kitab* as something that is above creation and eternal. Thus it is of divine essence.

Knowing these ideas that make up a Muslim's frame of reference helps us to better address the uniqueness of Jesus. We can explain to our Muslim friends that Jesus is not only of human nature, but also divine nature, since both the Bible and Qur'an refer to Him as God's Word. And we can remind them that though they revere their own Qur'an as God's Word, it is embodied in earthly paper and ink. Similarly, we regard Jesus as the Word of God, embodied in flesh in order to accommodate the nature of earthly beings.

The third item that the Qur'an speaks of is the Spirit of God, or the Spirit from God.

For such He (God) has written Faith in their hearts and strengthened them with a spirit from Himself (58:22)

In *The Holy Qur'an: Translation and Commentary* by A. Yusuf Ali, footnote number 5365 describes this "spirit from Himself" as "the divine spirit, which we can no more define adequately than we can define in human language the nature and attributes of God."

And so in the Qur'an as well, we can find evidence that points to a divine threesome—God, God's Word, and God's Spirit—each different, yet of the same divine essence, inseparable from one another.

In summary, avoid such words and phrases as *trinity* or *godhead of three persons* or anything else that would mislead your Muslim friend to think that you worship three separate gods. Remember, the Muslim can only think in terms of one God, and *only* one God. So try to speak of this one God in terms of His Word (Jesus), and His Spirit. Do not try to unravel the great mystery of the Godhead. Let the mystery remain; let God be God. Simply state your belief in one God whose will is revealed through His divine Word and carried out through His divine Spirit.

The Declaration *Jesus is God*

In your zeal to share the message of the gift with Muslim people, you will want to talk about the uniqueness of Jesus. Many times, you will find yourself drawn into a debate about Jesus and Muhammad, and the superiority of one over the other. With a feeling of triumph, you will be tempted to proclaim with a loud voice, "But Muhammad was only a man; Jesus is God." You may react in exultation, but a Muslim will react in shock.

Again, we need to consider the Muslim's frame of reference. Look carefully at the following Qur'anic passage:

> They do blaspheme who say, "God is Christ the son of Mary." But said Christ, "O Children of Israel! Worship God, my Lord and your Lord. Whoever joins other gods with God—God will forbid him the Garden, and fire will be his abode" (5:72).

Notice the line, "Whoever joins other gods with God." Whenever you refer to Jesus as God, you give the Muslim the impression that you worship at least two different gods—the god Jesus, and the god to whom Jesus prayed. For the Muslim, that is clearly two gods. To worship another god besides the one true God is to commit the unpardonable sin of *shirk*. This is the worst sin a Muslim can commit. It is the sin, the penalty of which is "the fire will be his abode." Of course, we don't believe in two gods, but that's the message we convey.

Without saying, "Jesus is God," we need to find ways to explain to Muslims why we believe Jesus is greater than just a prophet, and that He is even divine. The New Testament helps us in this regard. In various places, we find special descriptions of Jesus that point

210

beyond His humanity to His divinity, such as: "Word of God" (Revelation 19:13); "radiance of God's glory and the exact representation of his being" (Hebrews 1:3); "the image of the invisible God" (Colossians 1:15); and "the image of God" (2 Corinthians 4:4). These references speak of the one true God who is fully revealed in Jesus.

The Word *Cross*

Of course, one of the core themes that we are quick to include in the proclamation of the Gospel is that Jesus died on the cross for our sins. For Christians worldwide, the cross is the centerpiece of Christianity. When sincere Christians close their eyes and envision the cross, they think of words such as love, forgiveness, reconciliation, and peace. But when Muslims close their eyes to envision the cross, they think of completely different words. Words such as slaughter, cruelty, subjugation, and idolatry.

This imagery comes primarily from a historical frame of reference. During the eras of the Byzantine Empire, the Great Crusades, and Western Colonialism, the cross became the vivid icon of Christendom's conquest and expansion. Of course, war brings out the worst of evil from both sides of the battlefront. The conflicts of the Crusades were no different. From the chronicles of the Great Crusades, we learn that in the eleventh century, the Crusaders beheaded thousands of Muslims in the precincts of their mosque in Jerusalem. The term *Crusader* meant "bearer of the cross," but the cross these Crusaders bore was one that inflicted casualties, not healings.

Because of this historical frame of reference, when Muslims see the cross or hear the word *cross*, they envision a symbol that speaks of a religious enemy bent on destroying Islam. Therefore, it is helpful in the initial stages of contact to avoid the word *cross* and instead of speaking about Jesus "dying on the cross," speak of Him as "giving up His life as a sacrifice for the sins of the world." After all, it is not the physical cross made of wood that is critical to the gospel message—it is rather the suffering of Christ and its revelation of the long-suffering love of God on behalf of the whole world.

The Title *Holy Spirit*

In your conversation with Muslim people, you will inevitably want to talk about the Holy Spirit and its role in the life of the believer. A proper view of the work of the Holy Spirit is critical for understanding the transformation that takes place in the lives of people when their hearts are cleansed from sin. People need to understand that it is the Holy Spirit who encourages and empowers them to resist evil and become the kind of servants God wants them to be. Though the Qur'an mentions the Spirit in a variety of ways, there is no clear teaching on this matter because the references are vague. For the most part, Muslims avoid any discussion regarding the Spirit by brushing aside the issue as a mystery that God has chosen to conceal. When Muslims hear the term *Holy Spirit*, however, they generally concur in its meaning, which differs from the meaning given to the Christian's Holy Spirit.

Again we look to the Qur'an for the Muslim's frame of reference. Notice the following verses that refer to the matter of revelations to Muhammad:

> *Say (O Muhammad to mankind), "Whoever is an enemy to Gabriel—for he brings down the (revelation) to thy heart by God's will..." (2:97).*

> *Say, "The holy spirit has brought the revelation [the scripture of the Qur'an] from thy Lord in truth, in order to strengthen those who believe..." (16:102).*

From these verses, Muslims believe that Gabriel was the angel who revealed the Qur'an to Muhammad. Muslims also believe angels are ministering spirits as described in Hebrews 1:14. But Gabriel stands out among them all because he is the one who conveys God's message to humankind. In that sense, he is a very holy angel, or a holy spirit (*ruh-ul qudus*). With that frame of reference, Muslims think that you are referring to Gabriel whenever you use the term *Holy Spirit*. Of course, this can create confusion when you talk about the need of the Holy Spirit to rule in the hearts of believers. This can be avoided by referring to the Holy Spirit as the "Spirit from God" (*ruh min allah*), and explaining that whenever the term *Holy Spirit* is used in the Bible, it does not refer to Gabriel. Remember, the Qur'an helps us with this issue in 58:22: "He has written faith in their hearts, and strengthened them with a spirit from Himself."

Reflection

As you relate to Muslim people about your own faith, do not feel compelled to explain the mystery that surrounds the Godhead, and even the nature of Jesus. None among us mortals can fully comprehend that which is related to the divine. Whenever you discuss the identity of Jesus and the Holy Spirit, be careful not to diminish the simplicity of the Gospel. Sometimes we make the mistake of imposing difficult requirements of profound theological understanding that the Scriptures themselves do not require. Nowhere does the New Testament require a new seeker of God to completely understand the nature of Jesus or the mystery of the Godhead. Salvation is not based on our intellectual ability to fully disclose the secret things of God; it is based on a childlike faith of the heart that will gratefully reach out to receive the gift.

But now we must ask, "What really is the gift?" Yes, we know it is Jesus and salvation in him, but what exactly is it people need to believe about Jesus to be saved? This brings us to the issue of the core message of the Gospel, which we will look at in the following chapter.

<u>16</u>

Learning to Avoid Unnecessary Controversy

We give no offense in anything, that our ministry may not be blamed.

2 Corinthians 6:3

In most cases, Muslims will politely engage in casual conversation. However, Christians who are not careful will find themselves easily drawn into controversy. It is usually on the issue of Jesus that general conversations turn into heated arguments about whose prophet is greater and whose religion is superior. Heated arguments between Muslims and Christians can explode into unguarded accusations and verbal slander, unleashing hidden animosity and prejudice from both sides. Some Christians struggle to win arguments with clever debating skills, not realizing that winning arguments often destroys the potential for friendships. When you debate a person, you learn to focus on his vulnerability; you focus on his faults. You look for his weakness. You look for areas of conflict so that one by one, you can prove his assertions wrong and your assertions right. In the process of this kind of approach, the Christian will find himself condemning his opponent and everything he supports. But remember, Jesus, the Lord of our hearts, did not come to condemn. As a servant, he came to serve and to save needy people. As a priest, he came to identify with human brokenness, not to stomp upon it. With that in mind, let us take a look at how Jesus interacted with someone who represented a rival to his own religious community.

One of the most striking parallels we see in the Bible of Christian-Muslim rivalry is the strained relationship that existed between the Jews and the Samaritans. Both communities worshiped the same Creator God, and yet, were separated by a wall of prejudice and hatred. We already saw in a previous chapter how Jesus' close disciples were ready to call fire down from heaven to destroy a Samaritan village for denying them entry.

At another time, we find Jesus and his disciples in a Samaritan town called Sychar (John 4:4-42). It is on this occasion that Jesus provides for us a useful model for presenting the Gospel to a religious rival. This is the beautiful story in which Jesus leads a Samaritan woman to the well of living water. Here are some important points to ponder.

First, the story opens with Jesus clearly recognizing the need to include the Samaritans in the blessings of God. Thus, whereas the Jews always found a way to circumvent Samaria in their travels, the scriptures record that Jesus "had to go through Samaria" (4:4). Secondly, upon meeting up with the Samaritan woman at the local well, Jesus initiated the interaction by making himself vulnerable. He put himself in a position of needing her help by asking, "will you give me a drink?" (4:7). By this act, he condescended to the idea that he could benefit something from the help of a despised Samaritan. Then thirdly, and most critical to this discussion, Jesus avoided controversy. He remained focused on her most pressing need—the need for self-worth and restored dignity—the need to be loved by a pure love, not a love that was manipulative and degrading. To understand this more clearly, let us uncover the areas of potential conflict in the story, and see how Jesus could have made an issue of each one of them.

Man vs. Woman

The first area of potential conflict is that a strange man addressed a strange woman, and the woman responded in prolonged conversation. Similar to orthodox Islamic culture, it was improper for a woman to be seen conversing freely in public with a man other than her husband. This is why John records in verse 27 that the disciples were surprised to see Jesus talking like this to a woman. Jesus could have used this occasion to fault the woman for being so immodest. He could have condemned her for being seen in public at midday, when most women fetched their water in the early hours of the morning to avoid the company of men. Jesus could have praised his Jewish culture for having a higher standard of conduct in terms of mixed-gender interaction. But Jesus chose not to make this an issue of contention.

Jew vs. Samaritan

The next obvious potential area of conflict was the face-to-face meeting between a Jew and a Samaritan. Jesus could have easily reminded the woman of the inferiority of her people based on their historical past. The Samaritans were a mixed breed of the Children of Israel as a result of intermarriage with idolatrous foreigners, and therefore bore the stigma of a corrupted race. Jesus could have faulted her ancestors for failing to preserve the uniqueness of God's chosen people. But Jesus refrained from doing so.

The Children of Abraham vs. the Children of Jacob

The Jews of Jesus' day often identified themselves with Abraham (John 8:39), whereas the Samaritans identified with Jacob (4:12). Jesus could have argued that as the "Friend of God," Abraham was superior to Jacob. Furthermore, it was initially to Abraham that God made the promise of the seed of blessing of Genesis 22:18.

Mt. Zion vs. Mt. Gerizim

For the Jews, Mt. Zion was the mount of worship on which the Temple stood. However, the Samaritans revered a different mountain. It was Mt. Gerizim of Deuteronomy 11:29 from which the blessings of God were to be proclaimed. Jesus could have argued, on the basis of scriptural prophecy, that Mt. Zion played a far greater role in the scheme of God's salvation for the human race.

The Old Testament vs. the Pentateuch

This area of contention is not so obvious, but it is an important observation and critical to the understanding of Jesus' approach in the story. Jesus, as well as the Jews, accepted the entire Old Testament as we have it today, namely the Law of Moses, the Prophets, and the Psalms (Luke 24:44). The Samaritans, however, embraced only the Law of Moses. Jesus could have condemned the Samaritans for failing to accept the totality of God's revelations, but again, he avoided controversy.

Messiah the Savior vs. *Messiah the Prophet*

Here is another important observation which is likewise critical to the understanding of Jesus' approach. Because the Samaritans accepted only the Law of Moses, their understanding of the mission of the Messiah was limited. On the basis of the prophecy of Deuteronomy 18:18, the Samaritans expected the Messiah to be a prophet like Moses, through whom God would reveal His will. And because the Messiah, like Moses, would be a superior prophet, he would know all things and would teach all things. He would be the great Teacher.

What the Samaritans believed about the Messiah was true. The Messiah would indeed be a great prophet. But on the basis of the other prophecies of the Old Testament, he would be much more than a great prophet; he would be the savior who would redeem Israel and the whole world. He would be the promised blessing for all nations. On this point, Jesus could have reprimanded the Samaritan woman for having such a narrow understanding of the Messiah.

From what we now know, Jesus could have argued about many issues that differentiated the Jews from the Samaritans. But notice very carefully; Jesus did not focus on their differences. His objective was not to expose all the wrong things about the Samaritans and dwell on all the right things about the Jews. His objective was not to win an argument and defeat an opponent. His purpose was not to condemn; it was to serve. He was a servant and *"the Lord's servant must not quarrel; instead he must be kind to everyone, able to teach, not resentful"* (2 Timothy 2:24). Let us see now how Jesus uses what he knows to lead his audience to the gift of the good news.

In his interaction with the Samaritan woman, Jesus was careful to avoid controversy. But just as importantly, he was careful about revealing his full identity and mission. Notice that he began revealing himself at her level of understanding. In other words, as imperfect as it was, he began with her frame of reference. There was something in her frame of reference about the Messiah that was true. It was not the complete truth, but what she did know was true. And so Jesus started with that truth, even though it was limited. Remember, this Samaritan woman, like her peers, not only knew about the existence of the Messiah, but she knew that the Messiah would be a unique prophet. In fact, he would be so great that he would teach his people all things because he would know everything. Yes, this Messiah would know all things. Here was a gem of truth, and Jesus started with this gem of truth. He did so by revealing to this woman something about her life that no strange Jew could possibly know. The moment Jesus uncovered the secrets of her private life and her five husbands, she knew this was no ordinary Jew. She knew this was a prophet, and possibly the Messiah himself. She exclaimed, *"Come, see a man who told me everything I did"* (4:28). With this news, Jesus captured the attention and favor of her fellow Samaritans. In fact, *"they urged him to stay with them, and he stayed two days. And because of his words many more became believers"* (4:41). No doubt, during his stay, Jesus opened the eyes of his Samaritan hosts to a greater understanding of the Messiah's mission.

But now we come to a critical question. What exactly was it that Jesus wanted them to understand about his mission? In order to receive the gift of God's blessing, how were these people to view Jesus? The answer is in John 4:42: *We know that this man really is the savior of the world.* It is clear that what is most crucial for a person's understanding of Jesus and salvation to follow is that Jesus is the Savior of humankind. Notice, the verse did not read, "we know that this man really is the Son of God," or "this man is God," or "this man is the second person of the Trinity." And notice also that Jesus did not begin by immediately identifying himself as the savior. He did not begin by speaking of his sacrificial death for the redemption of humankind. Instead, he began by examining the woman's frame of reference; he began by identifying a trace of truth with which he could begin and progressively build upon with further enlightenment. He led the Samaritans from a general truth to a more profound truth. He led them from the Prophet to the Savior. In the following chapters, we will see how this approach applies to our concern for Christian ministry in a Muslim context.

Reflection

Reading this chapter you may have silently nodded as the example of Jesus and the woman at the well was explained step by step. Perhaps you began thinking of how you might apply the information to the Muslim person or family you have come to know.

Discussing one's faith with a non-believer takes spiritual maturity and practice. Opening this kind of dialogue is not really about you opening a discussion with a Muslim. It is about you opening a channel through which the Holy Spirit can travel. Drawing a non-believer to Christ is not a work of the flesh, but of the

Spirit.

Through reading this book you are preparing yourself to be a vessel of the Holy Spirit. The Muslim you are speaking to may not be receptive, even though your approach has been measured, Bible based, and scripturally sound. If you perceive that is the case, take counsel from 2 Timothy 2:1, 14 and *"be strong in the grace that is in Christ Jesus"* and do not *"strive about words to no profit, to the ruin of the hearers."*

Then pray and wait on the Lord. He will provide another opportunity. He covets the hearts of the Muslim people.

<u>17</u>

Keeping to the Core Theme of the Gospel
Preach the word.

2 Timothy 4:2

We know that the goal of evangelism is to proclaim the good news of the Gospel to people of all nationalities and religious backgrounds. And according to the angelic messages given to both Mary and Joseph (Luke 2:11 and Ma.1:21), the good news is that God sent the Savior to the world to save people from their sins. With that in mind, Jesus clearly revealed to his disciples the core message of the Gospel when he declared, *"Repentance and forgiveness of sins will be preached in his name to all nations, beginning at Jerusalem"* (Luke 24:47).

To see how this was carried out, we will examine the preaching of Peter, one of the first evangelists as recorded in the Book of Acts. We will note what he says and doesn't say in his proclamation of the Gospel.

224

The First Sermon, on the Day of Pentecost (Acts 2:17-36 and 38-39)

In explaining the outpouring of the Holy Spirit on the Day of Pentecost, Peter incorporates into his discourse the message about Jesus. Here are some of the issues he includes: the ministry of Jesus was confirmed by God through miracles (2:22); everything regarding Jesus took place according to God's plan (2:23); Jesus is the fulfillment of God's promise that a son (descendent) of David would rule forever on his throne (2:30); Jesus is the fulfillment of David's prophecy regarding the Messiah who would not be abandoned in the grave (2:31); the resurrected Jesus was exalted up to God where he received the promise of the Holy Spirit (2:33); Jesus was made Lord and Messiah (2:36); there is forgiveness of sins for those who repent in Jesus' name (2:38); and the Holy Spirit is available to all believers (2:39). We are told, "With many other words he warned them" (2:40); however, it is apparent that the words that are recorded in Acts are the words that gave substance to his sermon. Before we comment on what was not included in this revealed portion of Peter's discourse, let us examine Peter's second sermon.

The Second Sermon, at Solomon's Colonnade (Acts 3:12-26)

In this sermon, Peter attempts to explain the miraculous healing of the crippled beggar. In doing so, he again includes the good news about Jesus. These are some of the main points of his message: the God who glorified Jesus is the God of Abraham, Isaac, and Jacob (3:13); Jesus is God's servant (3:13); Jesus is the holy and righteous one (3:14); Jesus is the author of life (2:15); God raised Jesus from the dead (3:16); the miracle of healing took place in the name of Jesus (3:16); the Messiah suffered according to God's plan (3:18); repentance is a prerequisite to the removal of sin (3:19); God will send Christ back to earth to restore all things (3:21); and Jesus is the promised blessing of the lineage of Abraham that can turn people away from their sin (3:26). Later in his defense before the Sanhedrin, Peter went on to say that salvation is found in no other name but Jesus (4:12).

Peter's first two sermons are of particular interest because they both address a Jewish audience. Because orthodox Muslims bear a similar mindset to Jewish sensitivities regarding the oneness of God and polytheism, the context of Peter's messages is significant. With that in mind, we now want to focus on what Peter does not say. For example, nowhere does Peter refer to Jesus as the *Son of God*. Neither does he utter the statement, *Jesus is God*. He does not mention anything about a trinity. Nor does he use any terminology common to the discussion of atonement, such as "redeemed by the blood of the cross" or "Jesus died on the cross for our sins." He simply speaks of Jesus by beginning with a frame of reference with which the Jews are already familiar, such as the Old Testament patriarchs and related prophecies. Then he proceeds to speak about repentance and forgiveness of sins in Jesus' name. In his sermons, Peter does not try to solve the mystery of Jesus' nature, and he does not teach profound doctrine. He stays true to the simplicity of the Gospel by proclaiming salvation in Jesus. He preached exactly what Jesus instructed his followers to preach: "...repentance and forgiveness of sins will be preached in his name."

The Third Sermon, in the House of Cornelius (Acts 10:34-43)

In this message, Peter includes the following themes: *Jesus is Lord of all and through Jesus there is good news of peace* (10:36); Jesus is anointed with the Holy Spirit and the power of God to perform miracles and deliver people from the power of the devil (10:38); God raised Jesus from the dead (10:40); God appointed Jesus to be judge over the living and the dead (10:42); and there is forgiveness of sin for those who believe in Jesus' name (10:43). On this occasion, Peter's audience was a Gentile audience. But the sermon is similar to Peter's previous sermons.

We also notice again that Peter does not refer to Jesus as "Son of God," nor does he make the statement, "Jesus is God." He does not say anything about the triune nature of God. And he does not speak on the issues of doctrine, such as sanctification, atonement, and redemption. He simply extols the greatness of Jesus the Messiah-servant of God in terms of his divinely given authority and miracle-working power. And he concludes with the core message of salvation that, in Jesus' name, there is forgiveness of sins.

Of course, in other passages of the New

Testament, we do find Peter teaching about doctrinal issues such as atonement and redemption. But this teaching is in his epistles that are addressed to people who are already believers. For example, in 1 Peter 1:18, Peter discusses the issue of redemption through the blood of the lamb—the one without blemish or defect, referring to Christ, the "Lamb of God." Peter goes into greater depths regarding the nature and ministry of Christ. But we need to remember that he is directing this teaching to people who have already received the Holy Spirit to help them perceive the deeper spiritual truths of God's secret wisdom. In light of 1 Corinthians 2:6 and 10, Peter, in his epistles, is teaching a "message of wisdom among the mature, for God has revealed it... by His Spirit."

We certainly cannot expect Muslims to understand the secret wisdom of God without first receiving the Holy Spirit to enlighten them. Perhaps this is one consideration we have overlooked in our zeal to proclaim the Gospel to them. We are prone to preach doctrinal issues which deal with the mysteries and secret wisdom of God instead of remaining true to the simplicity of the Gospel. For the non-believer, we need only to exalt Jesus as the chosen one sent by God to be the Savior of the world in whose name there is forgiveness of sins. Indeed this is a simple message, and yet we so often make it a complicated one. This is especially true in the context of interacting with a Muslim whose mindset already bears a predisposition against such terms and phrases as "the blood of the cross," "Son of God," and "Trinity."

Now that we have established the core message of the Gospel, we need to consider how to incorporate that message into our interaction with Muslim people. We need to address issues that will lead us to our main objective—proclaiming the gift of salvation in Christ. In the discussion of Peter's second sermon of Acts 3:12-26, we noted that Peter used a frame of reference which was familiar to his Jewish listeners. He made reference to Old Testament prophecies, Old Testament Patriarchs, and Old Testament scriptures. We could easily do the same, except for one problem. We are dealing with a Muslim audience, not a Jewish one. The Bible, both Old Testament and New Testament, provides an expanse of material from which to select an appropriate frame of reference. But we run into a dilemma with people who reject the Bible and everything else related to Christianity. This is exactly the problem Christians face in working among Muslims.

For centuries, Christians have found it extremely difficult to evangelize Muslim people. It has been no easy task to break ground and soften the soil for the planting of Gospel seeds. The soil of potential harvest fields has become hardened over the years from prejudice, misunderstanding, and animosity that have led to fear and apathy on the part of Christians, and resentment and suspicion on the part of Muslims. Furthermore, to counter any missionary activity from the Christian West, Muslims have been traditionally preconditioned to believe that the Bible is corrupt, that Jesus was no more than an ordinary prophet, and that Jesus' message was limited to the Jews. Consequently, when a Christian reaches for his Bible and begins to proclaim the Gospel of Jesus to a Muslim, these preconditions immediately trigger a closed minded mentality that refuses to engage in any further dialogue related to spiritual issues of eternal significance. After repeated attempts and struggles of frustration, one is compelled to question if there is any other way to speak of spiritual truths without the initial use of biblical references. Perhaps there are other sources of religious teaching that a Christian can use without causing a Muslim to immediately become self-defensive. But the only religious book a Muslim will readily acknowledge is his own Qur'an. Is it even thinkable for a Christian to consider the use of the Qur'an to converse about the things of God? This question leads to other related questions, such as—is the Bible the only source of knowledge that reflects spiritual truths and universal principles? In a sincere desire to effectively relate the Gospel to people of different cultures and religious backgrounds, is the follower of Jesus restricted to the sole use of biblical materials—or is he free to look for other sources that might help to eventually lead his audience into biblical truths, once the ground has been broken?

Recognizing the Truths of God's Self-Revelation

It is imperative at this juncture to review the purpose of revealed scripture as it is found in the Holy Bible. The Bible is replete with spiritual truths and universal principles, but as a whole, it can be said that the Bible is unique in that it is the only book of scripture that specifically and clearly guides the human race to the gift of salvation. Truly, the Bible is a volume of scripture that accomplishes far more than simply revealing the truths of God's existence. But it is in regard to these truths of God's existence that we need to turn our attention.

The Bible itself bears witness that the truths of God's existence are not confined to the pages of biblical revelation, but are in fact revealed in all of nature. Romans 1:20 states, "For since the creation of the world God's invisible qualities—His eternal power and divine nature—have been clearly seen, being understood from what has been made." For this very reason, the Bible declares people without excuse for denying the existence of God. In reference to God and the nations of the world, Acts 14:17 tells us that God "has not left himself without testimony." It is apparent that God has revealed Himself in all of creation to all people, and that certain universal truths regarding His nature are therefore attainable, even for those who are without any biblical revelation. If God is the ultimate author of all truth, and if these universal truths as revealed in creation are accessible to all people of all cultures, then surely it is possible that the acknowledgement of such truths may have, from time to time, been recorded or expressed in some form of communication to ensure their preservation. With this in mind, it is reasonable to suggest there could be other sources that contain messages of truth, albeit they are not the message of complete truth regarding salvation, since the Bible is unique in that regard. And if such sources exist, then Christians should be able to avail themselves of these sources in an effort to lay a foundation for an evangelistic message with material that is acceptable and identifiable to the audience in question. Let us return to the Book of Acts to see if we can find any model of evangelism that can help us in this regard.

Paul's Message in a Greek Context

In Acts 17, we find Paul the Apostle in Athens interacting with educated Greeks who regarded his teaching rather strange. As a result, Paul made a concerted effort to find some commonality within their religio-cultural frame of reference in order to relate more meaningfully. He searched for something that was appealing to his audience, something which did not contradict biblical truth, and something which could serve as a mutually agreed upon starting point for further discussion. First, Paul referred to the altar of the "unknown God" and found this to be an opportunity to say whatever he wanted about the biblical "Lord of heaven and earth," knowing that nothing could be said to refute him since this God was unknown to his Greek listeners. But then, more significantly, Paul quoted a verse of the Greek poets: *For in him we live and move and have our being* (v.28). Paul discovered in the writings of these Greek poets a universal truth which he also believed about the supreme god. Thus, Paul was able to begin his discourse with a general truth taken from within the cultural framework of his audience which was neither alien nor threatening, and which kept their attention, for they countered, *"We want to hear you again on this subject"* (v.32). The fact that *"A few men became followers of Paul and believed"* (v.34) leads us to conclude that from this simple universal truth which was retrieved from pagan poetry, Paul was eventually able to lead his discussion into the biblical truths of salvation.

In view of Paul's approach with the Greeks of Athens, it will be helpful to make some important observations before considering such an approach for Muslim evangelism.

1) That Paul chose to quote the verse, *"For in him we live and move and have our being,"* indicates that he accepted this statement as a universal truth. Otherwise, Paul would not have used it.

2) The fact that this statement of truth was associated with idolatrous Greek poets did not render the statement any less true. Though this statement may have derived from a collection of poetry containing other statements reflecting an anti-biblical view of religious belief and practice, Paul did not hesitate to retrieve this nugget of truth and reset it into a biblical context. Remember that Paul perceived that all truths, no matter where they are found, and no matter how Satan may attempt to distort them, originate from God which therefore entitles God's people to make proper use of them.

3) Paul was not concerned about the moral character of the poets he quoted, or the possibility of

demonic influence in their lives, since he believed God to be the actual author of the truth in question.

4) Some of the Greeks could have accused Paul of trickery by quoting their poets and appearing to be one of them (the Greeks). But certainly, Paul was not trying to deceive anyone. Instead, he was attempting to find an effective approach to communicate and facilitate their understanding. In no way did Paul profess to be one of them in regard to their religious beliefs. He simply professed belief in a universal truth in an effort to lead to the truths of the Gospel.

5) In this approach, Paul took the risk of being accused by his fellow believers of giving the mistaken impression that by accepting any part of the teaching of the Greek poets, he embraced the whole of their teaching with regard to their religious views. Yet, Paul felt he was within scriptural bounds and demonstrated that he was just as much concerned about relevance as he was about correctness. Paul exhibited such a passion for souls that he was willing to use "all possible means" that he "might save some" (1 Cor.9:22).

6) It is particularly significant that Paul did not spend a great amount of words chastising his Greek listeners, or criticizing their poets. As a former strict Pharisee, Paul certainly knew of God's abhorrence of idolatrous worship. Yet, he recognized that it was not his mission to condemn. Rather, as an ambassador of Christ, engaged in servant-hood and priesthood, it was his mission to proclaim a message of love, forgiveness, and reconciliation through Christ, and to do everything

possible to ensure the faithful delivery and clear understanding of that message. That meant doing whatever necessary to keep the channels of communication open.

Returning to the matter of evangelizing Muslim people, many Christians have experienced the difficulty of making any inroads beyond a polite exchange of pleasantries and small talk about climate and cuisine. Unfortunately, some Christians approach Muslims with a planned strategy of razing Islam to the ground by attacking its scriptures and its prophet. No matter how sincere Christians may be, any statement perceived as slanderous against the religion of Islam, its holy book, or its prophet, does very little to produce an atmosphere conducive to follow-up and long-term relationships which are so vital for keeping the channels of communication open. In most cases, such an approach immediately closes the door to any serious introspection and raises the flag of self-defense. It reaffirms a Muslim's suspicion that any Christian discourse on the topic of love and compassion is merely a smoke screen to an underlying "Crusader" mindset bent on destroying Islam worldwide.

As you become increasingly involved with Muslims, you will get to know them as human beings with hearts and souls. You will form friendships and forge meaningful relationships. In the role of priesthood and servant-hood, you will eventually identify with Paul's passionate declaration to the Thessalonian believers when he said:

*We loved you so much that we were delighted to share
with you not only the gospel of God but our lives as
well, because you had become so dear to us.*
1 Thessalonians 2:8

Reflection

In your search for effective approaches, you will
undoubtedly come across Christian literature for Muslim
evangelism that focuses on the discrepancies of the
Qur'an and the life of Muhammad as a way to refute
Islam. However, if you desire to cultivate friendships
with the Muslim people of your area you will find this
approach to be unsuitable. For most Muslim people,
religious sentiments are very strong and deeply sensitive.
As messengers of the love of God, you will be careful not
to wound those sentiments. Instead, it will become your
desire to offer something far more meaningful that will
raise the consciousness of your Muslim contacts above
the level of religious sentiment. Thus you will want to
take a different direction, and Paul's model in Acts 17
provides you an alternative approach. In the next
chapter, we will learn to apply such an approach for
evangelizing Muslims.

As you study these ways to be sensitive to the
Muslims you speak to, you may wonder why so much
attention is being given to *how* you present the gospel to
Muslims. Is it really necessary to take such care? One of
the most basic principles of the Bible answers that
question: Do unto others as you would have others do

unto you.

If someone you met was going to tell you something that ultimately would fly in the face of everything you had ever believed, call into question your God and your faith, and have consequences that would alter your life forever, how would you want to be told? The great care to present the gospel in the least offensive way possible to Muslims is not because of who they are. It is because of who we are. We are ambassadors of Christ and vessels of His love. We are told in 1 Peter to do all things with gentleness and respect. We are to model Christ to them.

Will they see Him in you? Will they want what you have?

18

What Topics Can I Discuss that Will Build Bridges?

Then Paul stood in the midst of the Areopagus and said, "Men of Athens, I perceive that in all things you are very religious;"
Acts 17:22

On the basis of Paul's ministry in Acts 17, let's make a sincere effort to search for areas of commonality as opposed to differences. As we enter this venture, it will be helpful to open our minds to certain possibilities that would lend support to this approach. For example, it is possible that in some measure, and in some point in time, God revealed Himself to Arabs, directly or indirectly, and even to Muhammad, just as He seemingly did to the Greek poets of Acts 17. It is also possible that though the Qur'an differ from the Bible on some major issues, it may still contain scattered statements of truth or even shades of truth. And if Christian scholars are

238

accurate in their assessment that much of Qur'anic material can be traced to Jewish and Christian origins, then there is a greater likelihood for uncovering similarities in religious lore, motif, and culture. This possibility becomes even more tenable in light of the fact that Muhammad's ancestry stems from Semitic roots.

Thus, instead of searching for discrepancies in the Qur'an, or for moral failures in the life of Muhammad, let us begin to investigate the material of the Qur'an for any traces of truth. We especially want to focus on any passages which could help encourage a Muslim's faith in the God of Abraham, and arouse his spiritual hunger for the God of love. Furthermore, we want to identify any Qur'anic material which could serve as a valid starting point for a discussion leading into the truths of the Gospel message of the Bible. It is imperative to repeat at this juncture that we do not believe the Qur'an to be a book of spiritual salvation. That is precisely the reason we are engaged in a study like this. It is to help us proclaim the gospel of true salvation to the Muslim people who are eternally lost without Christ. We do, however, hold to the biblical position that God has revealed His existence and His nature in some measure to all of humankind. And on that basis, we believe that the Qur'an could very well contain such truths, which could be fully illuminated in the light of biblical teaching. In dealing with these truths, our major concern will not be the moral character of any prophet, or the possibility of any demonic influence. Our major concern will be to retrieve whatever truths or traces of truth can be found in the Qur'an, and address them in the context of biblical revelation. Because it is our conviction that all truth originates with God, we can feel justified in pursuing this approach.

As we carefully study the Qur'an for any possibilities, we make some interesting discoveries. We find there are some important general truths within its pages. First, the Qur'an is unequivocally clear in declaring that there is only one God, and that none beside Him is to be worshiped.

> *God! There is no god but He—the Living, the Self-Subsisting, Eternal.* (3:2)

> *And He is God: there is no god but He. To Him be praise, at the first and at the last.* (28:70)

> *God is He, than Whom there is no other god—Who knows (all things) both secret and open; He, Most Gracious, Most Merciful.* (59:22)

With this belief in one God are similar beliefs in angels, prophets, prophetic revelations, resurrection, Day of Judgment, and heaven and hell. In addition, according to the Qur'an, because God is merciful and compassionate, He has revealed through the Qur'an for humankind general guidelines that cover a broad range of human behavior and relationships.

Not only is the Qur'an replete with ethical teaching, but such teaching is strikingly parallel to biblical material. There are many Qur'anic passages that provide moral guidance that we as Christians can agree with. Such as, do good, believe in God and the Last Day, the angels, holy books and prophets. This can be seen in the following selections:

> *God commands justice, the doing of good, and liberality to kith and kin, and He forbids all shameful deeds, and injustice and rebellion: He instructs you, that ye may receive admonition.* (16:90)

> *It is not righteousness that ye turn your faces towards East or West; but it is righteousness to believe in God and the Last Day, and the Angels, and the Book, and the Messengers; to spend of your substance, out of love for Him, for your kin, for orphans, for the needy, for the wayfarer, for those who ask, and for the ransom of slaves; to be steadfast in prayer, and practice regular charity; to fulfill the contracts which ye have made; and to be firm and patient, in pain (or suffering) and adversity, and throughout all periods of panic. Such are the people of truth, the God-fearing.* (2:177)

> *O ye who believe! Do your duty to God, seek the means of approach unto Him, and strive with might and main in His cause, that ye may prosper.* (5:35)

The Qur'an also speaks of one's duty to one's parents. The fifth commandment of the Ten Commandments tells us to honor our father and mother.

241

The following selection is how the Qur'an instructs Muslims on that subject:

> *Thy Lord hath decreed that ye worship none but Him, and that ye be kind to parents. Whether one or both of them attain old age in thy life, say not to them a word of contempt, nor repel them, but address them in terms of honour. And out of kindness, lower to them the wing of humility, and say, "My Lord! bestow on them thy mercy even as they cherished me in childhood."* (17:23-24)

There are clear instructions regarding women and wives:

> *And among His signs is this, that He created for you mates from among yourselves, that ye may dwell in tranquility with them; and He has put love and mercy between your (hearts). Verily in that are signs for those who reflect.* (30:21)

> *Men are the protectors and maintainers of women, because God has given the one more (strength) than the other, and because they support them from their means. Therefore the righteous women are devoutly obedient, and guard in (the husband's) absence what God would have them guard.* (4:34)

As well as clear instructions regarding adultery:

The woman and the man guilty of adultery or fornication—flog each of them with a hundred stripes. Let not compassion move you in their case, in a matter prescribed by God, if ye believe in God and the Last Day. And let a party of the believers witness their punishment. (24:2)

The Qur'an also speaks of one's duty to children, neighbors, strangers, and the poor. And the consequences of those who disregard that duty.

Serve God, and join not any partners with Him. And do good to parents, kinsfolk, orphans, those in need, neighbours who are near, neighbours who are strangers, the companion by your side, the wayfarer (ye meet), and what your right hands possess. (4:36)

Those who (in charity) spend of their goods by night and by day, in secret and in public, have their reward with their Lord. (2:274)

Nay, nay! But ye honour not the orphans! Nor do ye encourage one another to feed the poor! And ye devour inheritance, all with greed, and ye love wealth with inordinate love! Nay! When the earth is pounded to powder, and thy Lord cometh, and His angels, rank upon rank, and Hell, that Day, is brought (face to face), on that Day will man remember; but how will that remembrance profit him? He will say, "Ah!

Would that I had sent forth (good deeds) for (this) my (future) life!" For that Day His chastisement will be such as none (else) can inflict. (89:17-25)

The Qur'an also has much to say about honesty and justice as well as identifying, what are considered abominations, such as drinking, gambling, and divination. And the consequences of sin are clear:

Leave alone those who take their religion to be mere play and amusement, and are deceived by the life of this world. But proclaim (to them) this (truth): that every soul delivers itself to ruin by its own acts. It will find for itself no protector or intercessor except God. If it offered every ransom, (or reparation), none will be accepted. Such is (the end of) those who deliver themselves to ruin by their own acts. They will have for drink (only) boiling water, and for punishment, one most grievous. For they persisted in rejecting God. (6:70)

And fear the Day when ye shall be brought back to God. Then shall every soul be paid what it earned, and none shall be dealt with unjustly. (2:281)

Surely, these and many other similar verses of the Qur'an reflect common moral standards which can help to create an atmosphere of mutual respect and appreciation between a Muslim and a Christian.

It is important to remember that sincere and god-fearing Muslims are sensitive about the appearances of cleanliness, godliness, and modesty. The influences of secularism and permissiveness which threaten to erode family values and faith in God cause them great apprehension. When it comes to issues like sexual immorality, violent crime, drug addiction, alcoholism, poverty, homelessness and corruption, devout Christians and devout Muslims share many of the same concerns. By identifying with Muslims on these critical issues, you will find opportunities to establish respectful relationships that can blossom into long-lasting friendships. And it is through these friendships that we often find the opportunity to introduce Muslims to the greatest Friend of all.

Aside from ethical teaching, the Qur'an also addresses the religion of the heart with verses that speak more to the issue of spiritual experience and nearness to God. This was the type of material that gave to Islam its prevailing influence of mysticism. The following represents some verses that have spiritual themes:

In their hearts is a disease. (2:10) (Muslims know that the disease spoken of here is sin.)

God loves those who put their trust (in Him). (3:159)

Then those who believe in God, and hold fast to Him—soon will He admit them to mercy and grace from

Himself, and guide them to Himself by a straight way.
(4:174)

O ye who believe! Do your duty to God; seek the means of approach unto Him. (5:35)

O my Lord! ...grant me from Thy presence an authority to aid (me). (17:80)

He [God] has written faith in their hearts and strengthened them with a spirit from Himself. (58:22)

But bow down in adoration and bring thyself closer (to God)! (96:19)

In just these verses alone, there is a wealth of material that can be used to initiate some serious discussion dealing with the spiritual dimension of life; the potential for intimacy with God; and the critical issue of divine mercy without which none can enter the holy presence of God. These Qur'anic passages can be easily enforced with biblical references to emphasize and even arouse a spiritual yearning for more of God.

Of course, we are curious to know if the Qur'an has anything to say about Jesus. Surprisingly, to both Muslims and Christians, the Qur'an has a lot to say about Jesus. But we will hold that discussion for the next chapter.

Reflection

This chapter presents a treasure chest of new information that can be used to build bridges with Muslims. Though you may not have read the Qur'an before and the Qur'anic verses may seem awkwardly worded, and you may not immediately see specific scriptural parallels, don't be overwhelmed.

Like any carpenter who is going to build a bridge, you need good tools. Consider buying your own copy of the Qur'an to use as a reference. If it's not in your budget, there is a digital library provided by the University of Michigan that offers an English translation of the Qur'an at http://quod.lib.umich.edu/k/koran. It also provides the ability to search with various criteria. And there is another translation that can be accessed by typing "Qur'an by Yusuf Ali" in your web browser.

Perhaps you have concerns about reading the religious book of another faith. But how can you prepare for an honest and thoughtful discussion of a subject if you have no idea of the other person's position? Remember Paul's example of relating to Greek poetry. He found something within their cultural context through which God had already revealed Himself in some measure. Pray for the Holy Spirit's guidance when you read Qur'anic passages and ask Him to give you wisdom as you prepare to build bridges of understanding. There is nothing new about such an approach. Paul said in 2 Timothy 2:23-25:

> *Don't have anything to do with foolish and stupid arguments, because you know they produce quarrels.*

And the Lord's servant must not quarrel; instead, he must be kind to every one, able to teach, not resentful. Those who oppose him he must gently instruct, in the hope that God will grant them repentance leading them to a knowledge of the truth . . .

The more prepared and yielded you are, the stronger the bridge you stand on.

19

From Jesus the Prophet to Jesus the Savior

Here is a trustworthy saying that deserves full acceptance:
Christ Jesus came into the world to save sinners . . .

1 Timothy 1:15

In our search throughout the Qur'an for common ground, we are particularly interested to know whether or not there are any truths or traces of truth with regard to Jesus. We will discover that the Qur'an has much to say about him and provides for us a surprising amount of material to use as an effective frame of reference with Muslim people.

Most Muslims are already familiar with Jesus; however, what they know is limited or inaccurate. For example, Muslims believe that Jesus

1. is not a universal prophet
2. is presently in the second level of heaven (Muslims believe there are seven levels of heaven with Adam in the first level, Jesus and John the Baptist in the second level, Joseph in the third, Enoch in the fourth, Aaron in the fifth, Moses in the sixth, and Abraham in the seventh),
3. will return to the world.

In regard to his return to the earth, Muslims believe Jesus will

4. descend upon a mosque in Damascus,
5. lead Muslims in their prayers,
6. rule the world justly according to the Qur'an,
7. destroy all the crosses,
8. kill all the pigs,
9. kill the false Christ known as *Ad-Dajjal Al-Masih,*
10. marry and have children,
11. live for forty-five years,
12. die from a natural death,
13. be buried next to Muhammad,
14. and rise with everyone else on the Day of Resurrection.

This is a lot of information, but not one bit of it is from the Qur'an. It all comes from Islamic tradition. As we will see, the Qur'an gives an entirely different picture of Jesus. For example, part of 4:171 reads as follows:

> *. . . Christ Jesus the son of Mary was (no more than) a Messenger of God, and His Word, which He bestowed on Mary, and a Spirit proceeding from Him.*

From this description, Jesus is the Messiah, the Word of God, and a Spirit from God. Thus Muslims know Jesus by the following titles: *Isa Al-Masih* (Jesus, the Messiah); *Isa Kalimatullah* (Jesus, Word of God); and *Isa Ruhullah* (Jesus, Spirit of God). Each one of these titles is a nugget of truth. Jesus is indeed the Messiah, *the Anointed One*. He is indeed the *Word of God* on the basis of John 1:1-18. In fact, he is called by this title in Revelation 19:13, *"...and his name is the Word of God."* As for the title *Ruhullah*, though we do not speak about Jesus as a spirit, 1 Corinthians 15:45 refers to Jesus as "the last Adam, a life-giving spirit." Indeed, Christ Jesus does breathe into the lives of his followers eternal life. Though many Muslims will argue that Jesus was no different than other prophets, just this verse alone points to the uniqueness of Christ. But the Qur'an has more to say about this one whom the Bible also identifies as the son of Mary (Mark 6:3). What follows is a list of Qur'anic references that contain significant ideas and phrases as indicated by the bold print. You will notice the use of "We." In these verses it is the "plural of majesty" for God. Common to both the Arabic and Hebrew languages. When an authoritative figure speaks to his subjects, he uses the first person plural.

251

1. *We gave Moses the Book and followed him up with a succession of apostles. We gave Jesus the son of Mary clear (Signs) and* **strengthened him with the holy spirit.** *(2:87)* [Note: Mary is the only woman mentioned by name in the Qur'an]

2. *Behold! the angels said, "O Mary! God giveth thee glad tidings of a* **Word from Him.** *His name will be* **Christ** *Jesus, the son of Mary,* **held in honour in this world and the Hereafter** *and of (the company of)* **those nearest to God.** *(3:45)*

3. *Behold! God said, "O Jesus!* **I will take thee** *[cause you to die] and raise thee to Myself and clear thee (of the falsehoods) of those who blaspheme. I will make those who follow thee superior to those who reject faith, to the Day of Resurrection. Then shall ye all return unto me, and I will judge between you of the matters wherein ye dispute." (3:55)*

4. **The similitude of Jesus before God is as that of Adam; He created him from dust, then said to him, "Be," and he was.** *The Truth (comes) from God alone, so be not of those who doubt. (3:59-60)*

5. *That they said (in boast), "We killed Christ Jesus the son of Mary, the apostle of God"--- but they killed him not, nor crucified him; but so it was made to appear to them. And those who differ therein are full of doubts, with no (certain) knowledge, but only conjecture to*

follow. For of a surety, they killed him not. Nay, **God raised him up unto Himself; and God is Exalted in Power, Wise.** (4:157-158)

6. *And in their footsteps We sent Jesus the son of Mary, confirming the Law that had come before him. We sent him* **the Gospel; therein was guidance and light,** *and* **confirmation of the Law** *that had come before him—* **a guidance and an admonition to those who fear God.** (5:46)

7. *Then will God say, "O Jesus the son of Mary! Recount My favour to thee and to thy mother. Behold!* **I strengthened thee with the holy spirit,** *so that thou didst speak to the people in childhood and in maturity. Behold! I taught thee* **the Book and Wisdom, the Law and the Gospel,** *and behold! Thou* **makest** *out of* **clay,** *as it were, the figure of a bird, by My leave, and* **thou breathest into it and it becometh a bird** *by My leave; and thou healest those born blind, and the lepers, by My leave. And behold! Thou* **bringest forth the dead** *by My leave. And behold! I did restrain the Children of Israel from (violence to) thee when thou didst show them the clear Signs, and the unbelievers among them said, 'This is nothing but evident magic.'"* (5:110)

8. *She[Mary] said, "How shall I have a son, seeing that no man has touched me, and I am not unchaste?" He said, "So (it will be). Thy Lord saith, 'that is easy for*

*Me; and (We wish) to appoint him as a **Sign unto men**
and a **Mercy from Us.**' It is a matter (so) **decreed.**"*
(19:20-21)

9. *But she pointed to the babe. They said, "How can we
talk to one who is a child in the cradle?" He said, "**I am
indeed a servant of God.** He hath given me revelation
and made me a prophet. And **He hath made me
blessed wheresoever I be**, and hath enjoined on me
prayer and charity as long as I live. (He) hath made me
kind to my mother, and not overbearing or miserable.
So peace is on me the day I was born, **the day that I
die**, and the day that I shall be raised up to life
(again)!"*
Such (was) Jesus the son of Mary; **(it is) a
statement of truth,** about which they (vainly)
dispute. (19:29-31)

10. *And **We made the son of Mary and his mother
as a Sign.** We gave them both shelter on high ground,
affording rest and security and furnished with springs.*
(23:50)

11. *And (Jesus) shall be a **Sign (for the coming of)
the Hour** (of Judgment). Therefore have no doubt about
the (Hour), but follow ye Me; this is a straight way.*
(43:61)

It is remarkable that the Qur'an has this much to

say about Jesus. Most of the information is extremely significant and true. But now we need to determine how to use this material in order to say what the Qur'an unfortunately omits—that Jesus is the Savior of the world in whose name there is forgiveness of sins.

Identifying From the Qur'an a Common Frame of Reference For a Muslim Context

Rather than searching the Qur'an for extracting contradictions and devising arguments, we have attempted to look carefully for bits and pieces of truth, believing that God has left a witness of Himself and His purpose in all cultures. In that search, we have found traces of truth, albeit not the whole truth. But instead of faulting this limitation, let us see how we can apply the model of Jesus' approach with the Samaritan woman. We have looked at many Qur'anic verses that are about Jesus or in some way relate to Jesus which are of special interest. We see that they provide for us a frame of reference that is acceptable to the Muslim because it is composed of Qur'anic material. But now it is necessary to determine if we Christians can use this frame of reference. We do so by supporting each of the significant points with biblical references.

1. Jesus is strengthened with the Spirit from God (2:87)

Acts 10:38 ...God anointed Jesus of

Nazareth with the Holy Spirit and power

Isaiah 42:1 Here is My servant...., I will put My Spirit on him

2. Jesus is honored in heaven (3:45)

Acts 2:32-33, 36   God has raised this Jesus to life.... Exalted to the right hand of God

Acts 3:13 ...the God of our fathers has glorified His servant Jesus

3. Jesus has power to perform healing miracles (3:49)

Acts 2:22 Jesus of Nazareth was a man accredited by God to you by miracles, wonders and signs

Acts 3:16 It is Jesus' name...that has given this complete healing

4. Jesus is attributed creative power (3:49)

Acts 3:15 You killed the author of life, but God raised him from the dead

1 Corinthians 1:45 ...the last Adam, a life-giving spirit

5. Jesus is similar to Adam (3:58)

1 Corinthians 15:45 ...the last Adam, a life-giving spirit.

Romans 5:14 ...as did Adam who was a pattern of the one to come.

6. Jesus was raised up to God Himself (4:158)

Acts 2:33   Exalted to the right hand of God

Philippians 2:9   Therefore God exalted him to the highest place

7. Jesus is a sign to humankind (19:21)

Acts 2:39   The promise is for you and your children and for all who are far off

John 8:12   I am the Light of the world.

8. Jesus is a mercy from God (19:21)

Acts 10:43   ...everyone who believes in him [Jesus] receives forgiveness of sins in his name

Jude 1:21   Keep yourselves in God's love as you wait for the mercy of our Lord Jesus Christ to bring you to eternal life.

9. Jesus is born of a virgin (19:20-21)

Luke 1:26-27   ...God sent the angel Gabriel...to a virgin.... The virgin's name was Mary

Luke 1:34   "How shall this be," Mary asked the angel, "since I am a virgin?"

10. Jesus is a holy son (19:19)

Acts 3:14   You disowned the Holy and Righteous One

Hebrews 4:15   ...we have one who has

been tempted in every way,…yet was without sin.

11. Jesus is a servant of God (19:30)

Acts 3:13 …,the God of our fathers has glorified His servant Jesus

Acts 4:30 Stretch out your Hand to…perform miraculous signs…through the name of your holy servant Jesus.

12. Jesus is blessed wherever he is (19:31)

Acts 3:25 He [God] said to Abraham, "Through your offspring [Jesus] all peoples on earth will be blessed."

Acts 3:25 He [God] sent him [Jesus] first to you to bless you

13. Jesus is a sign of the Hour (43:61)

Acts 10:42 …he [Jesus] is the one whom God appointed as judge of the living and the dead.

Matthew 24:30 At that time the sign of the Son of Man will appear in the sky,… They will see the Son of Man coming on the clouds of the sky with power and great glory.

14. Jesus' lineage of Abraham, Isaac, and Jacob was chosen for a special purpose (38:45-46)

Acts 3:13 the God of Abraham, Isaac, and Jacob…has glorified his servant Jesus.

Acts 3: 25 And you are heirs of

the…covenant God made with your fathers. He said to Abraham, "Through your offspring all peoples on earth will be blessed."

Notice how we were able to verify many of the Qur'anic statements related to Jesus with material from Peter's sermons in the Book of Acts. This should help us to see how useful Peter's sermons can be in our desire to interact with a Muslim audience. Now that we have substantiated this Qur'anic material with biblical support, we have at our disposal an abundance of material to incorporate into our discussion of Jesus. We have retrieved this material from an acceptable frame of reference for the Muslim. Rather than beginning with the typical "Son of God who died on the cross" approach, we are able to come down to the level of the Muslim's context, arouse his interest in Jesus, and hopefully inspire him to respond with the words, *We want to hear you again on this subject* (Acts 17:32).

Getting From *Jesus the Prophet* to *Jesus the Savior* of the World

Let us examine a couple of examples to see how we can apply the above approach in a practical manner. One of the Qur'anic references that is especially helpful is 19:21 in which Gabriel informs Mary that she will have a son:

He said, "so (it will be). Thy Lord saith, 'That is easy for Me; and (We wish) to appoint him [Jesus] as a sign unto men and a mercy from Us.' It is a matter (so) decreed."

First of all, this verse helps us to refute the idea that Jesus is merely a national prophet, not a universal prophet. In other words, many Muslims insist Jesus was a prophet only to the Jews. But this verse confirms that he is a blessing from God for all humankind. Secondly, the phrase, "a mercy from Us [plural of majesty for God]," is especially significant for our desire to get to the core message of the Gospel. It is clear from this verse that Jesus' mission is connected to God's mercy. But now we need to see how this can help us to get to the Gospel of forgiveness of sins in Jesus' name. In the Qur'an, God's mercy is often linked to God's forgiveness of sins. For example, in the Qur'anic narrative of Adam and Eve, we find these amazing words of repentance:

Our Lord! We have wronged our own souls. If Thou forgive us not and bestow not upon us Thy Mercy, we shall certainly be lost. (7:23)

This passage is significant for several reasons. First of all, throughout the Qur'an, these are the only words that come from the mouth of Adam and Eve which means they are the first words spoken by humankind. Secondly, the passage reveals to us man's greatest problem (his lost-ness in sin); man's greatest need (God's forgiveness); and man's greatest hope (God's mercy). Thirdly, and pertinent to our discussion, God's forgiveness is available through His mercy.

Even more compelling is the fact that in several Qur'anic references, God's attributes of mercy and forgiveness are interlinked, such as in 2:218: "They have the hope of the mercy of God; And God is Oft-forgiving, Most Merciful." Other references that link these two attributes are 4:25, 5:74, 15:49, 16:119, and 39:53. From this observation, we want to draw the conclusion that the mercy from God spoken of in 19:21 not only relates to the forgiveness of sins, but links the forgiveness of sins to Jesus, the Sign of God's mercy for all humankind.

Another very useful reference from the Qur'an is the passage that speaks about the miracle power of Jesus. In 3:49, Jesus says the following:

> *I have come to you, with a Sign from your Lord, in that I make for you out of clay, as it were, the figure of a bird, and breathe into it, and it becomes a bird by God's leave: And I heal those born blind, and the lepers, and I quicken the dead, by God's leave; and I declare to you what ye eat, and what ye store in your houses. Surely therein is a Sign for you if ye did believe;*

First of all, notice the description of Jesus and the creation of the bird. Some scholars believe this story came from an early Christian legend. Our interest is not in the origin of the story, but in the fact that the Qur'an attributes to Jesus creative power. Yet there is something even more significant in this description. Notice the three important elements of this creation; 1) clay; 2) the molding of the clay; and 3) the life-giving breath. These are the very three elements the Qur'an uses to describe the creative act of Almighty God!

> *Thy Lord said to the angels: "I am about to create man, from sounding **clay**, from mud **molded** into shape. When I have fashioned him and **breathed** into him of My spirit, fall ye down in obeisance to him.* (15:28-29)

Secondly, and more importantly, we find in this passage that Jesus has the power to minister to the immediate needs of people. This is a very crucial observation because the Qur'an attributes this kind of ministry, such as healing, to no other prophet.

So often in our approach to Muslim people, we preach a message that simply does not relate. Over and over again, we try to interest our Muslim audience with the message of eternal life: "if you believe that Jesus died on the cross for your sins, you can have eternal life in heaven!" That becomes the standard message of the good news. But for most Muslim people, the message of eternal life does not scratch where it itches! If a mosquito bites you on the left arm, and the bite begins to itch, it does no good to scratch the right arm. Most Muslim people are preoccupied with physical and pressing needs, or with the *jinn* of the spirit world. For example, a mother holding her baby dying of malaria, or a father trying to find a cure for his demon-possessed son, is in need of a source of power to bring deliverance. For either one of them, our message about eternal life does not scratch where it itches. They are in desperate search of a solution for the emergency at hand. But knowing that the Qur'an speaks of Jesus' healing power, we now have a helpful frame of reference. Instead of John 3:16 that speaks about eternal life, we begin at the Muslim's level of understanding by sharing a more relevant portion of scripture such as Acts 10:37-38 of Peter's sermon at Cornelius' house:

> *You know what has happened throughout Judea, beginning in Galilee after the baptism that John preached—how God anointed Jesus of Nazareth with the Holy Spirit and power, and how he went around doing good and healing all who were under the power of the devil because God was with him.*

On the basis of the Qur'anic frame of reference which we have already established, we remind our Muslim friends that Jesus is still alive, because God raised him up to Himself (4:158). Furthermore, Jesus still has the power to perform extraordinary miracles because God honored him in heaven as he did on earth (3:45), which tells us that God never withdrew this power and authority from Jesus. With this in mind, it is important to pray with our Muslim friends who may be in need of healing, and to encourage them to believe for a miracle in

Jesus' name. In many cases, this kind of miracle can lead a Muslim from *Jesus the healer* to *Jesus the savior*.

Remember the story of the lame man of Luke 5 who was lowered through the roof. His immediate need was for healing. Even though Jesus knew that the spiritual need is always greater, he nevertheless began at the level of the man's expectation. But notice what Jesus said when he performed the healing:

> *But that you may know that the son of Man has authority on earth to forgive sins..., I tell you, get up, take your mat and go home.*
>
> Luke 5:24

In the accounts of the Gospel, Jesus often first ministered to the physical need in order to increase an individual's faith for spiritual deliverance. The same is true with Muslim people today. Those active in evangelizing Muslims know that Jesus often begins with a physical healing so that once a person recognizes the power of Christ to heal the sickness of the body, he is inspired to believe in Jesus' power to heal the *disease of the heart* (Qur'an 2:10). Forgiveness of sins is the greatest healing Muslims could ever receive, and the material we have just reviewed in the Qur'an helps us to lead them to that blessing.

Reflection

It is the anointing and activity of the Holy Spirit that changes the heart of man. As you have read this book you have learned many practical things to prepare you to further God's Kingdom. All of them use Christ and His disciples as models. As you reflect on the examples given, you will realize that you are being called to surrender to the power of the Holy Spirit and the purposes and plans of God, who desires that none die lost. You are agreeing to become His vessel.

If you have never personally had that experience, consider spending some time in prayer telling God you offer yourself as a living sacrifice to Him and His purposes in this matter. That you surrender your own will to His will. And that if He is calling you to be His witness, you will answer without reservation, "Yes, Lord."

20

Leading a Muslim to the Lordship of Christ

*Therefore go and make disciples of all nations,
baptizing them in the name of the Father and of the Son and of
the Holy Spirit, and teaching them to obey everything I have
commanded you.*

Matthew 28:19-20

One of the most exciting aspects of ministry is to sense the Holy Spirit working in the heart of an unbeliever whereby he or she becomes deeply moved by the message of the Gospel as well as by the message of your life. Though questions and uncertainties persist, you know the individual is seriously thinking about all the issues you have shared with him when he continues to be drawn to you for more teaching and more prayer. It is extremely important during this time to be sure that the Muslim inquirer is hungering for greater contact with God and not with an established American citizen who could possibly be a source of material benefit for himself

266

or his children. It is easy especially for immigrants from marginalized societies to become mesmerized by all the glitter and glamour of Western society and to think that becoming a Christian in America is a sure guarantee for employment, loans, and sponsorships. Of course we want to help these people as much as we can with their daily problems. However, we don't want them to think in terms of becoming a follower of Jesus for purely material gains. It is at this point that spiritual discernment is critical.

If, after prayerful consideration, you discern that a Muslim inquirer is truly absorbing the spiritual truths of the Gospel message, then it is important to make him clearly aware that he has some life-changing decisions to make. He has to decide whether to accept the gift or reject the gift. He has to choose whether or not to really believe in the message that Jesus is the Savior of the world and that in his name there is forgiveness of sin and assurance of salvation. Then he has to decide for himself whether or not to embrace Jesus as his own personal Savior and Lord. That means total allegiance to Christ. It also means a lifelong commitment to live a spiritually transformed life according to the teachings of Christ as outlined in the Injil (the Gospel; the New Testament). It must be made clear that there is no guarantee of a life free of hardship and suffering. In fact Jesus clearly warned his disciples that they would face persecution and trouble. However there is the guarantee that Jesus will enable his followers to persevere in this life and rejoice forever in the life to follow. If you sense that the

Muslim inquirer is ready to embrace Christ with this understanding, then on the basis of Acts 2:38, you need to share with him the meaning and importance of repentance and baptism.

The Need for the Muslim Background Believer to Repent

Muslims are familiar with the idea of repentance from the use of the Islamic term *tawba*, which generally means turning away from sin. However, the Muslim must understand that for this repentance to be genuine and acceptable to God, he must feel more than social guilt; he must sense inner guilt from the realization that his sinful deeds are against God Himself. This can only happen when he embraces the truth that God's predominant attribute is love, not power. If the Muslim is truly convicted of his sin and realizes that his sins are acts of disobedience against the very One who created him, loves him, and cares for him, then the Holy Spirit will bring forth from within his heart a feeling of deep remorse. As a result, he should truly feel sorry for his sins, and that sorrow will lead to tears of repentance bearing witness to his sincerity. The scriptures speak of this godly sorrow in 2 Cor.7:10:

> *Godly sorrow brings repentance that leads to salvation and leaves no regret.*

The Muslim must also demonstrate a determination in his heart to rid his life of any sinful

268

habits or practices. Of course he will not be able to accomplish this in his own human strength. However, he will need to be encouraged that as he yields his life to Christ, Christ will help him.

If you sense by the leading of the Holy Spirit that a Muslim is ready to commit his life to Christ, then you can help him to initiate this commitment by leading him in a prayer of repentance, such as the following:

O God, the Merciful One, the Compassionate One. All praise be unto You, Lord of heaven and earth. I prostrate my heart to You, for You alone are the Almighty and Holy One. I come to You in the name of Isa Al-Masih. Because I have now become a follower of Al-Masih, I claim the promise of the Injil that declares, *"everyone who believes in him* [Al-Masih Isa] *receives forgiveness of sins through his name"* [Acts 10:43].

O God Most High, I humbly come to You to confess that I am a sinner who has committed many sins. I realize now that not only have I sinned against people, but much worse, I have sinned against You, the Holy One, the Loving One. O God, You are the One who is so kind, patient, and lovingly concerned about my life, and yet it is You whom I have grieved the most by all my terrible deeds. I am sorry for this. In my sin, I have dishonored You. I have violated Your holiness. Please forgive me; please be merciful to me, for without your mercy, I am eternally lost.

Please cleanse my heart from sin; wash away all guilt and condemnation in the name of Isa Al-Masih, so that I may be free to worship You in true adoration and devotion.

O Mighty God, thank You for hearing my prayer and granting me the joy and assurance of forgiveness and salvation. Thank You for sending Isa Al-Masih into the world to personally reveal Your mercy and compassion for all people, including a sinner like me. Help me from now on to have the spiritual power to overcome the urge to sin. Strengthen me by Your Spirit. Protect me from the whispers and attacks of *Shaitan*. And enable me to submit to Your will at all times, as it is revealed in Your Word. For he who is *Kalimatullah* (Word of God) is now the Lord and Savior of my life. O Sovereign Lord, may You, the Living God, and Isa, the Living Word, be exalted in my life forever and ever!

Amin

The Need for the Muslim Background Believer to Take Water Baptism

According to the record of evangelism by the early apostles, such as Acts 10:34-48, the next major issue that we must deal with is the ritual of water baptism. When ministering in an Islamic context, it is helpful to know that for many Muslim people, conversion to the Lord

Jesus Christ is a long-term process, not an instantaneous event. Remember, even the close disciples of Jesus were not able to immediately convert every aspect of their lives to the teachings and lordship of Jesus. Some habits and attitudes required additional time. However, at the onset of this process of spiritual transformation, the new believer should be baptized. The ritual of baptism helps to mark the transition from evangelism to discipleship. When a person repents and accepts the gift of God's mercy, and when he makes the decision to follow Jesus, he must then be taught as a disciple. He must learn how a follower of Jesus lives and behaves in both public life and private life.

In regard to baptism, it is extremely important that the new Muslim Background Believer understand that this is not a ritual to indicate a person's abandonment of one community for another community. Rather it is a deeply symbolic ritual by which *an individual identifies himself as a follower of Jesus.* Through this ritual he finalizes or seals his decision to give allegiance to Christ for the rest of his life, even at the cost of danger, suffering, and death. It is also a means by which a person proves the sincerity of his commitment, because this ritual is meant to be a testimony to others. If a Muslim is truly sincere about this decision, then he should not be ashamed to publicly profess his faith in Christ. It is best that he be baptized in the presence of at least two or three believers so that his commitment to Christ can be verified by others. It is important for the Muslim believer to understand that this ritual symbolizes a spiritual change, and not necessarily a cultural change. It does not mean that he must change his name or his cultural identity, or even his cultural practices except for those that violate the teachings of Jesus. This is one area where so many Christians have made it extremely difficult for Muslim people to become Jesus' disciples.

Many Christians have the idea that when a person is "born again," he or she is born into the local Christian community. Of course every community has its own local culture and therefore Christians identify themselves according to their own distinct cultural traits. Thus when a Muslim chooses to become a follower of Christ, the local Christians think of him as a convert who is expected to convert from all Muslim cultural practices to the practices of the local Christian community, which often reflects a purely Western culture. For example, they expect Muslims to first of all change their names from Muslim names to Christian names. Karim must now become Peter and Ayesha must now become Elizabeth. Then Christians require Muslims to discard their prayer caps and veils. They expect them to keep their shoes on during worship, sing the songs of the local church, and pray as the local Christians do. Furthermore, the local Christians expect new Muslim Background Believers to embrace their Sunday attire, eat their food (including pork), and celebrate their holidays. For the local church, this is what identifies a Muslim as a new follower of Christ—a Christian—one who is completely extracted from his community and transplanted into the Christian community. But does all of this truly reflect scriptural teaching?

First of all, when Jesus spoke about being born again, he did not mean being born into a local community; but rather into the Kingdom of God! This is the context of John 3 and the "born again" experience. Because we are born into the Kingdom of God, we are born into a spiritual kingdom whose residents are identified by spiritual traits. Notice the teaching of Romans 14:17:

> For the kingdom of God is not a matter of eating and drinking, but of righteousness, peace, and joy in the Holy Spirit, . . .

The people of the Kingdom of God are not identified by their cultural practices, such as what they eat or drink, but by spiritual qualities which are basically the fruit of the Spirit, the first being love. How did Jesus say people would recognize his disciples? Was it by the clothes they wear, the food they eat, or the way they pray? No! It was not by way of cultural identification. Instead he said, *"By this all men will know that you are my disciples, if you love one another"* (John 13:35). It was by love! That is not a cultural trait; it is a spiritual trait. It is a fruit of the Spirit that grows in the garden of the Kingdom of God!

If a Muslim is forced by the local church to completely abandon his culture and community, how can he be a daily testimony to his family and friends? How can he be "salt of the earth" (Ma.5:13)? It is important to understand that when Muslims hear of one of their own being baptized as a Christian convert, they take it to mean that he or she has completely rejected the God of Abraham and embraced a Western culture which they view as godless. To avoid that kind of misunderstanding, it may be preferable to speak of these new believers as Followers of Jesus or Muslim Background Believers (MBBs)—Muslims who have not deserted their community but continue to live in their community as long as possible as a testimony of the transforming power of the Gospel.

What a Muslim really needs to understand is that by pledging his allegiance to Christ through water baptism, he has joined an additional community—a spiritual and universal community made up of fellow believers from a wide variety of cultural backgrounds, such as Muslim, Christian, Hindu, Buddhist, and others.

The Need for the Muslim Background Believer to Understand the Symbolism of Water Baptism

It is also important for the Muslim to understand the scriptural symbolism of baptism. On the basis of Romans 6, his immersion into the water is a symbol of burial. This is to remind him that his sinful ways are now viewed as dead. They are all buried in the past so that there is no longer any guilt or condemnation. Sin no longer has a grip upon his life. It is important that the Muslim realize that his sins are not merely covered, as in his previous worldview, to be viewed again on Judgment Day. Instead, they are completely erased by the work of

Christ. They are dead, never to be raised again.

His coming up out of the water of baptism is a symbol of resurrection. It is to remind him that his inner spirit has been revived. In his sinful state, his spirit was as dead. But now the condemnation of sin is gone. The heart has been washed and fully cleansed. In this state of purity, he now enters a completely new experience in which God's Spirit connects with his human spirit to make him spiritually alive.

Let's take a brief look at the method of baptism. When Jesus commissioned his close followers to go into all the world to preach the Gospel and baptize believers, he instructed them to baptize in the name of the Father, Son, and Holy Spirit (Matt. 28:19). Note that this formula is in the context of the Gentile world—all the nations outside the Jewish community. This meant people who knew nothing about the God of Abraham. However, the method of immersion in water was already a practice known to the Jews including John the Baptist. And in the scriptural accounts of the miraculous growth of the community of Christ's followers, the new believers are at times described as being baptized "into the name of Jesus Christ" (Acts 8:16 and 19:5). From this observation, it is evident that for the Jews who already believed in the God of Abraham, it was critical for them as new believers to understand that their new identification was marked by their faith and allegiance to Christ as Savior and Messiah. Thus to avoid confusion regarding the mystery of the Trinity, which is a very sensitive issue for Muslim people, it may prove helpful in some cases to baptize believers with the formula: *By the authority of God the Merciful One, the Compassionate One* [the Father], *Who reveals His will through His Word* [the Son], *and strengthens the heart of the believer by His Spirit* [the Holy Spirit], *I baptize you into the worldwide community of believers of our Lord and Savior, Isa al-Masih* [Jesus the Messiah]. This reworded formula helps to keep the Muslim's focus on his new identity in the body of Christ. As for the timing of baptism, it is strongly recommended that once a Muslim acknowledges his readiness to embrace Christ, he be baptized as soon as possible. There are some Christians who disagree with this view, arguing that he should first be taught the doctrines of the church. Then he will know for sure whether or not he wants to carry through with his decision. In this view, only after he is discipled does he qualify to become a disciple by baptism. The scriptural pattern, however, appears to take the opposite approach. When people responded to Christ, they were without hesitation baptized. Examples are the Ethiopian eunuch of Acts 8; Saul of Tarsus of Acts 9; Cornelius of Acts 10; and the Philippian jailer of Acts 16:33 which says, *"immediately he and all his household were baptized."* If Muslims are baptized immediately upon confirmation of devotion to Christ, then the ritual becomes much more meaningful and significant. By ritually taking on the mark of a disciple, Muslims are then ready to embrace the teachings of Christ.

When Muslims become followers of Christ, we now realize that their true identity is of a spiritual nature. The change that first takes place is of the heart. When one becomes a new creature in Christ, he or she becomes a new person whose heart and mindset undergo transformation. We learned that one of the mistakes we make is the demand we place upon Muslims to discard everything in their Islamic culture, including their names! Now we know that biblically, this is not a prerequisite for becoming a follower of the Lord Jesus. Of course, all sin must go, but cultural expression is negotiable. There are many Muslim cultural forms and practices that can be retained. In fact, much of orthodox Islamic culture is reflective of biblical culture. However, there are some aspects of Islamic culture that cannot be retained, and that is what we must now deal with. To do this, we will review the similar problem that affected the church of the New Testament.

In the Book of Acts, we find the story of the miraculous growth of the church. Initially, the church was composed of Jewish Background Believers who continued in their Jewish culture. Their beliefs and practices revolved around the prescriptions of the Mosaic Law. The new believers became identified as the followers of the Way. It is evident that even though they became followers of Jesus, they held on to their religious cultural practices that reflected the Mosaic Law. These practices included circumcision and animal sacrifice. Notice when Paul arrived in Jerusalem for his last visit, James, the church leader, advised him to join the other believers in their purification rites. These rites, which included head-shaving and animal sacrifice, were requirements of the Nazarite vow of Numbers 6:13-18.

Paul agreed to join them in these rituals (Acts 21:26). The animal sacrifice, of course, no longer pointed forward, but pointed backward, as a symbol representing the true Lamb of God. Similarly, if a Muslim Background Believer chooses to continue the animal sacrifice for the Eid-ul Qurban celebration, he must do so only with the realization that this sacrifice is merely a symbol pointing back to Jesus, the true redeeming Sacrifice. He must understand that the sacrifice of an animal in itself is of no value for the cleansing of the heart. Only Christ and the sacrifice of his life qualify in that regard. Furthermore, he must realize that the animal sacrifice is never to take the place of the sacrament of the Lord's Supper or Communion. The Lord's Supper must become a part of his worship and fellowship with other believers because this is exactly what Jesus commanded his followers to do in memory of his sacrificial death.

Returning now to the early church of the Book of Acts, the Gospel message did not remain confined within the walls of Jerusalem. It spread throughout the surrounding regions of Asia Minor and beyond. Consequently, many non-Jews (Gentiles) of an entirely different culture likewise embraced Christ as Savior and became devoted followers. That is when cultural conflict erupted. The Jewish followers of Jesus wanted the non-Jewish followers to adopt their Jewish culture. They wanted them to celebrate their holidays and adopt their practice of circumcision. This controversy became so heated that the church leaders in Jerusalem were compelled to hold a special council. They had to make an important decision. According to the teachings of Jesus, must non-Jews who became believers give up everything in their culture and completely adopt Jewish culture? Were they able to retain any of their Gentile practices? If so, what could they keep and what couldn't they keep, and on what basis would such a decision be made? This was a difficult situation because most of these non-Jews came out of an idolatrous background which had a widespread influence upon their culture.

Fortunately, the church leaders realized that the true mark of one's identity in Christ was the spiritual transformation of the heart. Salvation was not based on the observance of a culture that revolved around a system of religious works. It was clearly based on faith in the work of Christ. As a result, when the council concluded their deliberation over the matter, James, the leader of the church, made the following declaration: *It is my judgment, therefore, that we should not make it difficult for the Gentiles who are turning to God* (Acts 15:19). James' judgment was influenced by the guidance of the Holy Spirit. He mentioned this in the letter that he and the church elders sent out from Jerusalem to the Gentile churches. Part of that letter, stating their decision, is as follows:

> *...It seemed good to the Holy Spirit and to us not to burden you with anything beyond the following requirements: You are to abstain from food sacrificed to idols, from blood, from the meat of strangled animals and from sexual immorality. You will do well to avoid these things.* Acts 15:28-29

From this letter, it is evident that the Gentile believers were free to retain many of their cultural practices—but not all. Some they had to discard. A close examination of the list of prohibitions from the church leadership tells us something important. The practices that are mentioned in the letter are related to idolatrous and witchcraft practices. This included sacrifices to idols and the promiscuous behavior of the temple priestesses. These practices were non-negotiable. They had to be totally discontinued.

This biblical model helps us in our consideration of Muslims who become believers. This book has been primarily designed with orthodox Muslims in mind. We have determined already that many of their practices can be retained—but not all of them. No matter the degree of orthodoxy, most Muslims are involved in some measure with witchcraft practices and devices. Therefore, when they become believers, they must get rid of anything related to amulets, talismans, divinations, astrology charts, and the wide assortment of practices used to ward off evil spirits. Furthermore, if certain Muslims associate any demonic intervention with the sacrifice of animals during any of their festivals, then they should discontinue these sacrifices as well. They can simply observe the Lord's Supper to commemorate the sacrificial death of Christ.

It is imperative that the new believers in Christ clearly understand that Christ is above all powers, and that he came, not to simply manipulate or appease the evil spirits, but to defeat them. Christ came to utterly destroy the works of the devil (1 John 3:8)! We must be diligent to eliminate any witchcraft practice as a demonstration of faith that Jesus rules supreme, and that his name is indeed above all other names—including the names Muslims use to invoke the powers of the spirits. The believers must realize that if we are the followers of Jesus, then we do not need amulets, talismans, magic squares, incantations, and astrology charts to help us. For truly Christ is our Protector; and the Holy Spirit is our guide. This is sufficient to live a life completely surrendered to God—holy and acceptable unto him.

Reflection

As your relationship deepens with your Muslim friend, you may find yourself revisiting this chapter, going over the words of the prayer of repentance, or fanning back to other chapters looking for reassurance as you sense the person being drawn by the Spirit. You may suddenly feel completely inadequate for the task before you. Praise the Lord. That is right where you want to be!

If you are witnessing for Christ with any reliance on yourself, stop. You are off track. *Trust in the Lord with all your heart and lean not on your own understanding. In all your ways acknowledge Him and He will make your paths straight.* This is His work, you are only a vessel. You possess no quality, talent, or turn of phrase that can change the heart of man. Only the Holy Spirit can draw men and women to Christ. Your part in this is obedience to God.

Can you imagine the day that you lovingly lead a Muslim in a prayer of repentance? That day is coming. Release the outcome to Him.

21

Discipleship for Muslim Background Believers

If you love me, you will obey what I command.

John 14:15

In the newness of life of a new believer, definite changes will take place. These changes however will first be internal. According to Romans 12:2, the new Muslim believer will no longer live according to the ways of the world and the carnal flesh, but will be transformed by the renewing of his mind. In other words, he will see things differently; his attitudes will change. A transformation will take place in his worldview, and in some cases, as the Holy Spirit leads him, it may compel him to make necessary changes in his cultural practices as well. But the focus is first internal, then external.

Because Jesus referred to himself as "the way," his early disciples became known as Followers or People of the Way. In many Muslim settings, the label Christian has a very negative connotation. Thus, one solution is to encourage Muslim believers to identify themselves as Followers of Jesus or to take on the biblical identification, "People of the Way" (*ahl-al-tariqa*). They become pilgrims on a spiritual journey in which Jesus leads them ever deeper into the presence of God. Along the path, Jesus has placed markers to help the pilgrim reach his destination. These markers are words of guidance; they are teachings that help the pilgrim stay true to the path. They provide the guidelines for following the example of Jesus. Jesus said to his followers:

> *If you hold to my teaching, you are really my disciples. Then you will know the truth, and the truth will set you free.* John 8:31

> *Whoever has my commands and obeys them, he is the one who loves me. He who loves me will be loved by my Father, and I will love him and show myself to him.* John 14:21

It is important for the new disciple of Jesus to know what these commands or teachings are. They are interwoven in the words of Jesus. The discussions that follow represent some of the major issues which are particularly important for Muslim Background Believers.

Receive the Holy Spirit
When God raised Jesus from the death of the

cross, Jesus appeared to his disciples and did something strange. According to John 20:22, he breathed upon them and said, *"receive the Holy Spirit."* Just as God breathed into Adam the breath of physical life, so also did God want to breathe into humankind the breath of spiritual life. Jesus commissioned his disciples to proclaim the Gospel throughout the world, but instructed them not to begin until they received the help of the Spirit of God who would come into their lives to fill them and to strengthen them for their noble mission (Luke 24:49). This spiritual power would give them boldness and authority to preach the Gospel and perform miracles in Jesus' name. The Muslim needs to know that this infilling of the Spirit of God actually took place on the Day of Pentecost as recorded in Acts 2.

It is very important that the Muslim Background Believer realize that such an experience is possible even for him! In his previous mindset, such a link with God was reserved only for the prophets of God and Muslim saints. But he must come to understand that in this new spiritual order that begins with Christ, all of God's people are eligible and needful of this spiritual empowerment. The record of the Gospel confirms that this was God's intention as prophesied in Joel 2:28-29. Furthermore, according to Acts 2:38-39, this empowerment of the Holy Spirit is a gift from God for all those who repent and are baptized in Jesus' name.

The Muslim needs to be reminded that to follow Christ who is the holy servant of God, he likewise must live a holy life of servanthood. He can no longer continue in sinful acts or habits and simply excuse them away as marks of human weakness and forgetfulness. Nor can he continue to play with sinful acts thinking he can cancel them with good deeds. God, who is most holy, does not negotiate with sin through a system of merit and demerit. The believer must reject sin totally. When temptations come, the Holy Spirit is present to strengthen his heart and help him overcome those temptations.

Also, when the Holy Spirit comes to indwell his life, the Muslim believer must recognize that he is expected to rise above the carnal human plane to a higher plane where he participates in the divine nature. Through the channel and connection of the Holy Spirit, he must learn that the holy attributes of God are to reflect from his life therefore allowing absolutely no room for ungodliness. Thus not only is he gifted with the strength of the Spirit, but with the fruit of the Spirit of Galatians 5 that speak of the traits of godly character, such as love, patience, kindness, and self-control.

When the new believer receives the Spirit of God, he needs to understand that his own human spirit which was dead in sin has now become alive, giving him a new spiritual nature. In this way he has become a new creature in Christ. He has become linked to God by the touch and connection of the Spirit of God with his human spirit. As a result, he has become a member of God's heavenly household. He has become a member of the royal Family of God in which God now becomes his heavenly "Father" and he becomes God's spiritual child, born by the Spirit of God. It is important for the Muslim to understand the implication of John 1:12 that speaks about the right of becoming "children of God" for all who have embraced Christ. He must begin to think in terms of spiritual sonship as revealed in Romans 8:13-16. From his previous worldview, he could only think in terms of a Master-slave relationship with God. But as a new disciple of Christ, he must understand that he has an even more profound relationship now that he is a spiritual child of God. When he experiences this truth which is born out of a God whose predominant attribute is not power but love, he will arrive at a completely different outlook in regard to worship and service. It is one thing to serve as a slave; it is completely another to serve as a child. The slave serves out of fear of punishment; the son or daughter serves out of concern and love for the father. This leads to the next important matter for the disciple of Jesus—the matter of true worship and devotion to God.

Worship in Spirit and in Truth

According to the Scriptures, God created humankind for the purpose of worshiping Him. But when the human spirit is dry, human worship is also dry. As a result, worship for many Muslims is a rigorous exercise that fulfills a religious duty but offers little in terms of meaning and spiritual experience. Even the prayer ritual becomes an empty form of mechanical posture and outdated tradition. Muslims are particularly disillusioned when they hear their religious leaders speak on the issues of piety and yet live secret lives of immorality and corruption. Of course religious leaders also fail when they lack the inner power of the Spirit of God to overcome the temptations of evil. Such people do not worship in spirit because the Spirit of God is not in them. Furthermore, they do not worship in truth because what they practice in real life is contrary to what they preach in religious life.

When religious people recognize this inability to maintain internal purity, the emphasis of religion begins to shift to the outer forms of purity. Thus the orthodox Muslim is well acquainted with the importance placed on external forms and purification rituals, for it is easier to wash the hands and feet that are smeared with dust than to wash the heart that is smeared with hatred, greed and arrogance. However, when it comes to worship, most Muslims do not think in terms of knowing God intimately in a spiritual sense, simply because the Spirit of God is not within them. Therefore, there is no real sense of relationship or communion with God. Instead, most Muslims know God only as a task master who, as a God of vengeance, will severely punish those who fail to fully adhere to His laws. With this view, most Muslims observe the rigor of religious ritual and worship, not to draw near to embrace God's love, but to keep distant to escape His wrath.

For the new Muslim believer, his former experience of worship may have been dominated by a sense of fear and dread rather than a sense of love and anticipation. Rather than worshipping God for who he is, he may have worshiped God out of fear, out of tradition, or out of self-righteousness. But when he becomes a follower of Christ, and a transformation begins to take place in his heart and mind, he comes to know God as a God of love. On the basis of 1 John 4:15-19, he should now understand that God first revealed His love by sending Jesus to be his Savior. Furthermore, as a result of this love, and his acceptance of it, the punishment for his sin is gone. And if the punishment is gone, then the fear is gone! Now within his heart, in place of fear and dread, there should only be love and appreciation for the One who loved him first.

Only by perceiving God as a God of love can a Muslim worship God in spirit and in truth. It is divine love that opened for him the door to a relationship with God in which God is his heavenly Father. It is divine love that freed him to enter and embrace the presence of the Beloved One. Unlike before, the Muslim believer can worship God in spirit because he now has access to the Spirit of God, and he can worship God in truth because the Spirit of God will enable him to put into practice the teachings of Christ.

One important issue in the regard of worship is the motive of worship. Muslims are led to believe that performing "good works" according to their religious law can gain extra merit. This merit can then tip the scale of "good works" vs. bad works in favor of salvation. Thus there exists the preponderance of "good works" all for the sake of future reward. Religious rituals such as prayer, fasting, and giving of alms, become self-centered and are seen as necessary practices of worship for countering the punishment for sins. When a Muslim becomes a believer, this view of worship needs to change. When he understands that God is a God of love; that his sin is first and foremost against God; and that according to Genesis 6:6, God's heart is grieved and filled with pain, then he should realize that there is nothing in all the world he can do to heal the broken heart of God. There is no human work big enough or good enough to atone for such a sin. All that he can do is simply hope in God's mercy. And God's mercy responded through the life, death, and resurrection of Christ. It is so important for the Muslim believer to grasp the impact of Ephesians 2:8-9 which reminds us of God's gift, and that salvation can only be through God's grace, never through human works. The only work we can do to receive the gift of salvation is to believe! When people asked Jesus, *What must we do to do the works of God?* Jesus responded, *The work of God is this: to believe in the one He has sent* (John 6:28,29).

In the discipleship process, the Muslim must come to clearly understand the scriptural teaching on justification and righteousness as it relates to "good works" and the law. This is now the time to teach about the atonement of the cross and the redemption of the blood of the Lamb. This is the time to talk about the work of the cross and the righteousness of Christ that becomes our righteousness when we believe in him. The Book of Romans deals with this issue as follows:

But now a righteousness from God, apart from the Law, has been made known, to which the Law and the Prophets testify. This righteousness from God comes through faith in Jesus Christ to all who believe. There is no difference, for all have sinned and fall short of the glory of God, and are justified freely by His grace through the redemption that came by Christ Jesus. God presented him as a sacrifice of atonement, through faith in his blood. He did this to demonstrate His justice...
Romans 3:21-2

...that I may ...be found in him, not having a righteousness of my own that comes from the law, but that which is through faith in Christ—the righteousness that comes from God and is by faith.
Philippians 3:8-9

Muslims are correct in asserting that righteousness is the keeping of God's laws. The problem is our carnal fallen nature which prevents us from perfectly fulfilling these laws. And so we need an alternative path of righteousness, one that is not based on law. According to the Scriptures, God provided that alternative. There is another way to be reckoned as righteous in the eyes of God. It is the way of faith in the work of Christ—the death of the cross.

When this realization sets in, the Muslim should understand that with God's mercy there is no room for boasting and outward show of piety. There can only be room for humble gratitude for God's unconditional love. Therefore, when he worships God, he should no longer do so for the sake of merit. It is important for him to believe that through the work of Christ and the complete burial of past sin, he has already received the guarantee of eternal reward. And because he has learned that God is a God of love, he should now worship God not out of religious obligation, but out of sincere desire. He should now be able to worship God for who He is—the God of mercy and compassion—the God of love.

The Muslim who chooses to follow Christ is no longer a slave of fear subjected to man-made religious demands and empty ceremonies. Instead he is a true slave of God, and a slave of no other. In fact, he should be more willing to obey and serve God because there is now the urge within him to love God with all his heart. From now on, when he prays; when he keeps the fast; or when he gives alms, it should no longer be for the sake of religious merit. It should no longer be for outward show or for the sake of tradition. He should do all of this with a willing heart for the sake of expressing his love and appreciation to God for first loving him. His acts of worship should now be compelled by love. Only as he learns to worship and adore God as a *child of God* will he be able to humbly and obediently serve God as a faithful slave. Without such love, obedience remains mechanical and self-seeking; but with such love, obedience is indeed purified!

It will be important for the Muslim believer to understand that when the Spirit of God is in him, the love of God will also be in him, because "God is love" (1 John 4:8). This love will want to flood his inner being like a river rushing to overflow into the hearts of others. When he begins to truly worship God, he will realize that true worship remains incomplete until he begins to lovingly care for others, just as God has lovingly cared for him. This brings us to the next important subject—the matter of loving one another.

Love One Another

When Jesus realized that his earthly mission was about to reach its climax, he spent some private moments with his close disciples. During that time, he tried to prepare them for his eventual death. He lovingly tried to encourage them with words of hope and assurance that their grief would turn to joy. It was then that he especially focused on the love of the Father, and his own love for them, the disciples. He left them with this very important instruction, which has been the distinguishing mark of his true followers ever since:

> *As the Father has loved me, so have I loved you. Now remain in my love. If you obey my commands, you will remain in my love, just as I have obeyed my Father's commands and remain in His love.... My command is this: Love each other as I have loved you.* John 15: 9,10,12

As you share the teachings and deeds of Jesus with the new believer, help him to see that everything

Jesus did and said revolved around his love for God and humankind. And as for the divine law, he taught his disciples that they could fulfill all the requirements of the moral law by adhering to the law of love.

> *"Love the Lord your God with all your heart and with all your soul and with all your mind." This is the first and greatest commandment. And the second is like it: "Love your neighbor as yourself." All the Law and the Prophets hang on these two commandments."*
> Matthew 22:37-40

For example, the Law (of Moses) forbids idolatry and the slanderous use of God's name. However, if the disciple truly loves God with all his heart, then he will have no desire to worship any other. Furthermore, he will be careful to treat the name of God with utmost reverence. The Law also forbids such things as murder, theft, and giving false witness. However, if one truly loves his neighbor, he will not want to kill him, steal from him, or tell lies about him. Romans 13:8-10 elaborates on this point:

> *Let no debt remain outstanding, except the continuing debt to love one another, for he who loves his fellowman has fulfilled the law. The commandments, "Do not commit adultery," "Do not murder," "Do not steal," "Do not covet," and whatever other commandments there may be are summed up in this one rule: "Love your neighbor as yourself." Love*

does no harm to its neighbor. Therefore, love is the fulfillment of the law.

When the Muslim becomes a follower of Christ, he must not only have a right relationship with God, he must also have a right relationship with the people around him. Both of these relationships are to be established in the bonds of love for the sake of serving both God and humankind. Love must help his relationships to transform from self-seeking and self-benefiting contacts to genuine feelings of regard and concern for others. This pertains to both God and people. The passage of 1 John 4:20, 21 clearly warns that the believer cannot claim to love God if he is unwilling to love fellow beings:

> *If anyone says, "I love God," yet hates his brother, he is a liar. For anyone who does not love his brother, whom he has seen, cannot love God, whom he has never seen.... Whoever loves God must also love his brother.*

Performing Works without Love

The Muslim believer will know of people in his community who pride themselves in religious piety and are quick to display their regimen of "good works." However, he will need to be reminded that unless these "good works" are motivated purely by love, they become showpieces of hypocrisy. Many religious people perform "good works" only to be seen by others or to earn religious merit for themselves. Neither is acceptable in the eyes of God who is able to uncover the hidden motives of the heart. God desires from him a much purer love. He desires a genuine kind of love, a love that is transformed as a result of becoming a disciple of Christ and being filled with the Spirit of God.

> *Now that you have purified yourselves by obeying the truth so that you have sincere love for your brothers, love one another deeply, from the heart.*
> 1 Peter 1:22

Share the love chapter of 1 Corinthians 13 over and over again with the Muslim believer so that he begins to understand how this love is demonstrated and lived out. We should not be surprised that for many Muslims, it is the love of the Gospel which draws them to Christ. We believe that because God is love, and because humans are created in the image of God, every human being has the inherent yearning to be loved by a perfect love—divine love! It is important that this love begin to influence the thoughts and deeds of the new believer whose life was previously influenced by a "God of power" mindset that can make a person into an authoritarian figure bent on control and vengeance. He must see his role as changing from a power-wielding figurehead to one of a loving humble servant.

Preaching Love without Works

Besides people who perform "good works" that

are void of genuine love, there are others who preach about genuine love but fail to do good works. Remind the believer that according to the scriptures, it is simply not enough to teach about love. If we truly are to love one another, then we must show it. And this love is to be demonstrated to people outside the family as well as to people inside the family. Our words and our faith must be backed up by our actions. Otherwise our love is false. It is not the kind of pure love that Jesus speaks about to his followers. Christ proved his love by the act of giving his life for others. His followers must also prove their love by acts of selflessness on behalf of others.

Sometimes in our effort to convince the Muslim that salvation is by faith in God's grace, and not by works, we give him the idea that the duty of "good works" is no longer an important issue. From his former Islamic perspective and teaching, works was an essential requirement for salvation. That's why he was caught up in good works. But when he becomes a follower of Christ and continually hears the emphasis of God's grace, he may become inclined to dismiss any further need for good works. That's when it's important to help him see that good works are still very significant. The difference is that in his new life in Christ he no longer performs them as a prerequisite to salvation; he performs them as an outflow of salvation. The love that now fills his heart flows outward to others and expresses itself in tangible ways. The following scriptures will help him to see that becoming a follower of Christ does not do away with "good works," rather it purifies "good works."

If anyone has material possessions and sees his brother in need, but has no pity on him, how can the love of God be in him? Dear children, let us not love with words or tongue but with actions and in truth. 1 John 3:17, 18

What good is it, my brother, if a man claim to have faith but has no deeds? Can such faith save him? Suppose a brother or sister is without clothes and daily food. If one of you says to him, "Go, I wish you well; keep warm and well fed," but does nothing about his physical needs, what good is it? In the same way, faith by itself, if it is not accompanied by action, is dead. James 2:14-17

Relating to Fellow Believers

As a new follower of Christ, the believer's first priority of love is of course God, the Merciful One, the Compassionate One. All that he does should be motivated by his desire to love Him and serve Him with all of his heart. Next, he will feel a deepening love for Christ who led him into the wonderful experience of God's presence in the first place. Then he should begin to develop a special kinship and love toward other followers, who like him, are Muslim Background Believers. Just as he holds a special affection for his own true brothers and sisters, so also he should hold a special affection for his spiritual brothers and sisters. For many Muslims, however, this is a very difficult step.

It will also be extremely important to remind the Muslim disciple that the community of Jesus' followers is a universal community whose members come from a wide variety of cultural and religious backgrounds. Most of them will be culturally different from him and will come from a Christian background. It will be important for him to know that not everyone from the Christian community is a true and dedicated follower of Christ, just as many Muslims are not true devoted followers of Islam. But the true followers of Christ will often identify themselves as having experienced a spiritual rebirth and transformation of life. But even these true followers of Christ will differ from the Muslim Background Believer simply because they follow a different culture. They will dress differently, sing differently, eat differently, and even consume pork! They will celebrate different holidays and perform different worship rituals. Even more disturbing, their rules for gender issues and codes for modesty will be radically different. But he needs to understand that despite all these cultural differences, he is united to these people by one common identity. They are all followers of Jesus and they all seek to obey his commands which rise above culture and unite people on a higher plane—a spiritual plane; that of love: love for God and love for fellow human beings.

Because orthodox Islam places so much emphasis on the external, the new Muslim believer will be tempted to judge fellow believers on the basis of their outward appearances and cultural practices. This same situation arose when the first disciples of Jesus began proclaiming the Gospel message. Many people from the community of the Jews responded. But many more responded from neighboring pagan communities!

When the two communities met, there was a clash. Some of the new believers from Jewish background were criticizing the new believers from the pagan background because they were not observing Jewish religious formalities. They began to reject the believers from the non-Jewish community on the basis of their cultural practices. But according to the teachings of the Gospel, this reaction was wrong. Jesus clearly taught that we become members of the Kingdom of God not by what we do, but by the condition of our hearts and our relationship to God. God searches for spiritual purity and not the purity of outward customs and rituals. God looks for the heart that has been transformed from the old person to the new person! According to the scriptures:

Neither circumcision or uncircumcision means anything; what counts is a new creation. Galatians 6:15

The LORD does not look at the things a man looks at. Man looks at the outward appearance, but the LORD looks at the heart. 1 Samuel 16:7

The following scriptures provide further teaching to help the new Muslim Background Believer to respect and accept others of a different background, and to focus on the more important issues of the Spirit.

Therefore, do not let anyone judge you by what you eat or drink, or with regard to a religious festival, a New Moon celebration or a Sabbath day.... Since, then, you have been raised with Christ, set your hearts on things above, where Christ is seated at the right hand of God. Set your minds on things above, not on earthly things.
Colossians 2:16; 3:1,2

The man who eats everything must not look down on him who does not, and the man who does not eat everything must not condemn the man who does, for God has accepted him. Who are you to judge someone else's servant? To his own master he stands or falls. And he will stand, for the Lord is able to make him stand.

One man considers one day more sacred than another; another man considers every day alike. Each one should be fully convinced in his own mind. He who regards one day as special does so to the Lord. He who eats meat, eats to the Lord, for he gives thanks to God; and he who abstains, does so to the Lord and gives thanks to God.... You, then, why do you judge your brother? Or why do you look down on your brother? For we will all stand before God's judgment seat.

Therefore, let us stop passing judgment on one another.... For the Kingdom of God is not a matter of eating and drinking, but of righteousness, peace and joy in the Holy Spirit,... Let us therefore make every effort to do what leads to peace and mutual edification. Romans 14: 3-6, 10, 13, 17, 19

May the God who gives endurance and encouragement give you a spirit of unity among yourselves as you follow Christ Jesus, so that with one heart and one mouth you may glorify the God and Father of our Lord Jesus Christ. Accept one another, then, just as Christ accepted you, in order to bring praise to God. Romans 15:5-7

The Master's Words of Comfort

When a Muslim becomes a follower of the Lord Jesus, you can be sure he or she will face great persecution from his family and community. His heart will become filled with doubts. The pressure will be so great that he will be tempted to revert to Islam. This is when he will need the Lord's encouragement.

Just as Jesus spoke words of comfort to his close disciples, the believer must realize that these same words are spoken to him. He needs to claim these words as promises of Jesus that will help him to stay true to the end:

The Holy Spirit, whom the Father will send in my name, will teach you all things and will remind you of everything I have said to you. Peace I leave with you.... Do not let your hearts be troubled and do not be

302

afraid. John 14:26,27

> *I have told you these things, so that in me you may have peace. In this world you will have trouble. But take heart! I have overcome the world.* John 16:33

Assure the Muslim Background Believer that in the power and authority of Christ Jesus, he shall overcome the spiritual struggles of the world. Salvation is certain. Encourage him to praise God for the wonderful holy scriptures that remind him each day of the heavenly blessings that he has found in Christ.

> *Praise be to the God and Father of our Lord Jesus Christ! In his great mercy He has given us new birth into a living hope through the resurrection of Jesus Christ from the dead, and into an inheritance that can never perish, spoil or fade — kept in heaven for you, who through faith are shielded by God's power until the coming of the salvation that is ready to be revealed in the last time.*

> *In this you greatly rejoice, though now for a little while you may have to suffer grief in all kinds of trials. These have come so that your faith — of greater worth than gold, which perishes even though refined by fire — may be proved genuine and may result in praise, glory and honor when Jesus Christ is revealed. Though you have not seen him, you love him; and even though you do not see him now, you believe in him and are*

filled with an inexpressible and glorious joy, for you are receiving the goal of your faith, the salvation of your souls. 1 Peter 1:3-9

Reflection

The need for discipleship after a Muslim becomes a believer and follower of Jesus Christ can not be stressed enough. There have been many instances of Muslim Background Believers returning to Islam because they could not find a church home or any kind of meaningful connection to Christians. Or, even worse, those who are sold out to Christ and are in fear of being killed can not find support either corporately or individually because of the danger associated with helping them. In some cases this has led to their deaths.

If you have helped lead a Muslim friend to faith in Christ there is much you can do to encourage his or her continued growth as a disciple. It is important to remember a new Muslim believer is still a Muslim culturally. He still views worshipping God as a holy act and will find churches with guitars and drums loudly playing upbeat praise and worship music at the beginning of a service unsettling. Also, seeing the Bible, the Holy Scripture, being set on the floor or being used as a "lap table" to write notes on will be viewed as disrespectful. You can help prepare him for the cultural differences by reminding him that God looks beyond human culture into the human heart.

It will also be helpful if you meet with your pastor and share with him about the new believer's background and the cultural issues that make this believer uncomfortable, even in a Sunday morning service. Especially issues that involve cross gender interaction such as enthusiastic handshakes and holy hugs.

If your church has home cell groups, this would be a wonderful way to introduce a new believer to other Christians. But again, a little preparation time with the group before he or she arrives will go a long way in making a smooth transition.

The whole concept of community is extremely important in the Muslim culture. A willingness to offer generous hospitality and the time that that requires is critical. In most instances MBBs must find a new community to be part of since they are no longer accepted by family and former friends. Their "new birth" requires many needs to be met. By making appropriate adjustments to fit the Muslim culture, we can help fill the voids their new faith has created. Informal gatherings, barbeques, picnics, and such are great venues to form new friendships and deepen existing ones. They will provide much needed opportunities for believers to fellowship and grow from the continued witness of the Gospel truths.

All of this must be covered in constant prayer and communion with the Holy Spirit. You may be thinking that the friendship ministry that is the heart of leading Muslims to Christ and nurturing their new faith is a daunting commitment of time and resources. You might be asking yourself if God is truly calling you to such an undertaking.

". . . . I tell you, open your eyes and look at the fields! They are ripe for harvest." John 4:35

Glossary

a'authubillah   literally, "I seek refuge in Allah;"   a phrase uttered to ward off evil spirits.

abdullah servant of Allah; a term used for Jesus in the Qur'an (19:30).

ablution   ceremonial, ritual washing before prayer, known in Islam as *wudhu*.

adab manners and customs that define Islamic conduct or behavior.

adhan the call to Muslims for their daily obligatory prayers; this prayer call resembles an Arabic chant and is issued by a Muslim through a loudspeaker from the minaret of the local mosque.

ahl-al-tariqa   literally, "people of the way;" this is a term that can be used to identify followers of Jesus.

al-hamdulillah literally, "praise be to Allah."

Allah Ta'ala   literally, "the God Most High;"   *ta'ala* being an honorific term for the use of Allah.

Allahu Akbar   literally, "God is Greater;"   no matter

what measure of power one can think of, Allah is always greater (i.e., Allah is the greatest, the most powerful).

amulet   an ornament, usually containing inside it an inscription of a Qur'anic verse or an Islamic magic word/phrase/number square, and worn on the body to cure or protect against evil spirits.

animistic   believing that plants, animals, inanimate objects, and natural phenomena likewise possess souls or spirits that interact to maintain balance and harmony in the universe.

aqiqa   the Islamic celebration of a birth of a child that involves the shaving of the head of the infant and the sacrifice of an animal.

Ar-Rabb   literally, "the Lord," a title often used for Allah in the Qur'an.

Ar-Rahman Ar-Rahim   literally, "the merciful one, the compassionate one."

as-salamu alai kum   literally, "peace be upon you," which is the typical Islamic greeting

bai'at   a term which refers to the initiation rite for Sufi disciples who are inducted into a Sufi order or brotherhood.

bismillah   literally, "in the name of Allah;" a common

phrase which is used to invoke God's name, such as at the commencement of a meal.

burqa the veil or covering used by Muslim women to conceal themselves when out in public.

carrion the flesh of a dead and rotting animal.

chador a cloak, usually black in color, used by Muslim women to drape around their body and head leaving only the face exposed.

cosmos the complete and harmonious system of the universe.

Crusader literally, a "cross bearer;" one who participated in the military expeditions (the Great Crusades) first organized by the Roman Catholic Church in the eleventh century for the purpose of wresting the Holy Land and Jerusalem from Muslim control.

culture the way people collectively act, think, and speak as influenced by their traditions, religions, geography, climate, and languages.

Dar al-Harb literally, "the abode of chaos, disharmony, war;" Muslims divide the people of the world into two major categories. This is the category all non-Muslims who do not submit to Islamic law fall into, just as all non-Jews fall into the category of Gentile.

Dar al-Islam literally, "the abode of peace, harmony;" this is the other of the two major categories that Muslims under Islamic law fall into.

dawah literally, "invitation;" this is the term Muslims use for their religious propagation activities since these activities are seen as the means of inviting non-Muslims to embrace Islam.

disco music music that is generally associated with the Western dance hall and that features electric guitars, electric keyboards, and drums.

divination the witchcraft practice of revealing the unknown of some past event, some present mystery, or some future decision.

du'a an Islamic term used to refer to personal prayer from the heart; extemporaneous prayer.

ego-centric self-centered.

Eid holiday the celebration of either Eid-ul Adha (Celebriont/Feast of the Sacrifice) or Eid-ul Fitr (the Celebration of the breaking of the fast of Ramadhan).

Eid-Mubarak literally, "Blessed Celebration!" or "Happy Eid!"

Eid-ul Adha the Celebration/Feast of the Sacrifice.

Eid-ul Fitr the Celebration of the breaking of the fast of Ramadhan.

Eid-ul Qurban the Celebration/Feast of the Sacrifice; *qurban* is the word often used to refer to the animal sacrifice.

ethno-centric comparing and evaluating cultures of other ethnic people groups on the basis of one's own culture, often with the idea that one's own culture is superior.

extemporaneously speaking or praying spontaneously, at any moment, without any pre-memorized words or prepared scripts.

extended family a household of people that includes more than just the members of the nucleus family of husband-wife and children, such as parents, grandparents, cousins, aunts and uncles, and in-laws.

folk Islam this is the term used to refer to the type of Islam that is heavily influenced by witchcraft and practiced by most Muslims in the world who are indifferent and unmoved by the classical teachings of orthodox Islam.

frame of reference a set of standards, principles, religious ideas, etc. that one can use as a basis of comparison when talking about people of another culture.

fundamentalist Muslim a Muslim who wants to restore, revive, and establish as law the pristine teachings of the Prophet Muhammad based on the materials of the Qur'an and the *hadith*.

godhead the state of deity; this term is often used when speaking about the tri-une nature or the three-some aspect of the state of deity, ie., the "three persons" of the Godhead.

hadith literally, "a narrative" or description; this term is used to speak of the collection of material that supposedly describes everything Muhammad did and relates everything he said about issues of lifestyle and religion. The *hadith* provides for the serious Muslim reliable traditions which portray for him in detail Muhammad's example known as the *sunnah*.

halal that which is lawful or permissible, such as meat from animals over which Allah's name has been invoked by the phrase, *bismillah allahu akbar* before slaughter.

haram that which is unlawful or forbidden, such as meat from animals over which Allah's name has not been invoked; or such as the consumption of pork.

hijab a term that often refers to a Muslim woman's clothing which is used to cover her head as well as to veil her face.

humanism a system of belief which exalts the potential of human ability to the exclusion of any need for a belief or a dependence upon a divine being.

Iftar the light and quick snack that breaks the daily fast of each of the days of fasting of Ramadhan. It is eaten just before the *Maghrib* (sunset) prayer.

imam literally, "a religious guide or model;" among the Sunni Muslims, the word *imam* generally refers to the local Muslim priest who leads Muslims in their prayers in the mosque. Among the Shi'ites, the word *Imam* has a much grander meaning; it refers to the one religious leader of the Shi'ite community at large.

Incarnation classically, the embodiment of Jesus Christ, the divine Word of God, in human flesh; the act of an individual of one culture embodying himself into the wrapping of another person's culture.

Injil the Gospel, or the whole New Testament which bears witness of the Good News of Jesus.

insha'allah literally, "if Allah wills;" this phrase is used when speaking of some future planned event; for example, "*insha'allah*, we will visit you again next week."

invocation a prayer invoking the name of God on behalf of some need; for most Muslims, this is a memorized prayer or phrase taken from the *hadith* as a prayer that Muhammad prayed.

314

Isa Al-Masih   the Qur'anic Arabic rendering for Jesus the Messiah.

Isa Kalimatullah   the Arabic rendering for Jesus the Word of Allah, from the Qur'anic phrase, *kalimatuhu* of 4:171.

Isa Ruhullah   the Arabic rendering for Jesus the Spirit of Allah, from the Qur'anic phrase, *ruh-un min hu* of 4:171.

jamat   assembly or congregation, usually of believers.

jinn   one from among the spirit beings who were supposedly created by Allah from pure fire as a separate race of beings on earth; there are both good *jinn* and evil *jinn*.

Jumaa Prayer   the Friday noon prayer held at the mosque.

khatnah   circumcision.

liturgy   a prescribed format for public worship whereby the participants take an active role; this could include such things as responsive reading and congregational prayer.

maghrib **prayer**   the obligatory prayer at sunset; the fourth of the five prayers.

mahfil   a meeting of people; a get-together.

masha'allah   literally, "that which Allah wills;"   a substitute phrase for "thank-you."

mahzar   the shrine site of a Muslim saint which is often the destination of a pilgrimage.

Middle Ages   a period of European history from about the eleventh to the fifteenth century.

munajat   non-obligatory prayer; a substitute word for *du'a*.

niggardliness   stinginess, miserliness.

nikah   wedding ceremony; marriage contract.

nominal   existing in name only; for example, a nominal Muslim is one who is a Muslim in name only, and cares little about the actual beliefs and practices of Islam.

orthodox Muslim   a Muslim who sincerely and strictly adheres to Islamic teaching, tradition, and practice.

paradox   a statement or idea that is seemingly contradictory; for example, the Biblical teaching that Christ the Son of God is the Servant of God.

Pentateuch   the first five books of the Bible which are traditionally attributed to Moses and grouped together as The Law (Luke 24: 44).

Pir   literally, "elder;"   a Persian term used by Sufi Muslims to refer to their Teachers or Masters.

power encounter   an expression used to describe the confrontation between the forces of evil and the power of the Kingdom of God. Followers of Christ praying for the deliverance of a demon-possessed person is an example of a power encounter.

qibla   the direction of prayer for Muslims; when Muslims pray, they face the direction of the *Kaaba* in Mecca.

qurban   literally, "a means of access" or "that which brings near;" this term is commonly used to refer to the animal sacrifice during the Eid-ul Adha celebration.

Rabbana   literally, "our Lord;"   this term is used exclusively for Allah.

rahil a book stand for the use of the Qur'an because it would be considered derogatory to ever place the Qur'an on the floor.

Ramadhan   the ninth month of the Muslim calendar; supposedly the month during which the Qur'an was first revealed, and therefore the holy month during which Muslims observe the month-long Ramadhan fast.

rites of passage   rituals that mark the critical events of an individual's life span such as birth, puberty, marriage, and death.

ruh-ul qudus   literally, "holy spirit;" a term interpreted by Muslims to refer to the angel Gabriel.

salat   the obligatory prayer for Muslims which must be observed five times a day.

salat-ul janazah   the funeral prayer.

salawat   the portion of the *salat* which invokes Allah's blessing upon Muhammad and his people just as Allah blessed Abraham and his people.

Sanhedrin   the Jewish supreme court in the time of Jesus.

sayyiduna   literally, "our lord;" an expression that can be used for Jesus instead of *rabbana* which Muslims use exclusively for Allah.

servanthood   the role of helping and benefiting others in a spirit of love and sacrifice.

Shah   literally, "a king:" a Persian word used to denote highest honor, and often used as a title for Sufi saints.

shahada   the Islamic confession or statement of faith which acknowledges the oneness of Allah and the

318

prophethood of Muhammad.

shari'ah literally, "a path leading to a water hole;" this term is used to refer to Islamic law which is based on the Qur'an, and the sayings and deeds of Muhammad.

Sheikh literally, "an honorable old man;" this is a title given to a person of authority or great honor. This is also a common title given to the leaders of Sufi brotherhoods.

Shi'ite Muslims one of the two major sects of Islam whose Muslims pay great homage to Ali, Muhammad's son-in-law, and Ali's son, Hussein. Shi'ite Muslims primarily look to their Imam for religious guidance.

shirk associating any other god with Allah or worshiping anything or anyone else besides Allah; this is the unpardonable sin of Islam and is the worst sin a Muslim can commit.

stereotype a commonly held preconceived and prejudiced opinion about someone or something.

subhannahu wa ta'ala literally, "glorified is He and exalted;" this is an honorific expression that follows the utterance or written form of Allah, and is often abbreviated in English as Allah(SWT).

Sufi a mystical Muslim who emphasizes the internal aspects of religion as opposed to the external aspects of religion.

Suhuf-un-Nabiyin literally, "the books of the prophets;" this term can be used to refer to the books of the Bible which are not included in the *Tawrat* (Torah), the *Jabur* (Psalms), and the *Injil* (the Gospel of the New Testament).

Sunnah literally, "example;" Muslims speak of following the *sunnah* or example of Muhammad as it is detailed in the material of the *hadith*.

Sunni Muslims the larger of the two major Islamic sects; Sunni Muslims historically recognized the first four successors to Muhammad as "the rightly guided *khalifahs*." Sunni Muslims look primarily to the Qur'an and the *hadith* for religious guidance.

Surat-ul Fatiha literally, "the opening chapter;" this is the title of the first chapter of the Qur'an and is often recited as a prayer.

talisman a religious object which is believed to possess supernatural power and is used as a charm in witchcraft practices to ward off evil.

tariqa literally, "a path;" a term used by Sufi Muslims to refer to a particular Sufi brotherhood or to the method prescribed for approaching the nearness of Allah the Beloved.

tauhid a term used by Muslims to speak about the

absolute oneness of Allah which is the most fundamental teaching of Islam.

tawba   repentance.

Tawrat   the Arabic Qur'anic term used to refer to the revelations received by Moses.

theocracy   a government that centers on God and the laws of God.

traditionists   Muslims who were involved in the collection and study of *hadith* material.

triune nature   a term used to refer to the trinity aspect of God and the three persons of the Godhead, namely the Father, the Son, and the Holy Spirit.

ummah   a community or nation of people.

Umm-ul Kitab   literally, "the mother-book;" this term is used to refer to the eternal uncreated Word of God or Book of God from which all the divine revelations for mankind descended.

waffat   death.

walimah   wedding feast.

Zabur   the Arabic Qur'anic term used for the revelations received by David, to whom Christians attribute most of the Psalms.

zakat   obligatory giving of alms by Muslims who have material possessions and whose debts do not exceed the value of their possessions.

Appendix A
Population Growth Comparisons
Welcome to Christianville
Population 80

| 60 Christian People | 20 Muslim People |
| 30 Christian Couples | 10 Muslim Couples |

	Birth Rate				Birth Rate	
Year			Year			
1	No children		1	All couples have a child	+10
2	No children		2	5 couples have a child	+ 5
3	10 couples have a child	+10	3	All couples have a child	+10
4	No children		4	No children	
5	All couples have a child	+30	5	All couples have a child	+10
6	No children		6	5 couples have a child	+5
7	No children		7	All couples have a child	+10
8	All couples have a child	+30	8	No children	
9	No children		9	All couples have a child	+10
10	No children		10	No children	
11	No children		11	No children	
12	No children		12	All couples have a child	+10

Total population: Children	70		Total population: Children	70
Adults	60		Adults	20
	130			90

Passing away of first generation	-60			-20
New population: **Christians**	70		**Muslims**	70

Second Generation Christianville
Population 140

| 70 Christian People | | 70 Muslim People | |
| 35 Christian Couples | | 35 Muslim Couples | |

	Birth Rate			Birth Rate	
Year			Year		
1	No children		1	All couples have a child	+35
2	No children		2	20 couples have a child	+20
3	10 couples have a child	+10	3	All couples have a child	+35
4	No children		4	All couples have a child	+35
5	All couples have a child	+35	5	All couples have a child	+35
6	No children		6	20 couples have a child	+20
7	No children		7	All couples have a child	+35
8	All couples have a child	+35	8	No children	
9	No children		9	All couples have a child	+35
10	No children		10	No children	
11	No children		11	No children	
12	No children		12	All couples have a child	+35

Total population: Children	80	Total population: Children	285
Adults	70	Adults	70
	150		355

Passing away of second generation	-70		-70
New population: Christians	**80**	**Muslims**	**285**

324

Third Generation Christianville
Population 365

80 Christian People		285 Muslim People
40 Christian Couples		142 Muslim Couples

	Birth Rate			Birth Rate	
Year			Year		
1	No children		1	All couples have a child	+142
2	No children		2	100 couples have a child	+100
3	15 couples have a child	+15	3	All couples have a child	+142
4	No children		4	All couples have a child	+142
5	All couples have a child	+40	5	All couples have a child	+142
6	No children		6	No children	
7	No children		7	All couples have a child	+142
8	All couples have a child	+40	8	No children	
9	No children		9	No children	
10	No children		10	All couples have a child	+142
11	No children		11	No children	
12	No children		12	All couples have a child	+142

Total population: Children	95	Total population: Children	1,094
Adults	80	Adults	285
	175		1,379
Passing away of third generation	-80		-285
New population: Christians	**95**	**Muslims**	**1,094**

NOTE: Town name changed from Christianville to Islamville

325

Appendix B

The Ninety-Nine Islamic Names of God

The Beautiful Names
al-asma al-husna

According to the Qur'an, the most beautiful names belong to God. In the earlier centuries of Islam, a number of Islamic scholars independently searched the Qur'an and *hadith* material in an effort to compile a list of these names. Today, most Muslims refer to these names as the "ninety-nine names of Allah." Some Muslims recite these names by memory as a part of their worship. These names help Muslims to understand in some measure the attributes of Allah. There is not one standard list. This is because different scholars at different times compiled their own lists. What follows is an example of what the ninety-nine names look like. Most of the names and definitions are taken from the list by Imam Ghazali, a famous Islamic scholar of the 11th century. A partial translation of Ghazali's treatise on these names can be found in the work entitled, *Ninety-Nine Names of God* by Robert Stade (Ibadan, Nigeria: Daystar Press, 1970).

1. **AR-RAHMAN**. The Merciful One. **1:1** (Qur'anic reference; chapter 1, verse 1)

2. **AR-RAHIM**. The Compassionate One. **1:1**

3. **AL-MALIK**. The King. **20:114**

4. **AL-QUDDUS**. The Most Holy One. **62:1**

5. **AS-SALAM**. The Sound One. **59:23**

6. **AL-MUMIN**. The Author of Safety and Security **59:23**

7. **AL-MUHAYMIN**. The Protector and Guardian **59:23**

8. **AL-AZIZ**. The Incomparable and Unparalleled One. **59:23**

9. **AL-JABBAR**. The One who Compels. **59:23**

10. **AL-MUTAKABBIR**. The One Supreme in Pride and Greatness. **59:23**

11. **AL-KHALIQ**. The Creator. **59:24**

12. **AL-BARI**. The Maker. **59:24**

13. **AL-MUSAWWIR**. The Fashioner. **59:24**

14. **AL-GHAFFAR**. The Very Forgiving One. **39:5**

15. **AL-QAHHAR**. The Dominating One. **13:16**

16. **AL-WAHHAB**. The One who Gives Freely. **3:8**

17. **AR-RAZZAQ**. The One who Provides all Sustenance. **51:58**

18. **AL-FATTAH**. He who Opens all Things. **34:26**

19. **AL-ALIM**. The Omniscient One. **2:32**

20. **AL-QABID**. The One who Withholds. **2:245**

21. **AL-BASIT**. The One who Provides the Means of Sustenance as He wills. **2:245**

22. **AL-KHAFID**. The One who Abases the unbeliever. **56:3**

23. **AL-RAFI**. The One who Exalts the believer. **56:3**

24. **AL-MUIZZ**. The One who Rasises to Honor. **3:26**

25. **AL-MUZILL**. The One who Abases. **3:26**

26. **AS-SAMI**. The All-Hearing One. **3:35**

27. **AL-BASIR**. The All-Seeing One. **17:1**

28. **AL-HAKAM**. The Arbiter. **6:62**

29. **AL-ADL**. The Just One. (no reference)

30. **AL-LATIF**. The Subtle One. **6:104**

31. **AL-KHABIR**. The All-Cognizant One. **34:1**

32. **AL-HALIM**. The Forbearing One. **2:225**

33. **AL-AZIM**. The Great One. **2:255**

34. **AL-GHAFUR**. The Most Forgiving One. **12:98**

35. **ASH-SHAKUR**. The One who Expresses Thankfulness. **35:30**

36. **AL-ALI**. The Most High One. **22:62**

37. **AL-KABIR**. The Grand One. **13:9**

38. **AL-HAFIZ**. The Preserver. **11:57**

39. **AL-MUQIT**. He who is Cognizant and Capable of Providing His Creation with everything it needs. **4:85**

40. **AL-HASIB**. He who Satisfies the Needs of all Creation. **4:6**

41. **AL-JALIL**. The Sublime One. (no reference)

42. **AL-KARIM**. The Selflessly Generous One. **24:116**

43. **AR-RAQIB**. The One who Watches All. **4:1**

44. **AL-MUJIB**. The One who Responds to every need. **11:61**

45. **AL-WASI**. The One whose Capacity is Limitless. **2:115**

46. **AL-HAKIM**. The Ultimately Wise One. **2:32**

47. **AL-WADUD**. The Objectively Loving One. **11:90**

48. **AL-MAJID**. The Most Glorious One. **11:73**

49. **AL-BAITH**. The Quickener. **22:7**

50. **ASH-SHAHID**. The One who Witnesses and Knows Everything Manifest. **2:282**

51. **AL-HAQQ**. The Real One. **22:6**

52. **AL-WAKIL**. The Ultimate and Faithful Trustee. **3:173**

53. **AL-QAWI**. The Perfectly Strong One. **11:66**

54. **AL-MATIN**. The Firm One. **51:58**

55. **AL-WALII**. The Patron. **42:28**

56. **AL-HAMID**. The Ultimately Praiseworthy One. **22:64**

57. **AL-MUHSI**. The Absolute Reckoner. **58:6**

58. **AL-MUBDI**. The Originator. **85:13**

59. **AL-MUID**. The Restorer. **85:13**

60. **AL-MUHYI**. The One Responsible for Life. **30:50**

61. **AL-MUMIT**. The One Responsible for Death. **2:28**

62. **AL-HAYY**. The Absolutely Perceptive One. **2:255**

63. **AL-QAYYUM**. The Self-Subsisting One. **2:255**

64. **AL-WAJID**. He who Has No Needs. (no reference)

65. **AL-MAJID**. The Glorified One. **11:73**

66. **AL-AHAD**. He who is Uniquely One. **112:1**

67. **AS-SAMAD**. He to Whom one turns in every emergency. **112:2**

68. **AL-QADIR**. He who Acts as He Pleases. **17:99**

69. **AL-MUQTADIR**. He who Refrains from Action as He Pleases. **18:45**

70. **AL-MUQADDIM**. The One who Causes People to be Near. (no reference)

71. **AL-MUAKHKHIR**. The One who Causes People to be Distant from Him. (no reference)

72. **AL-AWWAL**. He who is First. **57:3**

73. **AL-AKHIR**. He who is Last. **57:3**

74. **AZ-ZAHIR**. The Manifest One. **57:3**

75. **AL-BATIN**. The Hidden One. **57:3**

76. **AL-BARR**. The Dutiful One. **52:28**

77. **AT-TAWWAB**. He who Constantly Turns People to Repentance. **2:37**

78. **AL-MUNTAQIM**. The Avenger. **43:41**

79. **AL-AFUW**. The One who Erases Sin. **22:60**

80. **AR-RAUF**. The Very Indulgent One (full of pity). **2:207**

81. **MALIK-UL-MULK**. The One who has Perfect Power over His Kingdom. **3:26**

82. **DHUL-JALAL-WAL-IKRAM**. The One Possessed of Majesty and Honor **55:27**

83. **AL-WALI**. He who has Charge over All. (no

reference)

84. **AL-MUTA-ALI**. The Highly Exalted One. (no reference)

85. **AL-MUQSIT**. The Ultimately Equitable One. **3:18**

86. **AL-JAMI** He who Combines all Things to accomplish His purposes. **3:9**

87. **AL-GHANI**. The Rich One. **22:64**

88. **AL-MUGHNI**. The Enriching One. **9:28**

89. **AL-MANI**. He who Repels Those Things detrimental to the universe. (no reference)

90. **AD-DARR.** He who is Responsible for Evil. **48:11**

91. **AN-NAFI**. He who is Responsible for Good. **48:11**

92. **AN-NUR**. The Light. **24:35**

93. **AL-HADI.** The Guide. **25:31**

94. **AL-BADI**. The Matchless, Unequaled One. **2:117**

95. **AL-BAQI**. The Everlasting One. **28:88**

96. **AL-WARITH**. The Inheritor. **15:23**

97. **AR-RASHID**. The Absolutely Judicious One. **11:87**

98. **AS-SABUR**. He who Times all Things Perfectly.   (no reference)

99.   **AL-WAHID**.   The   Unique   One.   **13:16**

About the Authors

Harry Morin is a foreign missionary with the Assemblies of God World Missions in Springfield, Missouri. For fifteen years, he and his family lived and served among Muslims in Asia. Presently based stateside, he travels overseas for the Assemblies of God World Missions organization, Global Initiative: Reaching the Muslim Peoples.

In this capacity he provides training for ministry related to Muslim outreach. Venues have included seminaries, Bible Schools, pastors' seminars, and Institutes of Islamic Studies in the Philippines, Romania, the Netherlands, India, El Salvador, and Columbia.

Since 1994 he has traveled to twenty-one different countries on four continents, completing seventy-two different teaching assignments. He has also spoken to hundreds of church congregations throughout the eastern United States.

He is the author of the independent study textbook, *Christian Ministry in a Muslim Context*, Global University, 2006, which is distributed by Global University, and used by missionary candidates.

He is also author of the texts, *Muslim Ministry in the African Context* by Africa's Hope, 2007, and *The Anointed One* (contextualized for the Muslim reader), Center for

Ministry to Muslims, 1993, as well as twenty contextualized booklets for the Muslim reader (published by Center for Ministry to Muslims).

He also has written over twenty five articles for *Intercede* (CMM prayer letter) and *Nur-ul Haq* magazine (a contextualized periodical for Muslim readers worldwide).

Nikki Arana is an award-winning author of women's fiction, essays, poetry, and magazine articles whose work has been published in the United States and Canada. She has won several national awards, including the American Christian Fiction Book of the Year for Women's Fiction, twice, and the Beacon Award. Her book, The Winds of Sonoma was named One of the Top 20 Books of the Year by Christianbook.com. Nikki is also the recipient of the Excellence in Media Silver Angel Award and the Jessie Cameron Alison Writer of the Year Award. She is an experienced speaker and has presented numerous, highly successful workshops on the craft of writing.

Though successful as a novelist, one's first impression might be that Nikki is a highly unlikely candidate to co-author a non-fiction book about evangelizing the Muslims. But while writing her third book, *The Fragrance of Roses*, God provided a highly unlikely resource to work with her for ten months on the medical aspects of her Christian novel. He provided a Muslim research scientist. Through this relationship the two found common ground. The Muslim doctor had a deep desire to help find the cure for childhood leukemia. Nikki had a deep desire to raise public awareness regarding the need for minorities to donate to bone marrow registries used by families of children with cancer. And so they worked together for a common cause. As the months passed a genuine friendship developed from the trust that was nurtured as they worked on the book. That friendship continues to this day.

It is this experience that has given Nikki a passion for the Muslim people. A very personal understanding that they are not only fellow human beings that we share this planet with, but they, like us, are a people who Christ died for. Through this book she hopes to empower other Christians to reach out to the Muslims living among us.

Acknowledgements

Harry Morin

I owe a debt of gratitude to award winning Christian author Nikki Arana for the publication of this book. It was an honor for me to receive her invitation to jointly author a book for providing American Christians with inspiration and practical helps for reaching out to the growing community of Muslim neighbors, co-workers, and fellow citizens. Her special gift for writing brought a spiritual and human touch to the manuscript which otherwise would have appeared overly academic. Her unyielding passion for the purpose of this book is especially felt in her chapter reflections, where she focuses on the heart matter of each issue and encourages the reader to process the material with an open mind and an open heart.

I am especially indebted to my wife, Vera, who spent over fifteen years with me on the mission field submerged in Muslim cultures both in Southern Asia and the Asia Pacific. Her steadfast faith and perseverance under difficult circumstances enabled me to contribute to this book from thirty years of experience. I also am indebted to my three children, Celisa, Troy, and Jodi, who by no choice of their own, lived their childhoods in an Islamic setting. I can only hope that the sacrifices of my family members will in some measure add to the growing family of God.

Nikki Arana

First, let me say that I am humbled and honored to read Harry's kind words about the small contribution I have made to the writing of this book. It is clear that God gave one of us a mission and one of us a vision, then brought us together to prosper what He ordained.

Others who contributed to this effort through their steadfast support are the Global Initiative: Reaching the Muslim Peoples, Natasha Kern, Susan Lohrer, and my spirit-filled husband, Antonio, who, other than Jesus, is the greatest gift God has given me.

I especially want to thank my prayer partners, Tex Gaynos, Dominic Daddato, and Renae Moore, who faithfully intercede on my behalf. They form a hedge around me so I can embrace with passion the call God put on my life when He gave me a heart for the Muslim people and a burden for the American Christian church.

To those of you who feel drawn to reach out in love and form friendships with Muslim people, you will want to know about another ministry that is dedicated to loving Muslims into the Kingdom, White Horse Ministry, Inc. You can learn more about their ongoing efforts at www.WLCati.com.